GRANTA 71

Shrinks

D0110027

FBC
.50
1/22

Acknowledgements are due to the following publishers for permission to quote from:
'The Love Song of J. Alfred Prufrock' from *Collected Poems 1909-1962* by T. S. Eliot,
reprinted by permission of Faber and Faber Ltd; 'To Speak of the Woe that Is in Marriage'
from *Life Studies* by Robert Lowell, reprinted by permission of Faber and Faber Ltd; *The
Oxford Dictionary of Superstitions* © 1989 Iona Opie and Moira Tatem, reprinted by
permission of Oxford University Press.

FEED YOUR MIND

with **Routledge Philosophy**

PHILOSOPHER: A KIND OF LIFE

Ted Honderich, Grote Professorship of Mind and Logic
at University College London, UK

'What marks this book out is its trueness to life. Usually autobiographies
have a rather neat narrative. But Honderich manages to convey the
contingency, the untidiness and a lot of the mystery of existence.'
Ben Rogers, author of A.J. Ayer: A Life

'A significant contribution to the cultural and social history of the last
half-century as well as a fascinating record of a particular life and of a
particular kind of life.' *Alasdair MacIntyre, author of After Virtue*

Honest, enlightening and entertaining, here is the story of Ted Honderich. In
the thick of it all as Grote Professor of Mind and Logic (a chair previously
held by A.J. Ayer), Ted Honderich reveals the actual world of working
philosophy and the real life of real philosophers. With Honderich's
philosophy goes rivalry, troubled academic relationships and a personal life
of friendships, marriages and affairs, and, yes, even travels with Elvis.

234 x156: 500pp: 32 b+w plates
Hb: 0-415-23697-5: £20.00   US: $30.00

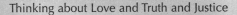

A COMMON HUMANITY

Thinking about Love and Truth and Justice

Raimond Gaita, Kings College, UK

'An absorbing read from beginning to end, its discussions are
memorable and in many places moving. A quite exceptional work.'
Tim Crane, University College London

'A wise and beautifully written book. It is a wonderful example of
how philosophy can still speak without any condescension to the
educated reader.' *Professor Simon Critchley, University of Essex*

'Clear, passionate, subtle and profound.'
Christopher Cordner, University of Melbourne

'Challenging and disturbing.' *Sydney Herald*

August 2000: 234x156: 328pp
Hb: 0-415-24113-8: £17.99   US: $27.95

AVAILABLE FROM ALL GOOD BOOKSHOPS

UK and Europe: to order direct call +44 08700 768853 or e-mail orders@routledge.co.uk

US and Canada: to order direct call 1-800-634-7064 or cserve@routledge-ny.com

www.routledge.com

THE EMOTIONS
ARE NOT
SKILLED WORKERS
Elliot Perlman

Sigmund Freud's study

FREUD MUSEUM, LONDON

He nearly called you again last night. Can you imagine that, after all this time? (*He* does. He imagines calling you or running into you by chance. Depending on the weather, he imagines you in one of those cotton dresses of yours with flowers on it, or in faded blue jeans and a thick woollen button-up cardigan over a check shirt, drinking coffee from a mug, looking through your tortoiseshell glasses at a book of poetry while it rains. He thinks of your hair tied back and that characteristic sweet scent on your neck. He imagines you this way when he is on the train, in the supermarket, at his parents' house, at night, alone, and when he is with women.)

He is wrong, though. You didn't read poetry at all. He had *wanted* you to read poetry but you didn't. If pressed, he confesses to an imprecise recollection of what it was you read, and anyway it wasn't your reading that started this. It was the laughter, the carefree laughter, the three-dimensional Coca-Cola advertisement that you were, the try-anything-once friends, the imperviousness to all that came before you, the chain telephone calls, the in-jokes, the instant music, the sunlight you carried with you, the way he felt when you spoke to his parents, the undergraduate introductory courses, the inevitability of your success, the beach houses, the white lace underwear, the private dancing, the good-graced acceptance of part-time shift work, the apparent absence of expectations, the ever-changing disposable cults of the rural, the family, the Eastern, the classical, the modern, the post-modern, the impoverished, the sleekly deregulated, the orgasm, the feminine, the feminist and then the way you cancelled with the air of one making a salad.

You would love the way he sees you. He uses you as a weapon against himself and not merely because you did. He sits in his car at traffic lights on his way out sometimes and tries to estimate how many times he has sat here, waiting at these traffic lights on his way somewhere without you, hoping to meet someone with the capacity to consign you to an anecdote, to be eventually confused with others. He thinks of you when the women lying next to him think he's asleep. It would not surprise you that there are many women. Do you remember you thought him beautiful? You never told him. He had to assume it. He was beautiful and is now, some nine years later, even more so. The years have refined him so that those once boyish good looks have evolved into a clean, smooth charm. Not always though. First thing in the morning or after he's been drinking the charm goes missing. The drinking is not really the problem at the moment, though, not right now. Of late it has been no more of a problem with him than it is with your husband, which is to say, of late the quantity itself is no cause for alarm. But there is a secret need in both men to have their inhibitors inhibited. In Simon's case this is merely the tip of an older and more fundamental iceberg. When did you stop seeing that in your husband it is some kind of repressed passion?

It is often almost too much for Simon to undertake even basic daily tasks; to shower and shave, to dress, to wash his clothes, to feed himself and Empson. He runs out of all but the most essential of foods and doesn't do anything about it until there's nothing for the dog. You couldn't know Empson. Simon got him as a puppy. He would be about three and a half now. He used to take him to school with him. This was the sort of thing he would do. The children loved Empson almost as much as they loved Simon. You loved him too. I can imagine he was a wonderful teacher. You might remember that Simon's father, William (or did you call him Mr Reynolds?), was disappointed that Simon was going to be a teacher, particularly a primary teacher. He felt that this was not a sufficiently manly occupation for his son and that Simon would be wasted. Ironically, though, had Simon still been teaching, William may not have felt the need to contact me.

It was very late one night. I could tell by his voice that William was embarrassed. He was at home and I was, of course, in my rooms scraping the last little bit of my dinner from the bottom of a cup. I don't know why he thought I'd still be there. He almost whispered into the telephone that he was calling on his son's behalf but without his knowledge. For all his embarrassment, and I have since learned that this is characteristic of him, he very soon got to the point. He told me he had a thirty-two-year-old son who lived alone with a dog in a flat by the sea in Elwood. He told me that his son, always obsessed with poetry, seldom went out since losing his job in the first wave of the downsizing epidemic. In getting directly to the point, William missed so many others. Simon has said that the reason his father has no time for poetry is that he is afraid of the messiness of life. Poetry feeds on all that spills over the boundaries of the usual things, the everyday things with which most people are obsessed, so William has no time for it. He cannot think of anything more unnecessary. What about you? What's your excuse?

The conversation must have lasted about half an hour—most of it taken up with William's examples of his son's lack of interest in things other than poetry and perhaps 'the damn dog'. He seems to have had no idea of Simon's continuing interest in you and everything about you. He told me that Simon was severely depressed, from which I concluded nothing much except that William wanted me to think that he thought his son was severely depressed. He told me that I had been well recommended to him by someone or other and that he was willing to pay for Simon to see me. I found that an interesting way of putting it. He was willing to pay for Simon to see me—as opposed to him being willing to pay me to treat Simon. His wife knew nothing about all of this and he asked me in advance to forgive him if she came into the room unexpectedly, and he was forced to hang up suddenly, without saying goodbye. William has spent much of his time planning to cope with people doing things *unexpectedly*. He would probably not recognize that he has ever done this, let alone the futility of doing it. He certainly would not recognize the utility of expecting just that little bit more—and planning for the unexpected just that little bit less. His wife didn't surprise him at all, not then.

At first there was nothing to be done because, as I explained to William, Simon had to *want* to see me. I couldn't call him up and say, 'Your father thinks you're disturbed in some way. How's Wednesday at four?' Since he had never broached the subject with Simon, I really didn't know what he thought I could do. We said goodbye and that, I thought, would be the end of it. Clearly, it wasn't.

About a month later William and Simon's mother, May, were out for dinner in Melbourne with Henry and Diane Osborne. You may remember the Osbornes; they are Simon's parents' closest friends. Simon assures me that Henry's contempt for poetry is probably second only to his father's. It was a Friday night and the Osbornes had taken Simon's parents to a French restaurant to celebrate William's retirement from the bank that very day. As they were leaving, having been fêted by the owner, a drunk Simon literally walked into his parents, apparently by chance, with his arm around the waist of a very attractive young woman. The two older couples, seeing the short-skirted advertisement for herself that she was, guessed her occupation fairly quickly and were clearly embarrassed. William started to apologize to everyone as though it was his responsibility. Henry tried to make light of it, asking the young woman if she had ever eaten at the restaurant before. Simon was trying to hail a taxi and the young woman, who said her name was Angelique, told him she had eaten there many times and that the owner was a client.

On Monday Simon called me. He told me the whole story and explained that it was a condition of the rapprochement with his parents that he arrange to see me. It was a brief conversation. He said that he would rather we didn't meet in my rooms and gave an address at which I was to meet him one evening. It was summer then and he said to come around the back into the garden where he would be waiting. I wouldn't normally ever agree to an arrangement like this, but something in his voice, an intelligence, and the honesty with which he told the story about his parents, the Osbornes and Angelique—a disarming honesty—made me agree. And, if I am to share the honesty I admired in Simon, I needed another full-paying private client. I still do.

It is quite well understood that a clinically depressed person will show little, if any, interest in constructive activity concerning future events or outcomes. In this respect, Simon has only flirted with depression in its definitive or clinical form. But if that is all that depression required, then I could say without much hesitation that Simon has always been, other than for short periods, too involved in things to be clinically depressed. William really knows very little about what's on his son's mind. What he and many people don't understand is that there is more to depression than a sometimes overwhelming feeling of inadequacy and hopelessness and profound sadness. When people are depressed they are sometimes very, very angry. They are not just quietly miserable. They can be filled with great passion.

Simon was sitting on a chair under a sun umbrella in a large well-cared-for garden with a swimming pool in the centre and birches and firs along the perimeter. He got up and we shook hands and introduced ourselves. I was struck by his clean handsomeness and by his calm. One rarely meets anyone who makes a better first impression than Simon. Do you remember? He thanked me for coming, saying he realized such a meeting was probably unusual. I said something banal about having to expect the unexpected in my line of business and then he quoted someone, some verse about surprises or chance, in that soothing voice of his. I don't know why, but I was a bit nervous. He asked me questions as though he was interviewing me and making mental notes; middle-aged, divorced, lives inner city, et cetera. I must have passed because he seemed to take a bit of a liking to me, albeit with some reserve. Perhaps I didn't fit his stereotype of a psychologist. I don't know. He told me not to ignore completely whatever it was his father had told me about him, saying his father's description of him no doubt contained what Simon called 'that dangerous element of truth', just enough to make me suspect that everything else his father had said, and would ever say, was true.

He was utterly charming, witty, and seemingly quite relaxed and intelligent. I was a little surprised he hadn't offered me at least a drink, but I didn't comment. We Europeans are instinctively better hosts, whether we have personality disorders or not. And I didn't want to interrupt him. I didn't know him and perhaps he would never again be so forthcoming. It's not that I expect patients to entertain me, but the circumstances here were quite unusually informal. Perhaps he felt a little uncomfortable offering me his parents' alcohol. I figured a place of that size, with the pool and the satellite dish, had to belong to his parents. They must have agreed to go out for the evening as part of the deal.

'I am a thirty-two-year-old, out-of-work teacher living on my own in a flat in Elwood,' he laughed. 'But just because I don't work doesn't mean I'm broken.'

Then, after some small talk, he started telling me about you. At first I didn't realize how long it had been since you had been together. It wasn't clear, so I asked him.

'It finished nine years ago,' he said, 'and you want to know why I'm still talking about it, right?'

'No, I didn't say that,' I replied.

'No, you didn't, but only because my father is paying you not to tell me I'm mad, or at least to tell him first. I think it's admirable what you guys do, but shit, it's embarrassingly primitive, wouldn't you say? What do you really know? And in any particular case, in my case, what do you really *want* to know? I'm afraid it won't make sense to you. I really mean that. I am genuinely afraid it won't make sense. I am not trying to sound casual or smug.

'Listen—all that she was then, all that she is now, those gestures, everything I remember but won't or can't articulate any more, the perfect words that are somehow made imperfect when used to describe her and all that should remain unsaid about her—it is all unsupported by reason. I know that. But that enigmatic calm which attaches itself to people in the presence of reason—it's something from which I haven't been able to take comfort, not reliably, not since her.

'It's like the smell of burnt toast. You made the toast. You looked forward to it. You even enjoyed making it, but it burned. What were you doing? Was it your fault? It doesn't matter any more. You open the window but only the very top layer of the smell goes away. The rest remains around you. It's on the walls. You leave the room but it's on your clothes. You change your clothes but it's in your hair. It's on the thin skin on the tops of your hands and people will ask you about it—and in the morning—it's still there.'

Now can you imagine it? I am sitting in a large, manicured garden at the back of someone's renovated turn-of-the-century symbol of success. The sun is getting ready to call it a day, but it is still quite warm. I thought I could see mosquitoes hovering over the edge of the pool. The outdoor furniture is comfortable, even if it is some of the ugliest I have seen. The air is still, so it's easy for me not to dwell too much on the prospect of the umbrella dislodging from the table and impaling someone.

This charming young man is eloquently expressing his quite legitimate doubts about the science or discipline that has brought me to him. He seems to have a fairly common and not necessarily unhealthy antagonism towards his petit bourgeois father, who seems to have your conventional authoritarian personality. They don't understand each other. They value different things, but not different enough for the father's alarm bells to ring hollow with the unemployed aesthete in front of me. It gets to him. But not as much as you do. He's a romantic, focusing on some idealization of the past. He could have offered me at least an iced tea, but I was getting paid and he was, after all, the kind we dream of—one of the incurably worried-well. He was a little melancholic but not completely without some justification. There was no reason why this could not go on for years. I thought he was normal, a bit unhappy—pretty much like everyone.

We heard someone walking up the side of the house towards us. Maybe it was more than one person. Suddenly Simon grabbed me, putting his hand over my mouth. He was quite surprisingly strong. There was a hysterical efficiency about him. I thought he was going to kill me. I didn't say a word. He dragged me behind some bushes near the edge of the garden where we both hid. He seemed to know where to hide, as though he had done it before. I was ready to jettison my first impressions of him. I was now convinced he was psychotic. We looked through the bushes at a man, your husband, entering the house with your son through the back door. It was your house.

Simon had meant to show me he was serious about you. He had been to your house many times without anyone ever knowing he was there. Taking me was his way of demonstrating that he was willing to take me seriously, or at least to try. When your husband and Sam were inside, Simon and I crept out. He took me to the Esplanade Hotel in St Kilda, opposite the beach. We went in his car. I had never been there before. We have since been there many times. That first evening was my initiation into Simon's life, the one he has kept hidden from his family. Within an hour I had witnessed a fight, heard a frenetic country singer ('rockabilly grunge' he said it was) and someone had tried to sell him what they promised were amphetamines. I had also been introduced to his friend Angelique.

When you left Simon he was angry with you. There was a tremendous sense of betrayal with the shock of your leaving. He could not understand your not wanting to share a common future in which, together, you would observe the world in all its sad and beautiful guises. The way he describes it, you could have been in different rooms and would have been able to predict the other's response to something because it would have been your own response. You respected the same things—aesthetically, politically, morally. He felt the two of you were co-conspirators. You wanted the same things and laughed at the same things. But ultimately you needed different things. Simon was a phase. You began to find his optimism, opinions and his touch too predictable and tiresome, stifling. You stopped wearing his T-shirts. You put them back. You pretended to be obtuse. Some nights no one could find you. Where were you? When his father, who never noticed anything, noticed your absence he blamed Simon and then, after a while, so did Simon himself. William was never so warm as he was to you when you had gone, while May would look out on to the street through the venetian blinds as though she were waiting for you. The other boys had gone, all good men, too, now with their own silent wives and good jobs, velour-clad children and brand new axes to grind.

Simon tried to find comfort in his reading, but one can only turn so many pages before the anaesthetic wears off. He had hoped the two of you could survive and maybe even correct a few of the world's imperfections. Perhaps his romanticism was always his biggest problem. Your inexplicable leaving was, literally, breathtaking.

William came home one night from work and found Simon speaking out loud to himself in his bedroom. It was nine years ago. At his desk, he was talking to himself. William stood at the door and listened:

> And would it have been worth it, after all,
> After the cups, the marmalade, the tea,
> Among the porcelain, among some talk of you and me,
> Would it have been worth while,
> To have bitten off the matter with a smile,
> To have squeezed the universe into a ball
> To roll it towards some overwhelming question,
> To say: 'I am Lazarus, come from the dead,
> Come back to tell you all, I shall tell you all'—
> If one, settling a pillow by her head,
> Should say: 'That is not what I meant at all.
> That is not it, at all.'

For a man so obsessed with words and language, it is interesting that Simon remembers perfectly what it was he was memorizing that night but not what was said between him and his father which so quickly led William to strike him. He remembers clearly the seconds before the force of his father's hand became a very personal heat in his lip and jaw. They said nothing more about it. He also remembers the breeze of his father's moving hand and the cold of his wedding ring. Not long after, Simon left home. You met your husband at about this time.

It was an accepted view for many years that pain avoidance and tension reduction were the major sources of a person's motivation. This was challenged (principally by Maslow) by the suggestion that more meaningful or more subtle conclusions with respect to human motivation could be reached by examining people's strivings for growth, for happiness and satisfaction. To this end, a distinction should be made between a person's deficit (or lower) needs and the growth (or higher) needs. The deficit needs are the more powerful and tend to take priority over the growth needs. A starving person will be little concerned at the possibility of other people seeing the lengths to which he may need to stoop in order to eat. However, the identification of a person's higher needs is more revealing. Moreover, any attempt by someone to satisfy his or her higher needs will suggest a state inconsistent with clinical depression. It is only when a person has at least partially satisfied most of the lower needs that they can begin to experience the higher needs and then attempt to gratify them. Such attempts at gratification are very likely to produce tension, but this tension is constructive; it is positive.

Not long after Simon left home, he started teaching. It was his first permanent class. He was so full of enthusiasm for his new life that sometimes he couldn't sleep. He had so many plans for his students and for himself. There was very little communication between him and William, although he spoke quite regularly to May. He still thought of you but the pain was not acute. He was contemplating a Master's in either Education or English. Education would have helped his career but there was still that unrelieved passion for literature and especially for poetry. He was thinking of writing something on the work of his hero, the literary critic William Empson. You might remember Simon going on about Empson, the author of *Seven Types of Ambiguity*.

Simon has tried to explain to me what is so fantastic about what he calls this landmark in the history of literary criticism (which, incidentally, is also the way it is described on the back of the book), but it's all lost on me. He bought me a copy of Empson's book but I couldn't get through it. I suspect he knows this as well. Essentially (and perhaps I am being too simplistic here for Simon), it sounds like an analysis of the effects which a writer may achieve, deliberately or unconsciously, through the use of *ambiguity*. (Everybody's got to make a living somehow.)

As wonderful as Empson's work may be, it was of greater interest to me that Empson, who was later knighted (possibly for his services to ambiguity!), published his outstanding work at the tender age of twenty-four and, more particularly, that Simon mentioned this several times. I think this is significant. But of course, as Simon told me, Empson had the fulsome encouragement of his supervisor at Cambridge. William denigrated Simon's efforts and early interest in teaching. His love of poetry was complete anathema to him. No one in the family, with the exception of May when he was a little boy, had ever encouraged Simon. You did for a while, didn't you?

Although the longing didn't stop, he had for a time forgiven himself for whatever it was that he had done to lose you. He had left home and it was impossible to stop him from talking to his friends about his children, as he called his students. He told May and even his brothers all about them, the twenty-two eight-year-olds in his charge, the noisy ones, the naughty ones, the scraggly ones with one jumper and two shirts, the fast ones in sneakers, the pretty ones with skinny legs who followed him everywhere and the very quiet ones who still were not used to having been born. There were twenty-two hopes to encourage and foster, little *people* to surprise and delight every day, to teach and to make happy with visits from Empson and, of course, to tell stories to. Can you imagine how they loved the way he told stories, with every word a song?

It did not take long till the parents came to see who it was that their children were talking about. Naturally, they fell for him too, some of the mothers quite literally. It would often begin with spurious concerns for a child's progress and end in a proposition. Simon delicately rebuffed all such offers. It wasn't that he regarded married women as sacrosanct. (Anyway, they were not all married.) It was more his commitment to the children. They were, each one of them, human beings, not devices for someone's gratification. They were the future, not theirs or his, but everyone's. You don't sully the future, knowingly.

Anyway, as you can imagine, his libido was being satiated elsewhere or, should I say, everywhere else. If one didn't know him, one would call Simon a liar, but everywhere he went, he was (and still is) almost inundated with propositions from women of all ages and backgrounds, many of which he accepted. He doesn't have to do anything. For all his charm and good looks, it is still quite remarkable. It's the stuff of movies. Indeed it quickly got to the point where he had difficulty telling his friends what he had been doing because an honest account would sound boastful. It seems he gets into conversations with women in shops, cafes and even on public transport. There is an exchange of telephone numbers and the rest is usually fairly predictable and not so interesting. It is of interest, however, that he never forms attachments with these women and never permits them to develop any legitimate expectations as to the future with him. He has a set speech, something like an emotional disclaimer, which he recites beforehand. Of course it does nothing to prevent recriminations on the part of the women, but it enables him to stake a claim to the high moral ground and, as long as he requires this (a higher, or *growth* need), he cannot be said to be clinically depressed. But, of course, it's of concern in itself that he is unable to form close emotional attachments with other women and that he needs the flattery. You remain unreplaced. You won't let him move on. His self-esteem is completely immune to his carnal successes but for some fleeting highs. It has no currency for him that isn't almost immediately devalued upon attainment.

It was both the complications from the casual trysts and a certain amount of guilt that led him to Angelique. You would like her. I do. They have been friends for a couple of years now. The night she met his parents and the Osbornes was not their first night together. They had previously struck an unusual arrangement. When they first met, she was working the streets and didn't really have what could be called regular clients. She was a refugee from a strict Lutheran Adelaide family who ran away when she got pregnant to a teenage football player. He denied being the father and broke off the relationship. Ostracized by her family and too proud to face her friends in the harsh light of certain Adelaide nightspots, she ran away to Melbourne's nightspots and lost the baby. When the free drinks and free passes ran out, so did her pride and she wound up working on the streets. Simon became one of her first regular clients. But it was very much on his terms, otherwise there would have been no point engaging a prostitute. He told her that she was never to stay the night, never to call him without him having called her first, and always to accept full payment at the time of her visit, no credit. His conditions were designed to avoid any complications or emotional ambiguity.

Simon discussed you with Angelique from the beginning. The very first time she came to his flat she saw photos of you and said that she thought you were beautiful. She knows all about you, even the story of how your father left his family in Italy to be with your mother. Simon recruited her as he recruited me.

She asked lots of questions about you and about William and May. She knows the stories of his childhood, his brothers and family holidays with the Osbornes in Sorrento. She loved hearing regular reports of Simon's students in the days before he stopped teaching. Angelique would like to be a mother some day. She too has been to your back garden. She has watched Sam play and thinks he is adorable. She has met your husband, too, and I'm afraid this was a coincidence. It wasn't through Simon.

Although perhaps even this, in a funny way, was through Simon. As you would expect, Angelique had some quite terrifying experiences on the streets, and despite the fact that Simon was trying to prevent any romance or dependency developing between them, he couldn't hide his concern. He eventually convinced her that she would be safer (marginally, in my opinion) if she worked through an agency and got off the street. I don't know the mechanics of this but I could ask her. It's not important. Presumably one goes for some kind of interview.

Maybe the more successful escort agencies use management consultants like you for this. Excuse me. I don't mean to be flippant. I really don't know. But I did learn, and this I must say surprised me, that some of the more upmarket agencies are on retainers to certain corporations. Not just small ones. It seems to be a prerequisite for being publicly listed. It is put on the company credit card like a meal or tickets to the tennis. The agency she's now attached to services several merchant banks and stockbroking firms. This is how Angelique first met your husband one busy Christmas. I'm sorry, but I really must tell you everything. It was quite an incredible coincidence without which everything would have happened differently, or perhaps not at all.

I won't ask you how much you already know. I don't wish to deal here with the grievances you have against your husband, even the fundamental ones. He is by no means the worst of her clients and, in fact, he is quite expansive. This may surprise you. You see, Angelique has no qualms about breaching your husband's confidence and we learn quite a lot more about you from him than we ever could from simply following you.

Of course, Simon did not always follow you. There was a time, a time I have spoken of earlier as a time of forgiveness, when Simon forgave himself for all that he was and all that had happened to him. He was teaching and knew he was good at it. He felt good about himself. Although he tried to fight against it, like most teachers (and parents), Simon had his favourites. Simon's favourite was a little boy, small for his age and very quiet. Whenever Simon brought Empson to school, this little boy was always the last to come and play with him. His name was Carlo. He was shy. Although not really disliked, he was too quiet to be popular with the other children and Simon thought he could see the beginning of a life of pain for him. He, perhaps arrogantly, thought he could change this. Simon likes to rescue people whenever he himself is not in need of rescuing. Do you remember?

Carlo's shyness made it difficult for Simon to assess his reading and comprehension skills accurately. He wasn't sure whether Carlo's slow reading was a reflection of poor ability or of his fear of reading out loud. He wanted to know what could make this little boy so afraid, anyway. He arranged for Carlo to stay back after school a couple of days a week. Simon would read to him, children's stories and rhymes. Afterwards Carlo would read back to him. Sometimes he even sang to him. Slowly Carlo was improving. Simon noticed he was even slightly more extrovert with his peers during the day.

Unfortunately, Carlo's story became public knowledge after this. You may not remember his name. Simon had always stayed in the classroom with him until his mother came to pick him up. Carlo's father worked nights and slept in the days. His mother worked in a clothing factory. There were other children in the family, but because of the private tuition Carlo got from Simon, they would leave earlier than Carlo and go home together. Carlo was the only one to be picked up by his mother after work.

One day Carlo's mother was working overtime. She instructed Carlo not to stay late with Simon that day but to leave with the other children. It will always haunt Simon. Carlo didn't leave school with his brothers and sisters but, saying nothing about his mother's overtime, he stayed back as usual with Simon. When they had finished their reading, the two of them went to check on Empson. Carlo wanted to go to the toilet. After about ten minutes, he hadn't returned and Simon thought the little boy might have had an accident and be too embarrassed to come back to the classroom. He gave it another ten minutes or so before starting to look for him. The little boy was not in the toilets, nor with Empson. Simon could not find him anywhere in the school yard. He ran around calling for him but the whole school was empty. It had never been so empty. As you probably know from the newspapers, he still hasn't been found.

This was the beginning of Simon's decline. He was devastated by the little boy's disappearance. He felt responsible for it. If anything, and you mustn't take this the wrong way, he actually felt a certain slight relief when Carlo's abduction turned out to be the first of that series of child kidnappings in Melbourne. In addition to the trauma and his sense of guilt, Simon was briefly, you might remember, the subject of some pretty tacky tabloid publicity. The other teachers even began to regard him warily. What had been initially regarded as admirable enthusiasm became an abnormal pedagogic zeal.

I found him very forthcoming about this whole period. It might have been at only our second or third session that he discussed it with me. I think he was rather hoping that this would be all that he had to tell me. But I think he was, in a way, glad he had it to tell me about. Have you ever expatiated on a particular experience to give a new acquaintance the impression of instant intimacy? It is not an uncommon form of flattery.

But I'm not so easily satisfied and Simon is not so easily intimate. In addition to you, and the disappearance of Carlo, he spoke quite easily about his father. It's fashionable. Simon rarely said anything much about May. One day I told him that I wanted him to tell me about his mother. He said there wasn't all that much to say. We were at his place, which was not unusual during his housebound, curtain-drawn days, and I insisted that he speak about her for an hour before I would listen to anything else. Simon said I was being ridiculous and that I could leave immediatcly if that was the case. I ignored him and got us both another beer from the kitchen and started playing with Empson. I gave him his drink and sat down. Then Simon talked for three hours. I didn't think it would work. My theatrics and feeble threats seldom work. I'm not much of a hypnotist, either, for that matter.

As a child, Simon found what was happening to his mother very frightening. She could at one moment be very loving, gentle and caring and then, seemingly quite suddenly, very angry. Or she would completely shut herself off. She just wasn't available. She would go into her bedroom and stay there. Sometimes Simon would creep in and hide under the bed or in a cupboard while she was asleep and just watch her, keeping his breathing as low as possible. She would not speak at these times. Her silences could go on for weeks. What happens to a child born to a mother who is depressed?

One woman in four becomes quite seriously depressed in the twelve months following the birth of a baby. But this went on well into Simon's childhood. His brothers seemed to be always outside breaking something or training for some event or else out camping. They were away. Simon was always there. He remembered, and it amazed him to remember, one summer afternoon in Sorrento with the Osbornes. William and May had been arguing fiercely. He doesn't remember what it was about. The older boys were on the beach playing cricket. William had stormed out. Simon had earlier slunk away from the screaming to shelter in his parents' bureau. He had

fallen asleep there and was awakened sometime later by the sound
of May's sobbing and heavy staccato breathing. He peeked through
the crack in the door and saw her lying on the bed in her half-opened
robe, her face and hair being caressed by Diane Osborne. Did he ever
mention this to you?

He is amazed that he could have forgotten this. He remembers
not understanding, being very frightened, but not being able to take
his eyes off his mother and Diane. There was, in that small space, the
extreme austerity of an almost empty mind colliding with something
sweetly frantic and wrong between the many breaths, and an
indifference to what he would be when the breathing was quiet again.
After a while, he could hear William coming down the passage. The
women were with each other and didn't hear him coming. Simon
didn't know what to do. He wasn't supposed to be there. He knew
things were in some way wrong but he was unable to speak. He didn't
know exactly what was wrong. Wasn't everyone a friend? William
pushed open the door and found the women together. He grabbed
Diane by her hair, pulling her off the bed, and hit them both, May in
the mouth and Diane in the stomach, knocking her to the floor. Then
he picked her up as though she were a piece of furniture and placed
her back on to his frightened wife who had fallen back on to the bed.
He madly exhorted them to continue.

Simon saw all of this from the crack between the bureau doors
before he passed out. His body pushed open one of the doors and
he fell to the floor. Everything went black. He has always felt
subconsciously that somehow none of this would have happened had
he not fallen asleep in the bureau. He wouldn't have seen it, and it
would not have happened. He wasn't supposed to be there. It was
never mentioned. Surely, he thought, this was what you did with
things that were never supposed to have happened. You didn't
mention it. Simon was crying when he finished telling me about his
mother. Then he asked me another one of those questions I'm never
sure I am supposed to be able to answer.

'What is it about men that makes women so lonely?'

When a child feels in danger, he or she will defend itself, hold
itself together, possibly withdraw. We do not spring fully grown into
the world. We have to develop or create our own sense of self. When

we have people around us who threaten us in various ways, perhaps by punishing us or leaving us, abandoning us, then our sense of self can seem to fall apart. That is the greatest, the most terrifying fear. We all experience it to some extent as small children and we grow up trying to defend ourselves against this fear. Some of us have to work harder at it than others. People won't talk about it. They think they don't have to and, often, they're right, unless it comes back.

Simon has tried on several occasions as an adult to reach May. He has done it as much for himself as for her. When the whole business with Carlo happened, Simon went to her. What could she say? A child disappears. It is so obviously a tragedy for those involved. But she couldn't understand the full extent of Simon's involvement. It wasn't so much what she could have said as the fact of her saying it, saying anything. But she hardly said anything that showed even the thinnest empathy and Simon felt rebuffed. Their relationship continued to consist of polite obligation-fulfilment. One Mother's Day he included a poem by Robert Lowell with his traditional card. Not long before this, May had confided to him that, with all her sons grown and gone, she was sometimes quite lonely. She said nothing about her marriage or about William directly, but he felt she didn't have to. For Mother's Day he copied out Lowell's 'To Speak of Woe That Is in Marriage' and gave it to her. Do you know it?

> The hot night makes us keep our bedroom windows open.
> Our magnolia blossoms. Life begins to happen.
> My hopped up husband drops his home disputes,
> and hits the streets to cruise for prostitutes,
> free-lancing out along the razor's edge.
> This screwball might kill his wife, then take the pledge.
> Oh the monotonous meanness of his lust...
> It's the injustice...he is so unjust—
> whiskey-blind, swaggering home at five.
> My only thought is how to keep alive.
> What makes him tick? Each night now I tie
> ten dollars and his car key to my thigh...
> Gored by the climacteric of his want,
> he stalls above me like an elephant.

Of course the parallels are very imperfect. The husband of the poem is almost as much one side of Simon as he is William. But Simon was hoping it might touch her in a way that could clear a new path for some kind of genuine dialogue or exchange. May never referred to it. Whatever she recognized or failed to understand, she said nothing about it, and Simon again felt foolish in front of her. He no longer minded looking ridiculous to William, who was ridiculous to him, but May was a disappointment. He regretted giving her the poem. He wondered how she could say nothing about it, even if it was just to say that the husband of the poem was not her husband at all. Simon would even have been heartened by some obvious and dutiful defence of William, some acknowledgement that William did not cruise the streets for prostitutes, that the lust of the poem's husband was not William's.

Simon still has that boyhood reluctance to talk directly, even in a psychoanalytic context, about his father's sexuality. I think you might know something about this from Sorrento, from that time at the beach house. Do you? It was towards the end, early one evening. Simon had taken the car to buy a few things before the shops closed. May was in the kitchen. You had just taken a shower. It was almost sunset. Do you remember? You were in the middle of putting on a change of clothes for the evening and you looked out of the window to watch the sunset. You were playing with a bracelet Simon had given you. There were problems with the clasp. Were you already planning to leave? Maybe that was what William was wondering as he watched you? The door wasn't completely closed. We know you did not know this. Obviously it was an accident not an invitation, but it enabled William to watch you there. And through the accident of the open door and the disposition of the light, the silhouettes of both of you were visible to Simon when his car pulled up. He saw you looking out of the window and he saw William watching you, everything was still and no one hurried to see less.

In the time I speak of as the time of Simon's decline, there was a change of government. The new government decided to stimulate the economy by terminating the employment of thousands and thousands of teachers. You may remember this. Your husband and

William voted for them. Perhaps you did too. Simon was stimulated out of his school. Given the size of the cuts, he would have stood a fair chance of losing his job, even had he not stood out within his school. As it was, after Carlo's disappearance, it was a certainty. His unemployment accelerated the decline. There were the bouts of drawn-curtain days and nights in bed. He slept and listened to the street sounds. His friends, who had kept their jobs and were trying to keep their marriages, had nothing in common with Simon any more. He didn't have the money to foster these friendships. They had stopped calling. May would call him occasionally but William could no longer bring himself to talk to Simon on a regular basis.

The sounds of his neighbours talking to each other, getting ready in the morning for the day, or of one of their dinner parties where the guests arrived with several bottles and well-rehearsed greetings; these sounds hurt him. How do they know so many people? Can you imagine, there was nowhere Simon had to be at a certain time every day, or any day. There were no certain times except those marked by his neighbours' sounds or by the birds announcing the end of another night he'd failed to sleep through.

Things wore out imperceptibly until they broke, one by one; the clothes drier, a heater, the collar of a shirt. And the neighbours would not shut up. He heard them, always laughing, as his bills came in, reformatted with their new corporate logos, the crowning achievement of micro-economic reform, and looking like invitations to a child's birthday party when they were really the philistine calling cards of the new society; the standard form ones and then, later, the threatening ones, threatening to withhold some or other service, or else to commence legal proceedings.

You wouldn't have wanted to see him this way. You don't know anyone like this. Your husband has seen to it. In the morning Simon would add a little milk to the scotch and at first it all seemed ridiculous, staying in bed till anytime, watching TV on the couch. But there was no contrast, no friction, nothing to call for any resistance. Two bowls of cereal and scotch and ice for one day can become one bowl, easily, and then just milk, scotch and a sliver of ice before lunch. No one said a thing and it wasn't ridiculous any more. It became unremarkable and surely that was false laughter, forced semi-hysterical laughter, coming from next door. He thought about you. He thought of killing the people next door. Would you hear that he was out of work? Would you ever be out of work? He decided that no matter how bad the economy became, you would never be out of work. When every last management consultant was trying to get work waiting on tables or mopping floors, you would still be many floors up in the city, surrounded by glass, perfectly pleated, going to meetings and making unfounded recommendations. Was he jealous? Certainly he was jealous, but more than that, much more than that, he was lonely. He was one of the loneliest people you don't see any more.

Again, it did not take long for him to blame himself. We spend our time watching things like this happen in other people's lives and attempting to divine what it is they have done to bring it on themselves, what it is that we would never do. So when it happened in his life, Simon was ready to accept that he had brought it on himself but he didn't know how he had done it.

It may be said that, in some sense, we create our own reality through the way we choose to perceive the external world and, like anything that is created or constructed, it can collapse. Does this mean anything to you? You think that you are happily married and then you discover that you are not happily married. Your whole perception of the outside world, as it pertains to you, just suddenly collapses. This is terrifying because our perception of ourselves within the outside world and our sense of self are the same thing. What was Simon in the world but a young man getting older on a couch, without a job, running out of time, running out of scotch, with all the cruelty of unrealized potential disguised as a home truth and the bitter aftertaste of misplaced hope? He walks into furniture at two o'clock in the morning. Outside the place next door there is a slamming of car doors and more wild laughter. Will they ever shut up? After a while you don't mess around. No ice. And surely it didn't have to be like this.

At that time Simon and I had not yet met, but I feel safe in saying that it was only Angelique that kept him from taking his life. She got involved. She breached the terms of their agreement and he was in no position to enforce it. Angelique would visit him without an appointment, without an invitation. At first he would send her away, explaining that she should not take it personally but he could no longer afford to see her. How can anybody not take something personally? As soon as you take it, it's personal. She didn't listen to him. She brought him food and cooked for him. She would ask him to read to her, insisting it was a new deal. He had to read to her in return for her company, no credit. She asked him questions about whatever he was reading to her, and in doing this she made him, in a small way, touch his former self. She held him when no one else was calling.

It might be easy for you to dismiss all of this between them as simply Simon taking advantage of her, using her. But he had gone out of his way to institute those artificial procedures to stop her from falling in love with him, relenting only at her insistence, and so it would be unfair of you to characterize it like that. Whatever blindness or timely self-deceptions led you into your husband's arms, you did not find yourself completely without hope of anything in your life ever changing for the better, and still you chose him or allowed yourself to be chosen by him. Your membership of society was never under any kind of review, and you never opened a newspaper to find the quintessence of your despair seasonally adjusted. Look at what was denied to him: love and work. It is asking a lot of a person to maintain a healthy self-esteem in the absence of both of these. And if his self-esteem is gone, how can you expect him to muster any reserves with which to make what are, after all, fairly subtle moral judgements and then to act on them, harming himself, perhaps fatally?

The period in a person's middle years between, say, twenty-five and forty-five is usually the period of greatest productivity. It is then that one establishes oneself in a vocation, brings up a family and creates a reputation in the community. The ability to work effectively, along with the ability to love, of course, is a sure mark of maturity. But Simon was living part of these prime productive years at a time when society denied him the opportunity to work in his chosen vocation, chosen, it must be said, with the most noble of intentions and in the face of his father's profound derision. So, yes, he permitted Angelique to cook for him and to hold him, to take him for walks.

He never permitted himself to tell her the lie she wanted to hear more than any poetry or prose. Despite this, she kept him going anyway, single-handedly, at least until I came on the scene.

One afternoon in bed, after a walk, she asked him how he could be so sure that he did not love her. Was she brave or stupid, do you think? Can you imagine you asking a question like that? Simon said that he *did* love her and that she should know it, but that he was not *in* love with her. You can forgive her, under the circumstances, for thinking he was off on another semantic frolic of his own. If he hadn't been so forthcoming she might have taken comfort in the ambiguity. He tried to explain.

'In spite of all that I unfortunately am now, or more accurately all that I am not, I am still far too cautious, too careful with you, to be in love with you. That's how I know, I suppose.'

'Now I *really* don't understand,' she said.

'You know you're in love with somebody when you wake up next to them, comfortable despite your breath smelling like week-old water at the bottom of a vase, when you are terribly excited to see them, to talk to them again, having missed them after all that sleep. You can fall out of bed into the shower and, still comfortable, burp or even fart while trying out various keys in which to sing the theme to a Peter Greenaway movie that you both hated and have never seen.'

When she asked who Peter Greenaway was, he could only say 'Yes' generally to the ceiling and run his fingers through her hair, all the way along her face and down until he had to alter his position in the bed. He would probably agree now that she saved his life. She loved him unconditionally and there is nothing more sustaining than that. But for herself there was nothing more dangerous. She was there for him no matter what he did and you were never there any more, no matter what he did.

All his warnings and strategies did nothing to protect her from falling in love with what was really just his *need*, and his diminished responsibility only enhanced his diminished sensitivity to her feelings. If I have been starving I am in no fit state to consider the needs of the hand that feeds me unconditionally and forewarned. Maybe Angelique needed to save his life but she could have done without much of the rest. Simon will admit this. I know her now, too, and we are agreed; with her strength, all her vitality and that almost naive optimism in spite of all she has seen, coupled with her methods of coping with all the shit that has littered her life, she is really a very special woman. Your husband would agree. I don't doubt it. He has taken great comfort from her.

She actually loves Simon to the point where she can become incredibly frustrated that she lacks the vocabulary to express it. She makes a lot of money now working for this upmarket agency. It's aimed at the corporate sector. Men like your husband unwind in her company and with her assistance. They pay her to dress in a manner that doesn't shame them and to undress in a manner that does. She would certainly be earning more than me now, but that's not terribly hard. Please don't underestimate her. She wants to get out of it too. She wants to be, of all things, a property developer when the market picks up, and a mother. She wants to be a mother when the market picks up! She's talked to Simon about having a child with him. Don't laugh. Whatever vestiges of middle-class sensibilities have stayed with Simon, and there are many, it is not these that keep him from Angelique. It is you, the myth of you. So please, don't laugh at him or at Angelique. You have, perhaps, become shy around empathy. It makes you uncomfortable now. You can live without it in the elaborately designed artifice that surrounds the swimming pool Simon and I have sat around. You do really live without it. Perhaps people ought to feel with more imagination.

Even before I started seeing him, Angelique had got him out of bed, out of his room. They went for long walks together, often taking Empson. They would talk about you. She told him everything that happened to her, everything your husband said. Simon's reactions varied. She could even make him laugh. After a while he was getting out on his own sometimes, shopping a little for basic foods or just walking around with Empson. Sometimes he would catch a train and stay on it for a couple of hours, reading or looking out of the window. You must understand how positive this was under the circumstances.

The circumstances and under them: he was in a shopping centre, walking by himself, when he saw you and Sam. It was afternoon. He had never seen Sam. You had just picked him up from school and the two of you went into the jeweller's on the corner. It is unlikely things would have turned out the way they have had it not been for his chance sighting of you and Sam that afternoon. Had you seen him things might have gone differently. But you didn't and this was no coincidence. He didn't want you to see him. From Sam's school uniform Simon could work out the school Sam went to and he figured that you must live in the area to be shopping there and sending your son to a local school.

He crossed the street and looked through the window from the side street. You were explaining something to the jeweller. Sam was turning a mobile watch display. It was taller than him. Given that Simon was afraid of your seeing him, he was undoubtedly taking an unnecessary risk in looking through that window. But it was not a calculated risk. It was as though nothing could match his fascination at seeing you interacting with the jeweller as an adult woman, a professional woman in a suit being served by the jeweller while your little boy played with whatever was on hand. For Simon time had stood still. He had heard that you had a little boy and had wondered what he would be like. What would he look like? His curiosity gave way to a kind of excitement.

Does it sound funny? Looking through the side-street window as you handed the jeweller your bracelet for him to examine, Simon watched you looking at your son. He was pleased to see you both together like that. The little boy came to you with something in his hand from the display, a watch. You gently admonished him and told him to put it back, all seemingly without sound in that darkened little corner shop. When Sam had done as you asked, you ran your fingers slowly through his hair and Simon thought that it must have felt good to Sam, to have done the right thing, to have known what to do and to have been able to do whatever would elicit even the briefest manifestation of the connection between you and him.

The jeweller took his time examining the bracelet under a desk lamp on the counter. He took what looked to Simon like a tiny screwdriver and began playing with the clasp on the bracelet, Simon's bracelet. You still wear it. You can imagine the effect on him when he realized this. He was desperate enough to take something like this as a kind of omen. Maybe this strikes you as sad? Perhaps it *is* sad, but before you close your eyes to him, I ask you to remember the last time you took something as an omen or saw something as a metaphor for something else? You can't remember, it was a long time ago? But you *are* functioning, aren't you? You're never in any danger. He took you, that elegant woman he saw in the jeweller's with her little boy, as hope, for him, for everyone. Sam was the future and here was the future looking to you for warmth and for guidance. If he put back the watch in the display cabinet, there would be no uncertainty about your response. He was loved unconditionally and, at least when you were with him, he knew it, it showed. Simon knew where you had come from and it filled him with hope that you and your young son could look the way you did now. After all, weren't you born together, you and Simon, back in your early twenties, summoning up all that you could from the first two decades or so of games and rehearsals before finally inventing yourselves as adults in each other's image?

You left the bracelet with the jeweller along with your name and telephone number. Sam wanted an ice cream. We don't know whether he got it. Simon remained undiscovered. He wanted to call Angelique and tell her about seeing you. She was often bringing news of your husband, no punches pulled, many times quite graphic, sometimes sad, seldom flattering. Now he had something to tell *her* and it was so positive. I told you that you would love the way he sees you. Are you going to tell me you don't understand any of this?

Angelique said you were cold. Simon wouldn't have it.

'You wouldn't say that if you'd seen her,' he said, pouring them both a drink. 'You're just going on her husband's need to rationalize his own behaviour. His infidelity needs a perception of coldness in her almost as much as it needs you. And the little boy, you should see the way she is with him, and the way he looks at her.'

'Sam, that's his name,' she said, unimpressed.

'Does he talk about the little boy?'

'Not much,' she said.

'You've never said he's said anything about him.'

'He hasn't said much about him. Think about the circumstances in which I see him. He's hardly going to bring out snaps of his family.'

'But he has said *something* about him to you, apart from merely that he has a son and what his name is, Sam. You told me.'

'He's six and very bright. Takes after her. He admits this,' she said matter-of-factly.

'Well, he certainly looks like his mother.'

'Simon, you saw him for a moment through the window of a darkened shop. You don't know what he looks like. You wouldn't recognize him in a group of kids.'

He's right, though, isn't he? Sam *does* look like you. We know this now. He's a very calm little boy, calm but inquiring, always investigating. Were you like this as a child? I suspect you were. Somewhere along the way, we lose our curiosity until we accept and then expect that we don't know, that we cannot really explain very much at all. Christ, I *can* go on, can't I? Just as he idealized you, Simon idealized your son and this is where it starts. Well, this is where the recent chronology starts, the one that leads me to you.

Simon began walking to your son's school in time for lunch, not always, but often, just to watch him while he played. He didn't do it every day. He wasn't able to. The downward mood swings led him back to his bed. The near euphoria he experienced seeing you by chance in the jeweller's was soon met with waves of its equal and opposite. A pedestal always doubles as a measure of sorts. If you invented your adult selves together, that is to say, if you were in some sense born at the same time, why was he following you and your son in this pathological way, humiliating himself to himself and, potentially, to you? What if you did see him one day? How could he explain himself, all that he had become? Would you blame him for it? What would he do if you looked at him with horror in your eyes? The papers tell it every day, there's no work anywhere and, anyway, teachers are just leeches on the public purse. Right? What if you bought this line too? You dress as though you do. Forgive me. I don't mean to be insulting. I simply want you to see yourself as he sees you.

If you weren't inspiring him, intriguing him and getting him up out of bed, you were destroying him, holding up to him the cruellest double-sided mirror imaginable. On one side there was the Simon as he was when you knew him, with all his promise—and on the other, a tentative man with no faith in himself and a sorry taste in late, liquid breakfasts.

On the days when one of us got him out, he went to see Sam. There is a definite calm about Sam. Simon keeps coming back to this. Sam is very comfortable with himself and this probably enhances his attractiveness to other children. At an age when boys are either trying to outdo each other, trying to be the boss of the game or else simply content merely to be included, it is extremely rare for the sheer presence of a little boy to have such an effect on the others as to have them nominate him their leader. But this has happened. Simon has seen it.

From just outside the school ground he saw some little boys attempt to arrest the natural chaos that threatened their enjoyment of a football. A boy, taller than the others, talked above the rest. Perhaps he owned the ball. He jumped excitedly as he spoke so that he seemed even taller than he was. He started the collective imagination with an idea. It must have seemed inspired; leave everything up to Sam. Soon most of the other little voices were nominating: Sam for captain, too. Sam, Sam. The way Simon tells it, they didn't fully understand the concept of a captain in the context of sport since they chose only one. He was to be the captain of both teams. They were crudely electing someone to organize them, to make the rules governing the use of the ball. They chose Sam as their captain. Why? It wasn't even his ball.

He is a handsome and capable little boy, not the fastest nor the tallest, nor even the smartest, but he is still tall, fast and smart. But more than this, he is quietly assured and very curious about the world around him. He likes to be able to make sense of things and, usually, he can. He is used to experiencing what he expects to experience. He has received more than the usual positive reinforcement from his teacher and from you and your husband, albeit all of you variously motivated. Simon attributes Sam's balance and calm to you. He said that the combination in Sam of an absence of both fear and arrogance is what marks him clearly as your son. You see how he remembers you? I told you. There is so much to be learned about someone from the little they remember and label 'the past'.

You have heard him read. You must have. Does anything strike you? Not about his reading, he reads well; does anything strike you about *what* he is reading, about its content? If you pick up the thin volumes from which children are taught to read, you will see short, simple sentences such as: 'Tom can run. Tom can jump. Run Tom run. Jump Tom jump.'

Think about this; the act of learning to read. A child is being made, almost certainly to some extent against his or her will, to sit still, pay attention and to concentrate on the symbols, the letters. The teacher, if at all successful, will have stimulated a certain curiosity in the child the satisfaction of which both requires and is the reward for his unnatural stillness. What does the child feel if he or she is obedient? What does he or she learn from the discomfort of the stillness and the concentration? Tom can run but he can't. Run, Tom, run. He has to feel discomfort in order to hear of someone else's good fortune. The words describe Tom being told to do something pleasurable which the young reader is being denied permission to do by the teacher.

Simon describes this as the first dichotomy in a child's education, the dichotomy between that which is *taught* as good or right and that which the child actually knows to be true in his or her experience. Of course, for a highly motivated child like Sam, this is hardly a problem. The praise he receives merely for the mechanical act of deciphering the symbols makes the effort worthwhile. But surely, after a while, he will have to become self-motivated. Hopefully his curiosity will be enough to keep him going. One day the praise won't be there.

Simon identifies another problem with these readers, or primers, as they used to be called. In the socialization of a child, the first people with whom he or she must learn to interact are the mother and father. Shouldn't it be the case then that these texts present realistic scenarios, encouraging legitimate expectations of parents in the child? What does the young reader get? There are never even the slightest differences between the parents. They never disagree. A child will know soon enough that something is wrong somewhere. There are two logically attractive alternatives. Either the stories are not true to life or else there is something wrong with the child's parents. In either case the difficult act of reading has let the child down; it was not worth it. The child was conned.

It is also one of the earliest sources of myth, the myth of eternal parental availability. Mother is always there. She is never preoccupied.

She has no job and no desire for one. Her role is a cross between that of God and a slave. She is never tired, never suspects her husband and never thinks that another man might just bring back the flavour she knew briefly, a little boy's lifetime ago, before Tom could run. She sees Tom run but he sees nothing and, you see, there's another lie.

Of course, nobody can always be there for a child. We have to leave them just to provide for them and—maybe even to sneak in some sort of a life for ourselves. Please believe me, I am not being critical. If you can afford it and your housekeeper is good with children, or not bad with them, even Simon wouldn't criticize you for taking some time for yourself. But of course it wasn't Simon or me that you were worried about.

Your husband doesn't always get told the whole truth. But Simon doesn't hold that against you either. It's just that gradually he has been gaining the impression that you have invoked Sam as a device for gaining some kind of secret autonomy from your husband. Simon's concern is that Sam is not benefiting from this. I'm sure you've rationalized this to some extent. Don't tell me. It goes along these lines; if *you* are happier this will somehow trickle down to Sam and maybe even to your husband; the *trickle down* theory. Well, of course, it sounds foolish once it's actually articulated. Simon didn't know exactly what you were doing on those days when your sister, your mother or housekeeper was picking up Sam from school. He couldn't be in two places at once, so he stayed near Sam, knowing that sooner or later you would return to him, smiling as though, *and* because, whatever had just happened had not happened.

But you don't need my doubtful insights to see the possible consequences of leaving Sam with others. Your housekeeper picked him up from school one day. They walked home. Sam was sucking on a frozen Sunnyboy she had bought for him. Do you remember Sunnyboys? Simon does. It was a hot day and Sam walked slowly, kicking cans and sticks as he walked, whatever was in his way. It takes longer to get from A to B if you do this, and by the time they had reached your house at the end of this particularly hot day, your housekeeper was just barely managing to hang on to her patience. Perhaps you have never seen her in this state. You should never hire somebody just because they smell like Johnson's baby powder. She told him to finish the Sunnyboy outside. It was melting and Sam was already sticky. He was really a bit of a mess with the sticky liquid on his hands and down the front of his school shirt.

When he was finished he carefully put the empty Sunnyboy wrapper on the grass near the edge of the pool and began kicking a plastic ball around the back garden by himself, back and forth. Simon felt tired just watching him. His energy seemed limitless, even in the heat. He kicked the ball from one end of the garden to the other and across, meeting it at the other end. He was puffing but showed no sign of stopping or even slowing down until, perhaps inevitably, the ball landed in the water. The momentum of the last kick took it away from the edge of the pool. He couldn't reach it.

It was obvious to Simon that Sam had been thoroughly warned about the dangers of going in the pool without the supervision of an adult. He was by no means a timid boy, but nevertheless, throwing off his clothes and retrieving the ball from the water himself was clearly not an option. He became increasingly frustrated. There didn't seem to be anything around that he could use to reach the ball even just to tap it to the edge. He called to the housekeeper but she was in the kitchen preparing dinner. The sliding door was closed and she had the radio turned up. Through an open window with the radio came the smell of onions frying. Sam rolled back and forth almost crying in frustration on the grass near the edge of the pool chanting your housekeeper's name. He picked up the torn Sunnyboy wrapper, tore the inside completely, making it a continuous piece, and leaned over the edge with it, moving it in the water in a scooping and paddling motion to create a current. The wrapper had no effect on the water so he threw it away and paddled with his hands. The ball began to move but it moved away from him so he ran to the other side of the pool and began the same scooping motion from there. He had created a current strong enough to start sending the ball against the earlier current and back again. He began to work faster with his hands, impatient for his ingenuity to reward him. The radio played Roy Orbison. Sam was still quietly chanting your housekeeper's name, angry with her, working furiously and breathing hard. The ball was nearing the other side.

Was it 'Only the Lonely'? Her name repeated in his voice, the heavy breathing and the angry little splashes of his paddling in the water gave way to a new fury of hands flat against the surface of the water, slapping the water. It was like this. He was in. He fell. His school shoes were certainly heavy on him. He swallowed in fear, in terror until the water surrounded him, inside and out. He had never known such distilled terror. Do you tell her what to cook each night in advance or is it ad hoc? Does she have a general idea of what's required? She's to prepare dinner and leave Sam alone to grow up—a separate person— like you, sink or swim. Only the lonely could know the way I feel. The onions were burning. She's in the fridge. She's somewhere. Where are you while your son is drowning in one of those tangible manifestations of the medieval bargain struck between your husband's accountant and your parents' ambitions for you?

He holds Sam upside down with one hand by his legs. He beats him on the back with the other hand. Nothing is happening. He beats him harder. The water comes out in spasms like projectile vomit. There is the faintest orange tinge to it. It keeps coming, Simon lays him down on his back. He wipes his mouth. Anything. In panic, he tries mouth-to-mouth but he doesn't know how.

Even if his estimate was inaccurate, it would still be interesting to know how long Simon *thinks* he waited before pulling Sam from the pool. Can you imagine him behind those trees in your garden? Initially frightened that the ball is going to lead Sam to find him, he watches Sam's frustration with the ball and with your housekeeper. He sees the splash or maybe just hears it, but he has no idea whether Sam can swim. He has no idea, from his vantage point behind the trees, whether your housekeeper has been watching constantly, intermittently, or at all. His own absurdity stings him in those inert moments between the thought that perhaps your son was drowning in front of him and his own stretching, pulling and gripping motion to reintroduce oxygen to the boy's lungs. However long Simon waited, it was long enough for it to dawn on him that Sam's rescue was not inevitable. Nobody knew Simon was there. If he had not been there, what then? Would Sam have died? And what about you and your husband?

He had Sam lying on his back with his head tilted back. He had breathed into his mouth. Sam was very quiet and he looked up into

Simon's eyes. He calmed very quickly, perhaps he was exhausted. Simon stroked his forehead and looked down into his eyes. He made some soothing sounds, they may not have been words, and found the parting in Sam's hair with his fingers.

'Lucky your mum asked me to have a look at the garden, my friend, or we don't know where we'd be. You're a bit of a tiger, aren't you?'

Sam looked up at him. Simon didn't think he had understood him but it didn't matter. The terror was going from his eyes and the sun was just beginning to dry his hair. They were your eyes. There was another song on the radio. Sam seemed about to cry. Something must have been added to the onions or they would have burned by then. There was a fresh sizzling of something from the kitchen, something with a lot of moisture in it.

'Sam?

'It's all right, just a big fright, that's all. You'll be all right, won't you?'

'Yes,' he said quietly.

'Mum will be home soon.'

'Why...are *you* here?' Sam asked.

'I'm here...for the garden.' He combed the boy's hair with a gentle rhythm.

'You can cry if you want to, Sam. It might be a good idea.'

He kissed the boy's forehead and left the garden.

I am sure you are thinking of several things. There is no need for you to be feeling guilty about this, if you are. Sam was all right. If you are feeling guilty, I would ask you to put it aside for now. Maybe there is a time for it but not now. Come back to me. We're not finished. Angelique almost convinced Simon to be angry with you. That says a lot about her, wouldn't you say? She thinks she'll handle her affairs differently when, having made it in property, she becomes a mother. I shouldn't be flippant but sometimes I am amused by the transparency of people's motives. Anyway, there's something noble, isn't there, in planning to protect your unconceived child from swimming pools. No, she wasn't just talking about swimming pools. Simon said that she was almost able to convince him to be angry with you because she spoke as an expert, about abandonment, the first signs of it.

The Emotions Are Not Skilled Workers

Have you ever taken a train at eleven o'clock on a weekday morning, a suburban train, and travelled for three hours back to the station where you got on? You have not, by all accounts, shivered with cold and self-loathing on a warm day, or looked out of the window of a train and wished the tunnel would never end. Have you ever affected a microscopic examination of the pattern on your automated teller machine card while you waited for the woman at the bank to confirm your closing balance?

Simon was shaken after the swimming pool afternoon. Although he had rescued Sam, he periodically felt somehow an accomplice. No, I can't readily provide an explanation for this, not one that wouldn't cause you to cast a truckload of aspersions on my particular version of a trade. He felt what is felt by many witnesses to accidents or traumatic events. Was there something he could have done? But what makes this so difficult to understand is that he did the very thing, the *only* thing, that stood between Sam and disaster. So, in what way could he possibly have been an accomplice?

It frightened him. His drinking picked up again. He didn't shave, couldn't sleep, kept irregular hours, generally approximated clinical depression. Perhaps it was in part the thought that, after all these years, he might have re-entered your life one hot day as the man inexplicably holding your drowned son. He's made much of the heat of that day when we've discussed it. I tried to find out more about this 'accomplice's guilt'. He would not always acknowledge it, changing his story. I asked him on these *denying* days why his drinking picked up so much at this time. He said it was a hot summer. It was. I remember. Simon had been out of work for some time by then. He said he found the heat humiliating.

Were you ever a silly girl with your head full only of laughter and serious boys who visited your attention with their stern adolescent dumbness? Try to remember. It would have been before you decided to choose between various styles and ideologies and well before the choice to stop choosing. You see, if you are now the finely-honed product of all those years of choosing, what were you before this, before choice? Can you remember how old you were when you ceased to be a tabula rasa? Maybe not precisely, but there had to be a time before the choice, the choice to speak in a certain tone, to mix a kind of polite forthrightness with a certain reticence. It would have been some time in early adolescence. Something, some event you may not even remember at first, would have launched you into the orbit of choice that led you to be the person you find yourself now. Perhaps you were greatly impressed by something you saw or someone you knew, something you felt? Was there a vaccine, some ampoule of humiliation, which immunized you against whatever it was that the girl no one chose to sit next to was riddled with? Do you remember when Sam began to define himself?

When did Sam start coming home with notes from his teacher and poor results? I caution you against putting too much store in the academic achievement of such a young child. It's far too early for ominous predictions, no matter what some of my colleagues may say. It's the reports of the change in attitude that I would want to remind you of and, in so far as the change in his academic results (if his school progress can be called that) is important at all, it is not the results but the change itself. He was (and is) clearly a bright little boy. He used to do well most of the time. By this I mean he was attentive and picked things up quickly. He was well liked by the teachers and the other children. Then, quite suddenly, he was failing most of the time, with only the occasional mediocre mark in maths and spelling. He stopped picking things up, he lost attention quickly. Why did he decide to fail? I am suggesting that it was almost a conscious decision, as rational as any decision you or your husband might make. I would hazard a couple of explanations, both of them perhaps equally obvious.

To learn means to grow up (as Bettelheim tells us). If a child stops learning, he can, in some way, retard his growing up. Why would he wish to do this? Many children see growing up as the incremental discarding of their mother and the need to be mothered. Why did Sam find himself craving you again like a very small child? This was the boy others chose to organize the game, a quietly industrious little boy running on his own success. Suddenly, he is disruptive, he is failing. Why? What is he feeling?

The decision to fail is often made in the pursuit of attention. It's a kind of depression in a way, too. (And don't, for Christ's sake, tell me children can't be depressed, or have you forgotten everything?) There is some anger that he is internalizing. He hurts you by hurting himself and if he hurts himself sufficiently, surely you will notice. I am broken. Look. Can you bear it?

It is probably clear to you by now that I do not provide Simon with much in the way of what might commonly be thought of as advice. It's not my role, not professionally, despite the popular view. I can't do it, anyway, not even as his friend. His thoughts come faster than my wisdom. I am hoping that I can't be blamed for this. Angelique can be judgemental. Most people can. It's usually disguised as something well-thought-of and called something else. My position has always been that the mere provision of a sounding board must be of some help. Simon has trusted me from quite early on. We have never experienced the problem psychologists call transference, where the patient develops a particular emotional attitude, positive or negative, towards the analyst. Perhaps it is the opposite. I wanted *him* to like *me*, not for his treatment—well, not only.

I have, I suppose, tried to guide him, but gently; he is able to resist. What is there to resist, my occasional sporadic outbursts of benevolent common sense? Nothing unusual, probably about as common as the estrangement of my wife from me, but with one notable exception. They return, these flashes of common sense, when Simon has finished moving me. Anyway, take note! He was hiding behind your husband's trees long before William ever called me. But I didn't try to stop him when I found out about it. That is true. I didn't know he planned a return visit to that jewellery store on the corner. How could I know that?

What was he thinking? Yes, that is supposed to be where I come in. Clearly, I don't know everything. Knowing everything is not my area. It isn't even supposed to be, I am supposed to be able to deduce the source of someone's unhappiness and, maybe, to say that I do not have sufficient information, even when I do. I don't know why you left him nine or so years ago. He doesn't know. We speculate. Some of at least one of my children's education has been paid for from the proceeds of speculating why you left him. He said it was sudden. But there's no other way to leave someone, is there? You are always with them right up until you're not. Yes, William's been paying for this wisdom. And he's supposed to be shrewd in matters fiscal.

How could I know he planned to return to your corner jeweller, let alone what would follow? He wanted to see the bracelet, to touch it, as though it were an abiding and tangible manifestation of the link between the two of you nine years ago, and now. Maybe it is. Why do you wear it? It's old and inexpensive with a clasp that you can't rely on. I am sure your husband would have courted you with much better pieces. But you wear it and when it breaks you take it to an elderly man with an accent in a corner shop and he makes promises to you for which you pay, willingly.

Does the bracelet remind you of Simon or of the person you were when you were with him? Perhaps you just like the bracelet, simple as that. You haven't been one for hanging on to things that have no use for you. Somewhere between my wife's place and my rooms there's a wall on which someone has painted: NOSTALGIA ISN'T WHAT IT USED TO BE! We are in heated agreement.

Even remembering his obsession, I don't know quite what he had in mind nor whether he had anything in mind. What would he have achieved by paying for the repairs to the bracelet and then depositing it secretly in your letter box or somewhere? He doesn't know, either, but this is not what happened anyway. When he went to the shop and enquired after the bracelet, the jeweller told him that it had been picked up. Simon was a little embarrassed and said that he hadn't realized you had already picked it up. But the jeweller told him, with old-world European discretion, that it was not you but a gentleman. Simon feigned a familiarity with your husband, even describing him for the increasingly uncomfortable jeweller, but no, it was another gentleman.

Simon was so taken aback that he momentarily forgot himself, becoming angry, and cross-examined the old jeweller as to what-the-hell you thought you were doing. The jeweller apologized, either on your behalf or, most likely, on his own behalf for giving this well-spoken young man news which so obviously distressed him.

Another gentleman. Nothing Angelique or I could ever say about you could make the sizeable dent in your pedestal that the jeweller made with these words. For a while it was all Simon would talk about. Angelique found him either expansive about it, in a pseudo-scientific way, or else steeped in a familiar melancholic reflection about whether or not you were seeing another man and, if so, why. Would you leave your husband for him and to what extent were your decisions informed by considerations of Sam's interest? Was it simply that he felt he had a grip on the concept of your husband, who he was, and, in some sense, that he even had his measure? A new man might threaten the order of things, even if that order had been dysfunctional. Yes, but I think it was more. There was a quite genuine concern for Sam. Was it better for him to grow up with dissatisfied parents in a sterile marriage, with or without infidelity (the fate of most of us), or with separated parents with all the attendant problems (the fate of the rest of us), but in an atmosphere not without a modicum of hope for the future?

As always, I tried to discuss the absurd with him with the utmost seriousness. It's not absurd to imagine that you are having, have had or are about to have an affair, nor even that, in spite of his wealth, your lifestyle, your child and the sheer bother of it all, you would some day leave your husband. What *is* absurd, I thought, was that Simon should imagine that he has some say in all this, some control. Most of us have to fight to gain some control over our *own* lives, and here is Simon, for whom it is sometimes too much to shave, to wash his clothes, to feed himself or to walk his dog, contemplating whether a woman with whom he has had no involvement for nearly a decade should or should not stay in her marriage. I don't laugh. I have never laughed. That's how we know I'm professional.

And isn't it interesting to see how bourgeois he is? For all his rejection of his parents and their rejection of him, he is at one with them in thinking there is something intrinsically sacred about marriage, even a sterile marriage, one in which the husband gets more warmth from the prostitute he visits regularly than from his wife, one in which the wife has been too successful in utterly repudiating everything she used to be before she managed to get everything her parents had taught her she had ever wanted. And Sam. Simon is angry that the possibility is left open that Sam may, in some sense, be abandoned as a consequence of your attempt to mitigate the damage of a hasty decision to marry a man as remote from Simon as you are now.

This, Simon told me, is what happened when Angelique walked into his flat one afternoon. The door was open and she found Simon sitting on his couch with the customary glass of scotch, listening to music and reading. At first she just stood there looking at him. Empson was asleep.

'Is this it? Are you just going to sit here for the rest of your life, listening to Stephen Cummings and getting yourself shit-faced?'

'I've got some Leonard Cohen somewhere around here.'

'Simon, OK, you *don't* have a job. It's not the end of the world. You sit around here drinking in this...museum or...shrine, you've built to an ex-girlfriend. That's all she is. Everyone's got them and everyone's out of work.'

'What's your problem today?' he interrupted.

'I don't have a problem. I've got plans instead. If I'm not happy with things I try to change them. Isn't that what you'd tell me to do?'

She stood with her hands on her hips.

'I never tell you what to do.'

'Well, that's bullshit for a start. You gave me all these *instructions* when I first started seeing you, how I wasn't to call you without you calling me first and all the rest of it.'

'You didn't listen to me,' he said.

'No, of course not. Who would listen to you? You're a boring old smart-arse with an alcohol problem and a thing for a yuppie girl you haven't spoken to for ten years. You're pathetic, Simon!'

'Why do you visit me, Angel?'

She sat on the edge of the couch and took a sip of his drink.

'I like your dog.'

She patted Empson, refilled Simon's glass and drank from it. Then she moved closer.

'And despite all this, I still think you're beautiful...and you're funny.'

Simon put his arm around her. 'Funny! In what way funny?'

'You make me laugh. You make things out of nothing...with just...words. You're entertaining and...' she gestured to the room around her, 'it's like a place I can escape to. You give me advice.'

'Yes, now is a very good time to get into property.'

She put the palm of her hand to his cheek.

'Simon! Look at the skin on your face.'

'No thank you.'

'It's all dry and...' she studied his face, 'you're so pale.'

'Wouldn't get much for me in my present state, I'll grant you.'

'You've got to start caring. You've really got to get some kind of life, get out more, drink less, eat better.'

'Now just a minute. I won't have a thing said against your cooking.'

'Simon, I'm being serious.'

He kissed her.

'Are you staying for dinner, Angel?'

'No. I'm on tonight.'

'Anyone I know, or everyone I know?'

She got up. 'It's your favourite client, among others. You know, I think he suspects.'

'Suspects what?' Simon asked.

'I think he suspects she's seeing someone else.'

He stood up. 'What makes you say that? You haven't said anything have you? Jesus, you haven't said anything?'

'You know she doesn't want any more children?'

'How do you know that?'

'He told me. How else would I know?'

'I can't *believe* the things he tells you!'

'Yeah, scandalous isn't it,' she said, taking another sip.

'Well, it's not that it's private, hell, it's all private...but it's irrelevant.'

'Irrelevant! Irrelevant to what?'

'How the hell can he screw you talking about his wife and child?'

'I've told you. It's not all that crap you see in the movies. I don't dress up in a uniform or any shit like that. Well, not for him. He's just one of those guys who spends every day talking non-stop about things that don't matter to people he doesn't like or people he's afraid of. He knows he can say anything to me. It's pretty common with the regulars. It's all part of it.'

Simon wasn't listening.

'He'd be another "only child"—lonely,' he said pouring another drink.

'Who?'

'Sam.'

'Yes, he would be, an only child in a broken home.'

'A "broken home"—what's that, Angel? It's just a cliché. Anyway, she won't leave him. She knows when she's on to a good thing.'

'He doesn't think so. He thinks she'll have an affair.'

'For Christ's sake, what do you two do—undress each other very slowly so there's time enough to speculate on *her* fidelity? I hope you charge him extra for the analysis.'

She ignored him and spoke very deliberately. 'He told me he thinks there's someone else. She's going away next week to some conference or convention or something.'

'Oh, he's crazy, paranoid. He's really crazy. You're both crazy. People go away to conventions all the time. Even teachers do these days, or used to. He's just trying to assuage his guilt, or maybe it turns him on talking about it with you.'

'Simon, will you relax? So what if she's going away with someone? It's *his* problem not yours.'

'This is just part of the shit he spins you, Angel. You don't believe it?'

She stood up and met his eyes.

'He said he'd leave her if she's seeing someone else.'

Simon realizes that maybe the penny has dropped for your husband—that your marriage is in trouble and that you've just found out. What kind of man is he? Will he try to save it or will he put on a brave face? Is putting on a brave face the only way he thinks he can save it? Or will he leave you?

Bravery. For better or for worse, men usually give it up after adolescence. Well, it's not really bravery at all, is it? It's a kind of childish pride that we, as a society, tend to idealize. We imbue our screen heroes with it, this 'cool'. And isn't it seductive—this apparent absence of vulnerability? It works. Don't women want to be desired by someone who doesn't feel pain, who isn't afraid?

But it's an act. Anybody who doesn't want or need something is dead. And anyone who does need something can be hurt. They can be afraid. We teach men this act, to perform it all the time. And subsequent to their emancipation, women now have to pretend too. But your husband is so well conditioned he's not aware it's an act. He's been doing it all his life. That's how he attracted you in the first place and, after years of marriage to you, he's still playing invulnerable. But is he right to? Is the only truly happy marriage one of detachment and respect? Your husband needs you so badly that he won't talk to you in the hope that you'll respect him all the more for his silence. What if he did talk to you? What if he told you the truth? What if he cried in the cinema and stopped flirting with the fifteen-year-old girl at the dry-cleaner's? He thinks the men that service his car break some new part every chance they get. When he can't open a window in your house at the first attempt, he contemplates his mortality. He regrets ever putting anything in your name. He wants you to watch him when your sister is around. He's not totally comfortable with the fact that your father is Italian. His eyebrows displease him, they always have, and sometimes he hastily stimulates himself secretly in the bathroom before going to bed with you so that he might keep up with you.

It's hard to be certain exactly where Angelique's fondness for your husband stops and her desire to taunt Simon with him starts. She is certainly fond of him. He makes her feel needed with his confessions and, as you can see, because of his confessions, Simon also makes her feel needed. For as long as Simon is obsessed with you, there will always be a place where your husband will be welcome. But if Simon was well, if he had a job, if he could forget about you and rejoin the nine-to-five rate-paying dinner-party guests, the commuters, the opinion-polled, if he was somebody's target market—where would Angelique and your husband be? And where would you be? Where will you be if you do leave him? Will Sam finally catch a first glimpse of some exhausted rapprochement between you and your by then ex-husband at his twenty-first birthday party, just before the speeches, when, as you stand together, you look honestly at this man with a shame you could never bear to put into words, a shame that only hindsight can deliver? And in the light of what your husband has become since you left him, in the light of his fall, will you regret your inability to say, 'I'm sorry I was not there to catch you'?

The need or striving for a sense of control is generally considered healthy. People's behaviour is often determined, to a large extent, by the amount of personal control the individual believes he or she has. Indeed, clinically depressed people do not attempt to alter their circumstances at all. And the longer they do not attempt to intervene the greater their problems become. But here is the critical point. To be healthy, it must be *their* circumstances that they seek to change. There is no merit in attempting to control other people's lives. I never counselled any kind of Machiavellian desperation. Simon came up with this on his own. In theory, we don't drum up business.

Was he looking out at the street through the venetian blinds when reason momentarily turned away from him as though it had become as tired of him as he had himself? To be honest, it was not really a flight from reason so much as a perverse confluence of events. Reason has always been an early riser. It's always the first to leave. Simon learned from Angelique that your husband had an early meeting nearly every morning, but there was one particular morning that especially interested him, the morning of the day you were to be flying out for your conference. If the meeting had been in the afternoon, or even later that morning, Simon might never have known about it. If Angelique had not woken him for breakfast he might have found out about it too late. But it was all as if it were on some kind of 'just in time' schedule.

Your husband was having a 'busy time', often working late, always starting early. You remember. Why don't you ever ask anybody questions? Well, I suppose you will now. Think about it. It's a depressed market. They're not going to pay people to work those kind of hours any more and you don't earn commission if the phone doesn't ring. There was no busy time at all except maybe with Angelique, but he did have a breakfast meeting that morning. Simon assures me that, one day, well-dressed people will start having breakfast at home again. But the dollar had been up to no good while your husband was with Angelique. It went down on him, through the floor, and this necessitated a lot of urgent consultation. There is, apparently, an excess of coffee but a shortage of croissants at these breakfast meetings, Angelique tells us. More importantly, Simon knew from her exactly when your husband would be unable to receive calls, so he could leave a message for him without the risk of speaking to him, a message from you. Your husband could have called you back and been put straight at any time throughout the day. Or you could have *really* called him, to clarify something or even just to say goodbye again, to say anything. Simon would not have known. He was taking a risk but, when you think about it, what was he really risking? What would have happened if your husband had not received Simon's message? He could not have recognized him even if he saw him.

In the event your husband didn't call you. He didn't need to, he had everything straight already—pick up Sam from school, take him to dinner at your parents', pick him up at lunchtime on Saturday, leave some money out for the housekeeper. The shopping had been done. It was only for a weekend. And you didn't call him either. Those midday calls are kept to a minimum. Instructions are issued in the morning and they tend not to be queried in the absence of any major ambiguity. You had your briefcase and your overnight bag already packed, sitting in the boot of the car at the bottom of the tower where you work. You could go directly from drinks to the airport. You weren't going to call him in the middle of the day—not this day.

Simon has yet another theory about children I haven't mentioned, theory no. 6017, which I would say has almost no validity but which, yet again, I found interesting. This one he formulated on the basis of his observations from the perimeter of a school ground but I don't think he really accepts it. (It has all the hallmarks of a psychological theory, doesn't it?) He says that, as a rule of thumb, one can correlate the amount of time a child spends on the school premises after the final bell has rung for the day with the degree of domestic dislocation to which the child is subjected. Why is a child still at school after school hours? If he or she is being detained on account of bad behaviour, who is the child rebelling against, or emulating? If the child is receiving extra tuition, why is it that he or she isn't able learn at the same rate as the others? If he or she is loitering around the grounds after hours, perhaps home is an unpleasant place to be.

It's pretty simplistic stuff and, as I said, I don't think he really believes it. What about after-school sport? And what about Art,

Craft, Music, Drama and smoking behind the bike sheds? All of this attracts them to school, for many a cross between a temple and a marketplace. This is where it all happens and we must be careful not to discount the importance to them of these things merely because we have forgotten about so much that was important to us.

There are brightly painted red and white posts in the ground that designate the beginning and end of children's crossings. Have you noticed how these posts subtly come to a point, but somehow it's not sharp, we can touch it, a palpable manifestation of our collective anxiety for our children. The wire-mesh fence inclines towards the school building with lush green foliage on the inside of it forming a raised plantation, ideal for jungle warfare and general hiding. The building itself is in different sections. The central part is just over a hundred years old, with reddish-brown bricks, a white border around the windows and a roof of slate tiles rising to a spire. Next to this are extensions such as the library, with much lower roofs and brick of different shades of red, reflecting subsequent spasms of public funding.

There is a sign on the wall of the library just below the guttering which reads: WARNING. KEEP OFF. THIS ROOF HAS A SECURITY CAMERA CONNECTED DIRECT TO A SECURITY COMPANY. TRESPASSERS CAN EXPECT IMMEDIATE ARREST. Out of the highest external brick wall comes a two-tiered wooden fire escape leading to an asphalt basketball court. There is an old rusted ring at each end without a backboard. Do boys play netball? Beside the court is a big green dump bin surrounded by smaller silver rubbish bins, some of which are chained to each other (presumably so that they can't escape). Others are dented, having been used at critical times to demarcate one area from another.

Not far from the bins are the cricket nets, the wire sagging at the ends, and next to them the small concrete field for the teachers' car park. The classrooms are of different sizes, each with a different feel inside according to the age of the class and the age of its teacher. Some have tiny plastic tables facing the blackboard and wooden chairs with denim and gingham chair-bags hanging from them. Others are lined with collages, animals-meet-fashion-models-and-dairy products. There are charts, Where Rain Comes From, Where

The Sun Goes. Nothing else sounds like the bell and the children spill out on its instruction at a rate that bears no relation to anything else.

In the seconds before the bell rings, the parents, grandparents and assorted guardians mill around the fence near the gate. They don't come in. Some talk, others just wait. It is interesting that children of the same ages are met by adults of such different ages and backgrounds: young women and much older men from Southern Europe, the Pacific and South-East Asia. How old are the children before they refuse to be hugged in front of their peers? How young are they when the accent of a waiting guardian engenders a shame they will, years later, remember with a fresh and much richer shame? Some of the children are not met by anyone. They might walk home alone or in groups. They try each other's bikes. Perhaps they are going to meet a parent at work? Some of them are in no hurry to end the day's commerce. They hang around.

Ball games start and children of all sizes are lost to them. There's a kid with crazy eyes and a big bag of marbles smoothing the ground in front of him. He's wearing a black T-shirt emblazoned with the image of a steroid-enriched bodybuilder, naked to the waist, with a sub-machine gun strapped to his chest. The kid holds a marble in the air between his thumb and forefinger and calls out, 'Hit it and you win it,' in a slow, dragging voice as though he were selling papers. The teachers' car park is emptying. The younger women, fresh from teaching college, are getting into their first cars, still with furry cartoon characters wrapped around the rear-view mirrors and stickers on the back advertising radio stations now in liquidation and seaside resorts the young women went to with their slightly older young men who drove bigger cars and gave them the stickers. The kid with the crazy eyes has a small crowd of boys in front of him, 'Hit it and you win it.'

Sam was thinking about it. He stood with his hands in his pockets watching the other boys, some of them older. His school bag was on the ground and he wasn't looking for anyone.

'Sam.' He heard his name called but ignored it. He was watching the boys and the marbles. Hit it and you win it.

'Sam,' Simon called again.

Sam turned round.

'Do you remember me?'

He shook his head.

'Yes you do. Do you remember that awful day when you fell in the pool at home?'

'You're the gardener!' he said.

'Yes. I'm the gardener. Do you like to play marbles?'

'Yes. Sometimes,' Sam answered, looking back at the others.

'Listen—Sam. You know your mum won't be picking you up today?'

'Yes. Dad will.'

'Well, he was going to, Sam, but he can't now. He's got something at his work that is going to make him late home. He asked me to come and tell you—and to look after you. Is that OK?'

'Yes.'

'Do you like chocolate milk? I do.'

Simon knows about empty school grounds, about looking in them for someone, calling out with a dry mouth and a machine-gun pulse. Your husband looked everywhere. He had only been there twice before. He went through his pockets looking for the message in the hand of someone else's secretary, the message from you that Simon had left for him telling him that Sam was on an excursion and would be back late. It wouldn't have helped anything to have found it but he felt he needed to see it. When he realized he didn't have it, he started to wonder whether he had dreamed the whole thing. You can imagine. The walk becomes a nervous trot. Can you picture it? He is still trying to deny what is happening. He loosens his tie and then he runs, unashamedly, in terror. Nothing could prepare him for this. He cries his son's name to stop the world, to pause it with the cry. You must know all of this by now.

Angelique was looking for the use-by date on a packet of drinking chocolate. The cupboard was filled with tins of soup, chocolate, canned fruit and packets of mashed potato, many of which she had bought for Simon over the last few months. There were some saucepans in the kitchen sink with the remnants of a tin of soup congealing on the sides. She was pleased to see this. It showed that he was getting through the supplies. There were some newspapers piled up on the floor and some empty bottles stacked neatly in a row beside the rubbish bin. There were not as many as there used to be.

'When did you buy this drinking chocolate?' she called to Simon in the next room.

'He doesn't want *hot* chocolate. There's some chocolate topping in there somewhere near the front. I bought it yesterday,' he called back.

'I was making it for *us*, but if it's stale I'll throw it out.'

'I didn't know drinking chocolate went off, but maybe the new improved stuff comes with state-of-the-art environmentally vindictive obsolescence. You can't stop progress you know...can't stop anything,' he added quietly.

She boiled some milk to go with the chocolate topping for two mugs' worth of hot chocolate and poured some more chocolate topping into a glass with ice cream and milk. There seemed to be so much milk.

'I don't know what these will be like. I've never made hot chocolate from topping before,' she said, carrying all three of the drinks into the room and placing them on the coffee table. The television was on, but turned low, almost inaudible. Sam was asleep on the carpet with a pillow underneath his head and a blanket over him. Empson was asleep next to him. Angelique sat down next to Simon with her hot chocolate.

'Do you think you know what you're doing?' she asked.

'Quite clearly I don't. But whenever I used to think I knew what I was doing, subsequent events proved that I *never* knew what I was doing. People who are certain they know what they're doing are very dangerous. I'm not dangerous.'

'You're crazy, Simon. What do you think is going to come of this? Nothing good, you know that.'

Simon put his mug down and got up to adjust the blanket around Sam. He knelt on the floor and made sure no part of him was uncovered below his chin.

'Angel, no doubt you're probably right, but like the guy said when he jumped off the Rialto building and got to the twentieth floor: so far so good.'

She smiled weakly. Empson sighed. The television showed a police car in a narrow alley. She looked around the room, for so long a cave of inert chaos, now sparely littered with several neat piles of mess, newspapers and books mostly. Her gaze came to rest on Simon with your sleeping son beside him.

'I want you to know—I love you, Simon. I know everything you've said. I know I am...*forewarned*, as you say, but please know it—remember it, no matter what—I love you even though... I know you're crazy. You're the softest man I've ever met. Too soft. *He's* smarter than you,' she said pointing to Sam, still sleeping.

'He may well prove to be smarter than me. He's already a lot wiser.'

'They're going to find him here. You know they will. They'll figure it out,' she said.

'They'll find him happy and safe if they do, with a chocolate moustache.'

'What do you mean *if*? They *will* find him, it's just a question of how soon. They'll both be frantic. It's not going to take them long.'

She got up and went over to him on the floor. He held her in his arms and they looked at your beautiful son gently breathing half into the pillow.

'When will they find him? They won't be that fast,' he said in a low voice. 'The emotions are not skilled workers.'

She repeated the line to herself after a moment's thought.

'Is it Eliot?' she asked. He shook his head.

'Dylan Thomas? No. Yeats, isn't it?'

'No,' he answered, running his fingers through her hair.

'Who wrote that, *The emotions are not skilled workers*?' She put her head in his lap.

'That's a story in itself, Angel.'

He looked down at the part of her face that was exposed.

'What is it?' She was crying silently. He held her closer against his chest. She took deep breaths, trying to get the air past her throat. Empson and Sam exhaled almost in time with each other. They were all of them on the floor in one corner of the room. The television showed the flag of an oil company blowing in the wind. This is how it all looked and this is what you would have heard in the last moment before the door was kicked in. They pushed it in with one kick, although it was locked. There were three of them, uniformed police, two men and a woman, with a warrant for Simon's arrest. They didn't need to kick the door in. He would have opened it. By the time they got to Simon's place you would have been well and truly contacted. Your husband would have reached you by then. How did you feel? I have never been paged at an airport. You know how it is. It's always someone else.

So this is where we are now—all of us *separate* people. William has been calling me but I haven't returned the calls. He hasn't gone to Simon yet. He's got to blame somebody before he does anything else. First things first. He's got me in his sights. And why not? He's got to get something out of this. I think he knows he can't get his money back. I don't have it. We drank it at the Esplanade. He probably wants me deregistered, if not arrested.

It had occurred to me that it would not be possible for Simon to get you out of his system without actually seeing you again, without establishing contact. My thinking was, with respect, that you could not help but disappoint him now. This would have hurt him very much in the short run. It might even have driven him back to his darkened bedroom. But after a while his despair over the reality of you, as opposed to the idealization of you, would evaporate, and with it a lot of other things. I told him this. I think he was coming around. I think it could have helped him. You could have—just by being the person you are, with whatever fears and weaknesses you have, just like the rest of us. You could have told him you remember it all fondly—at least that. It would not have taken much. He nearly called you several times. You weren't to know. He nearly called you last night.

They really do get one phone call, like on television or in the movies. He was scared. He called me from the police station yesterday. He said he didn't know whether they were going to keep him in the lock-up or send him to the remand centre so I don't know exactly where he is today. I don't know how they knew where to find Sam so quickly either. There's a lot I don't know—but I do know that your son has never been in less danger. And I also know that you're the only one who can help Simon now. You're the only one that can save him, Simon told me as much just now on the phone. He said you've got to tell them that he is your lover, that he had your permission to take Sam. That is the only course that can save him. Why would you want to save him? Because he's ill and because he's never stopped loving you. Among other things, he is ill *because* he's never stopped loving you. I'm not saying you owe him anything beyond that which we all owe each other but—when we are all finished being told that everyone out there must take responsibility for themselves—what's it like when we get home? What's it like inside? He had been cast out and he had never done anything wrong, till now. You think it would be the end of everything to help him like this but it would only be the end of some things. What are you going to do? You're involved. You are finally involved, after all these years, and there is no way out of it. There are a few people you can help now. I nearly called you last night. □

Royal Festival Hall
Queen Elizabeth Hall
Purcell Room

Poetry International 2000

6-14 October
www.poetryinternational.co.uk

Fleur Adcock
Yehuda Amichai
John Ashbery
Yves Bonnefoy
Volker Braun
Jean 'Binta' Breeze
Ciaran Carson
Billy Collins
Michael Donaghy
Carol Ann Duffy
UA Fanthorpe
James Fenton
Tua Forsström
Lorna Goodison
Lavinia Greenlaw
Marilyn Hacker

Clive James
Kathleen Jamie
Jackie Kay
Liz Lochhead
Christopher Logue
Michael Longley
Roddy Lumsden
Claire Malroux
Jamie McKendrick
Anthony Minghella
Adrian Mitchell
Edwin Morgan
Andrew Motion
Les Murray
Bernard O'Donoghue

Sharon Olds
Don Paterson
Brian Patten
Tom Phillips
Dorothy Porter
Dimitri Prigov
WG Sebald
Jo Shapcott
Penelope Shuttle
Matthew Sweeney
Haris Vlavianos
Daniel Weissbort
Hugo Williams
Dane Zajc

Box office 020 7960 4242
Book online www.sbc.org.uk

For a free programme email
Literature&Talks@rfh.org.uk
or call 020 7921 0971

Supported by
Royal Mail

BookBrain.co.uk

Funded by
THE ARTS COUNCIL OF ENGLAND

sbc

The first major biography of an anti-colonial icon: a thoughtful,
critical and moving account of Fanon's life and violent times.

FRANTZ FANON

A LIFE I DAVID MACEY

Published November £25 Hardback

Granta Books

Order now on **www.granta.com** or on
Freecall 0500 004 033 to receive a 30% discount

SHRINKS
Edmund White

The blessings of family life in the USA, c.1955

HULTON GETTY

In the mid-1950s, when I was fourteen or fifteen, I told my mother I was homosexual: that was the word, back then, homosexual, in its full satanic majesty, cloaked in ether fumes, a combination of evil and sickness.

Of course I'd learned the word from her. She was a psychologist. Throughout my early childhood, she'd been studying part-time for a master's degree in child psychology. Since I was not only her son but also her best friend, she confided everything she was learning about me—her live-in guinea pig—to me. For instance, I was enrolled in an 'experimental' kindergarten run by Dr Arlett, my mother's mentor in the department of child psychology at the University of Cincinnati. Dr Arlett, however, decided after just one semester that I was 'too altruistic' to continue in the school. I was dismissed. I suspect that she meant I was weirdly responsive to the moods of the female teachers-in-training, for whom I manifested a sugary, fake concern, just as I'd learned to do with my mother. No doubt I was judged to be an unhealthy influence on the other kids. But my mother, who chose against all evidence to interpret my vices as virtues, my defeats as victories, decided that what Dr Arlett really meant was that I was too advanced spiritually, too mature, to hang back in the shallows with my coevals.

My reward was a return to loneliness. We lived at the end of a lane in a small, rented mock-Tudor house. My older sister, who disliked me, was attending Miss Daugherty's School for Girls; she sometimes brought friends home, but she didn't let them play with me. I played alone—or talked to my mother when she wasn't at school or studying.

My mother wrote her master's thesis on the religious experiences of children. She herself was intensely spiritual; at least she spoke often of her inner life and said she prayed, though I never saw her pray. She'd been brought up a Baptist in Texas, but she'd converted to Christian Science, initially to please my father but later out of a genuine affinity with the thinking of Mary Baker Eddy. Like Mrs Eddy, my mother denied the existence of evil (except as it was embodied by my father's mistress). Like Mrs Eddy, my mother believed in thinking mightily positive thoughts. She had a pantheistic, nearly Hindu conviction that every living creature was sacred and formed a wave cresting out of, then dissolving back into, Universal Mind. When my mother was distraught, which occurred on a daily basis, she found consolation in bourbon and Eddy's *Science and Health with Key to the Scriptures*. Eddy's hostility to medicine my mother dismissed as an ideal beyond our grasp given our current state of imperfect evolution.

My mother detected signs in me of a great soul and highly advanced spirituality.

When I was seven my parents divorced. My mother had ordered my father to choose between her and his mistress (who doubled as his secretary); he chose the mistress. My mother was devastated. Although she had a giant capacity for reinterpreting every loss as a gain, even she couldn't find something positive in divorce.

It was a good thing she'd taken that degree in psychology because now, at age forty-five, she had to go to work to supplement her meagre alimony. She laboured long hours for low pay as a state psychologist in Illinois and Texas, and later in Illinois again, administering IQ tests to hundreds of grade school students and even 'projective' tests (the Rorschach, the House-Tree-Person) to children suspected of being 'disturbed'.

True to my status as guinea pig, I was tested frequently. She who was so often overwrought at home, given to rages or fits of weeping, would become strangely calm and professional when administering a test. Her hands would make smoothing gestures, as though the lamp-lit table between us were that very sea of mind that needed to be stilled back into universality. Her voice was lowered and given a story-telling sweetness ('Now, Eddie, could you tell me everything you see in this ink blot?'). I, too, was transformed when tested, but toward anxiety, since a psychological test was like an X-ray or a blood test, likely to reveal a lurking disease: hostility, perversion or craziness or, even worse, a low intelligence.

She wrote down everything I saw in each plate and exactly where in each ink blot I detected a tomb or a diamond. She then went off for a few hours and consulted her thick dark-blue-bound manual of interpretation with its burgundy label. I was afraid of the results, as absolute and inarguable in their objectivity as they were mysterious in their encoding and decoding.

My mother was nearly gleeful when she told me I was a 'borderline psychotic' with 'strong schizophrenic tendencies'. Apparently the most telling sign of my insanity was my failure to see anything human in the ink blots. All I saw were jewels and headstones.

What remained unclear was whether I was inevitably sliding over the frontier toward full-blown psychosis or whether the process was reversible. Did the Rorschach lay bare my essence or my becoming? Was I becoming better or worse?

There was nothing consistent or logical about my mother's thinking. She found me wise to the point of genius and often said she wanted to write a book about raising the Exceptional Child ('Let him take the lead—he will teach you what he wants to learn'). I was, she suggested, possessed of almost divine understanding and profundity. But then (and here, on alternating days, she could get on a similar roll) I was also half-crazy, dangerously unbalanced, suspiciously apt at imitating wisdom and understanding, a flatterer, a robot programmed to resemble a thinking, feeling human being.

In fourth grade, no matter how mentally ill I might have been, I continued to get good grades in every subject except arithmetic (we moved too often for me to be able to follow a coherent sequence of math courses). Perhaps the only public sign of craziness was my obsession with playing a king on stage. In third grade, in Dallas, I wrote and starred in *The Blue Bird*, a script I'd plagiarized from Molnár (my first piece of writing was a plagiarism). My mother rented a gold, bejewelled crown, a blue velvet doublet and white knee breeches from a costume shop.

When I was eleven, we lived for a year in the Faust Hotel in Rockford, Illinois, a grim industrial town where my mother worked as a state psychologist. For some reason she decided that the local state schools were good enough for my sister but not for me, a decision my sister bitterly resented. I was sent to Keith Country Day, where the classes were small—no more than fourteen students. One of my friends was Arnold Rheingold, perhaps the first Jew I'd ever met. His father was a psychiatrist. When I dined at Arnold's house I was impressed by the deference paid to their son by his parents just because he was a boy. And I was awed by the father, the first man I'd ever met who read books and sought out new ideas rather than preaching familiar ones. That he had migraines and had to nurse them in his darkened study after dinner struck me as the possible and certainly glamorous price he had to pay for living the life of the mind.

I wrote a play, *The Death of Hector*, in which I starred as the tragic hero; my best friend, a handsome jock, played the nearly silent, sadistic role of Achilles, who killed me and then, in a radical departure from classical tradition, mourned me with noisy, wordless wailing before, rather illogically, setting off to desecrate my corpse by dragging it around the walls of Troy behind his chariot (offstage action seen and reported by a leaden, talentless Chorus, a fat girl I knew and liked). It was a headily passionate range of emotions to assign to my blond, vacant-eyed Achilles who, in real life, seemed mainly baffled by me to the point of sheepishness; I could make him hang his beautiful, blond head and blush.

When I played with my two girl cousins in Texas or later with friends in Ohio or Illinois, I always had a single game in mind: king and slave. Like Jean Genet's lunatic servants in *The Maids*, I didn't much care which role I played so long as the drama of domination and submission got properly performed. There wasn't much to this pathetically static 'game' beyond procession and coronation for the king and bowing or even kneeling for the slaves. When my cousins Sue and Jean started giggling and became distracted, I re-dubbed them queens and ordered them to make the solemn entrance. I bowed obsequiously with a grand salaam designed as a silent reproach to their insufficiently serious servitude. I hoped they'd catch on, though they could never quite grasp the grandeur of the ceremony.

In sixth grade in Evanston, Illinois, I played a weak, nearly hysterical King Charles to a tomboyish St Joan and that summer, at Camp Towering Pines near Racine, Wisconsin, I wrote and starred in my version of *Boris Godunov*; I was imperially robed in the stiff red wool blanket from the Hudson Bay Company that my mother had bought to keep me warm on chilly northern summer nights. I conflated the coronation scene and the mad scene.

The formula emerges: I wanted to be a king, but I also needed to die, go mad or undergo humiliation for my arrogance, a scenario that resembled the plots of queer novels of the 1950s, though I'd never read one. (The only homosexual narrative I knew of was the life of Nijinsky which, to be sure, had devolved into madness and silence. My mother, who perhaps both feared and hoped for a strange destiny for me, had given me this biography when I was still a boy of nine or ten.)

That same summer at camp, the summer of *Boris Godunov,* I had my first sexual experience or rather tasted the first penis that wasn't my own. I put the matter so precisely because before then I'd wrestled for hours and hours with friends in Evanston, Illinois, where we lived when I was eleven and twelve, and while alone I'd actually managed to lick my own penis by lying nude on my back and throwing my legs over my head in the first stage of a backward somersault. By craning my neck upwards off the mattress and pulling my pelvis down with my hands I could just graze the glans with the tip of my tongue and catch one clear drop of liquid as sticky if not as sweet as the honey I liked to work up the honeysuckle blossom. Once I'd drunk long and hard at a big, smelly, teenage cock there at camp I no longer needed to tread the boards as a suicidal monarch. I stopped conspiring to bend everyone to my need to rule or serve; I discovered that I was happiest while serving, and serving under someone else's sceptre.

Happy? That's not the word.

Predestined and agonized. Abject. Bewitched. Perhaps that's closer.

I'd read in one of my mother's psychological manuals a long entry on homosexuality that I could scarcely understand. But I did take in that whereas adult homosexuality was an entrenched ego disorder caused by an unresolved Oedipus Complex and resulting in secondary narcissistic gains that were especially hard to uproot, in every early adolescence the individual, the *boy,* passes through a homosexual *stage* that is perfectly normal, a brief swirl around the Scylla of orality and the Charybdis of anality before surging to the sunny open seas of mature genitality. I could only hope that I was just passing through a phase.

I was afire with sexual longing and looked for partners everywhere. The same maniacal energy I'd devoted to playing a succession of dying kings right out of *The Golden Bough* I now consecrated to scoring. I haunted the toilets at the Howard Street elevated station, the one that marked the frontier between Chicago and Evanston. A few men let me touch them and twice a man drove me in a car full of children's toys down to the beach. I wasn't ugly but I *was* jailbait and life even for a part-time homosexual was hard enough during the Eisenhower years.

When I was fourteen my mother announced that she was thinking of marrying Mr Hamilton, a Chicago newspaperman. I had had sex with Mr Hamilton's twenty-year-old son Bob who had pretended he drank too much one night and was forced to stay over—in my room. Now with Wilde-like fatality I said, 'Then it will have to be a double wedding.'

Because of this quip my mother called up Bob Hamilton in a cold fury and denounced him—and the marriage to Mr Hamilton never came to anything.

Betraying my partners was something I felt drawn to. At Camp Towering Pines I'd let an older boy 'hypnotize' me and press my willing mouth down on his penis, but I couldn't resist informing my mother, nominally the camp psychologist, of what he'd 'attempted'. Did I hope to shift the blame for unhealthy desires and practices on to someone else? Or did I merely hope to stir up trouble, create a drama? Or was I trying to draw my mother's attention to behaviour I was horrified by the moment I'd ejaculated? Or was I angry with these young men for not loving me as much as they desired me? If they had loved me they would have attempted to run away with me, wouldn't they? Love was what I wanted, though I don't think I could have been loved any more than a porcupine can be embraced.

My mother sent me to a Freudian psychiatrist in Evanston for an evaluation. I had just read Oscar Wilde and was determined to be as brittle and brilliant as his characters. I sat on the edge of my chair, hectic red flowers blowing in my cheeks, and rattled on and on about my condition, my illness, which I was no more able to defend than Wilde could. All he or I had to offer was defiance and a dandified insolence. If we were pinned down, by a prosecutor or an examining psychiatrist, what could we say—that homosexuality was defensible? Neither of us was that clever; no one could escape his particular moment in history, especially since I, as an American living during the tranquillized 1950s, scarcely believed in history at all. For us nature had replaced history. What I was doing was against nature, anti-physical.

The psychiatrist told my mother that I was 'unsalvageable'. That I should be locked up and the key thrown away. My mother promptly reported this harsh, scary judgement to me, and to my father, though I begged her not to. Of course neither she nor I was capable of dismissing this diagnosis as a dangerously narrow-minded prejudice held by a banal little suburbanite in a brown suit. No, it came from a doctor and was as unquestionable as a diagnosis of diabetes or cancer. The doctor's level of sophistication or humanity was irrelevant.

My mother had a younger friend named Johanna Tabin who had studied with Anna Freud in London and was now practising as a psychoanalyst in Glencoe. We occasionally spent social evenings with her and her husband and two sons in their big suburban house or at our much smaller apartment beside the lake. They represented everything we aspired to—wealth and calm intelligence and respectability, social and professional importance and family love. Johanna's husband, Julius, had been a nuclear physicist and had become a patent lawyer for nuclear inventions.

Johanna's sons, a few years younger than my sister and I, were treated with elaborate respect by their mother. Whenever they would ask her a question or say something to her, she would immediately turn her attention to them, even if she was on the phone listening to my mother. This indulgence was very unhealthy, my mother decided, and she resented it as much as she disapproved of it. But Johanna was intractable. The second there was a treble squeak in the background, she'd put the receiver aside and say, 'Yes, darling, I'm listening. What is it, darling?' She analysed their dreams and games with an equal attentiveness. I remember when Geoffrey, the younger son, kept singing a song he'd made up about a tumbleweed, she'd decided that he was the little tumbleweed who makes the big horse, his father, rear back in fright—a perfectly normal desire to intimidate the patriarch, she said with a happy smile.

Rather mournfully I thought my mother was too self-absorbed

ever to have interpreted my behaviour so ingeniously, and if she'd managed to detect a sign of defiance in me she would have squelched it rather than nourished it. Now I can see that she was all alone in the world, poor and overworked and profoundly wounded by my father's rejection. Even though she called us the Three Musketeers, we were in fact painfully divided each from the other. My sister was convinced that our mother and I were shamefully bizarre. She herself was unpopular and withdrawn. I was obviously a freak. Only when my mother was administering a test or diagnosing a child did she feel calm and whole and professional.

She must have been jealous of Johanna's happy marriage, because she was always picking up hints of its imminent collapse. 'Poor Johanna,' she'd say. 'The poor little thing is terribly neglected by Julius. It's only a matter of days before he abandons her.'

Despite these dire predictions, Johanna's marriage continued to flourish stubbornly, her career to become more and more distinguished, her husband more and more successful, her sons increasingly brilliant. 'Poor Johanna,' Mother would croon. 'She buries herself in her work because she's so unhappy in her marriage.'

The only thing that amazed me was that Johanna remained so attached to my mother. Did my mother possess undetectable attractions? In a similar way I'd been disconcerted when I'd read my mother's thesis on the religious career of children and discovered in it so many big words I didn't know and had never heard my mother pronounce.

One evening at Johanna's, I talked to her about my homosexuality. I don't remember how the subject came up. Had my mother already set it up? All I remember was that we were seated briefly on the glassed-in sun porch just two steps down from the more brightly lit living room. Dinner was over. Johanna kept casting sunny smiles back at her boys, who were out of earshot and racing around the couch, but when she returned her attention to me she lowered her big sad eyes behind the pale, blue-rimmed glasses and a delicate frown-line was traced across her pure brow. She wore no make-up beyond a faintly pink lipstick. She didn't really follow fashion; she was content to appear neat, of which my mother, who got herself up as elaborately as an *onnagata* in the Kabuki, thoroughly disapproved. Johanna scrunched forward and rested her chin on her palm. She was as lithe as a girl. She had beautiful teeth (her mother was a dentist).

'I'm very worried,' I said. 'I don't seem to be moving out of the normal homosexual stage of development.' I was fifteen.

'Yes, dear,' she said, 'I can feel you're very concerned.' She had a way of reflecting through re-statement what her interlocutor had just said, a technique ascribed to Carl Rogers that my mother found insulting and maddeningly condescending but that I liked because it seemed so focused and non-judgemental. Johanna's life was so manifestly a success that I was happy to bask for an instant in her attention.

'Do you think I should see a therapist?'

She studied my face with her huge, sympathetic eyes and said nothing.

'Could I see you?' I asked. I knew that she received many patients a day in the soundproof office in the basement. My mother had also told me that Johanna had cured a lesbian who was now happily married to a New York writer.

'Have you,' she asked with a tentativeness that suggested a sensitivity in me I was far from enjoying, 'Have you, dear, ever actually...'

'Had sex?' I asked brightly. 'Oh, yes, many times.' For an instant I was proud of my experience until I saw my admission shocked and saddened her.

'I had no idea,' she said, shaking her head as if it suddenly weighed much much more, 'that you'd actually gone on to act out, to act on your impulses.' She looked mournful. Whereas Christianity had taught me that the thought was as bad as the deed, Johanna seemed to think acting out was much worse than merely desiring. By realizing my fantasies I'd—what? Made them harder to root out? Coarsened myself?

'You thought I just had a few fantasies?' I was almost insulted, certainly amused, although I could also see I should downplay the extent of my debauchery if I didn't want to break her heart.

She peered deeply into my eyes, perhaps searching for some reassuring signs of remorse or the pain I must undoubtedly be feeling. She shook herself free of her thoughts and said, 'I'm afraid I can't see you as a patient, dear, since we're all such friends. But I can recommend someone who...' Here she put her words together carefully, '...who might help you find your way toward a life that would fully express you, who you really are.'

With a brilliant flash of lightning over the dark landscape of my personality, I suddenly saw that homosexuality, far from being saturnine or interestingly artistic, was in fact a lack, an emptiness, a deformity preventing a full and happy development.

Already I hoped to be a writer but, as I was beginning to realize, successful writing entailed a grasp of universal values and eternal truths, which were necessarily heterosexual. Foolishly I had imagined I could transform the dross of homosexuality into the gold of art, but now I saw I could never be a great artist if I remained ignorant of the classical verities of marriage and child-rearing, adultery and divorce. But if psychoanalysis could convert me into a heterosexual, might it not at the same time ablate the very neurosis that made me want to write? Should I tamper with my neurosis?

I began to read books about psychoanalysis—Freud himself, especially the *Introduction to Psychoanalysis* and *The Interpretation of Dreams*, but also the softer, less pessimistic American adaptations of his thought by Erich Fromm. I learned that making art was an act of neurotic compensation and sublimation—although Theodor Reik made his unorthodox mark by arguing that art was the highest form of mental health. I couldn't find much about homosexuality in any book, but enough to know it was sterile, inauthentic, endlessly repetitious and infantile.

Somewhere I came across the theory that homosexuality was caused by an absent father and a suffocating mother. Perhaps my mother herself had been the one to suggest that my father's absence had queered me, for she was always eager to work out the multiple ways in which his desertion had harmed us all. To bring me the benefits of a suitable father figure she was eager to remarry—but no man was willing to take on the burden. I was sent to live with my father for one year back in Cincinnati, but he ignored me—and I had sex on a regular basis with the neighbour boy.

When I realized that I wasn't getting any better, that I was just as obsessed with men as ever, I begged my parents to enrol me in a boys' boarding school. My reasoning was that if I was homosexual because I was suffocated by my mother and deprived of male models, then a tough, almost military school would be sure to shape me up. Reluctantly they complied, but after a year away from home, when I realized I was more besotted with boys than previously, I asked my father to send me to a shrink.

I had one all picked out. Half the students at my school, Cranbrook, outside Detroit, Michigan, were day boys and half were boarders. We boarding students were occasionally allowed to spend a weekend with a day boy's family if we got written permission from our parents. I was invited home by Stephen Schwartz. His family played classical music (the Mozart Clarinet Concerto, Bach's cantatas) on a stereo that was piped into every room of the compact wood house which, to my eyes, looked half-Hopi, half-Japanese. He was a shaggy-haired mouth-breather, arty and intelligent, who was neither scandalized by nor interested in my perversion. He liked to write and knew a lot about jazz; he was neither a grade-grubber nor an athlete, the only two admissible types at Cranbrook. He had a crazy sense of humour. All the grim striving of his fellow students and the severity of our anti-intellectual, martinet masters only made him laugh. We worked together on the student literary magazine, to which he contributed satires.

His father was a psychiatrist who recommended me to James Clark Moloney. I made an appointment with Moloney and my mother wrote a note granting me permission to take a taxi to his office in a Detroit suburb. I wrote about Moloney in *A Boy's Own Story*, published in 1982, more than two decades after the event, though I was still angry with him.

My father was reluctant to take on the expense of regular psychiatric fees, which amounted to fifty dollars an hour at a time when a good dinner at a restaurant cost five dollars, for instance, and a general practitioner charged only ten dollars a visit. Someone wealthy at that time earned seventy or eighty thousand dollars a year. Dr Moloney wanted to see me three times a week, which came to six hundred dollars a month, a sum that exceeded my mother's alimony by a hundred dollars.

My father also objected just as strenuously to the whole notion of psychoanalysis, which he saw as a form of soak-the-rich charlatanism, an ineffectual and dangerously self-indulgent stewing over problems engendered by idleness and entrenched through the principle of the more you scratch the more it itches. As a good businessman he made me put all my arguments for psychoanalysis in clear, terse letters, which he countered in short missives printed in his neat hand on stationery that read 'From the desk of E. V. White.' He addressed me as 'Dear Ed V.,' (I was Edmund Valentine White III, a dynastic custom typical of even quite ordinary families in the South). I wrote to him explicitly about my unsuccessful struggle against homosexuality and about the smothering-mother, absent-father aetiology, intended as an indirect reproach against him. I knew the divorce was a sore spot, since he considered it a blot on his rectitude, not because he loved my mother (he didn't) but because he believed divorce under any circumstances was morally reprehensible. He was privately an eccentric, even violent man, but he could tolerate no demerit on his public record. He wanted to appear, if not actually be, irreproachable.

I had no idea what to expect at Dr Moloney's, but I certainly thought he'd be a small man with a varnished pate and an inky comb-over, many books (some in German) and in his waiting room the sorry smell of old tobacco. I was in no way prepared for the cages of shrieking birds, the Papuan deities and, in the garden as seen through a plate-glass window, a gilt statue of a meditating *bodhisattva*. I fancied myself a Buddhist but of the austere Theravada sort, and I sniffed at Dr Moloney's idolatry, even though I'd come here precisely because I sought a compassionate intercessor, a *bodhisattva* of my own.

He didn't have a secretary. Another patient let me in and we sat uncomfortably staring at each other, rigid with sibling rivalry. At last Moloney stumbled out, escorting a sniffing little woman. He appeared surprised that he'd double-booked his next hour.

'Don't worry,' he said to me. 'There are enough teats to suckle the whole litter.' He chuckled, revealing neatly spaced teeth in a handsome red face. He cocked an eye at me.

He had a leonine mane of white hair, a bulbous nose with a sore on one side, close to the tip, which he kept vaguely clawing at, as an old dog will half-heartedly try to free itself of its collar. He wore sandals on big, yellow-nailed feet, shapeless trousers held up with a rope, a short-sleeved Hawaiian shirt. He licked his lips constantly. He made me feel very prim, especially since I'd put on my favourite Brooks Brothers sack suit with the brown and black twill. I didn't like the idea that he'd already decided I was a famished pup before I'd said even a word.

He chose to see the other patient first, though not for a full hour, he explained, but more for a patch-up. If I sat in the inner waiting room I could hear the drone of the patient's voice and the grunt of the doctor's. Not their words, just the rhythm and intonation of their voices, but the mere possibility of eavesdropping frightened and attracted me.

Moloney had but one master theory and he proposed it to everyone as an answer to every ill. He believed in the introjected mother. Every infant has the right to expect and enjoy unconditional love from his mother, at full throttle and all the time. Modern American women, however, are deformed by societal inhibitions and their own deprivations as children. They are incapable of giving complete, nourishing love; when I told Dr Moloney that my mother hadn't breastfed me because she had inverted nipples, he slapped his knees, let out a great cry and leaped to his feet. 'You see!'

The emotionally starved, alienated child decides to mother himself. The faint, elusive image of his mother's face and warmth he incorporates into his inner pantheon. Now he is no longer dependent on her vagaries, caprices and eclipses. Now he can beam her up whenever he needs her. If he sucks his thumb he is nursing himself. He has become a closed circuit—with only one crucial disadvantage: such total independence is virtually synonymous with madness. He has lost all vital connection to the outside world. He's self-sufficient, but at a terrible price. When he thinks he has fallen in love with a real woman, in point of fact all he's done is to project his mother's *imago* on to a neutral screen. He is enamoured of half of his inner cast of characters. Since he's not relating to a real person in all her shifting specificity but instead to the crude, fixed outlines of the introjected mother, he cannot interact with the flesh-and-blood woman. If she should break through his defences by smiling her real smile, breathing her real breath on his cheek, he will panic and break it off. As an infant he learned how dangerous it was to open up to an actual, autonomous Other.

I was taught all this during my very first hour with Dr Moloney—or rather my first ninety minutes, since he was eager to prove to me he was not like one of those goddamn tightass Freudians with their finicky, fucking fifty-minute hours. He also needed to lay out his entire theory during our first encounter so that it could begin to sink in.

As I learned in session after session, Dr Moloney had served in the Pacific as an army doctor. There, in Okinawa, he had observed that infants were fearless and happy because they never left their mother's side; they were carried everywhere, papoose-style, bound to their mother's back, their heads looking out *above* hers—'That way they feel united to her but in charge.' Once I saw an elegant young father on the streets of Birmingham, a baby peering out at the world from his back, and I recognized one of Dr Moloney's Michigan Okinawans.

Moloney gave me his books to read and even one of his manuscripts to improve. 'Don't think I'm a castrating asshole like your father, an anal perfectionist who can't admit that another man can help him. I need all the help I can get.' He loved to insult my parents, whom he'd never met and who were not at all the straw men he'd set up. They were as eccentric as he—impoverished rural Texans unprepared for the world they'd created for themselves by earning money and moving North. Moloney cursed them for being uptight patricians, unfeeling aristocrats, but in fact they were self-made crazy people, all too full of dangerous feelings. I would never sink to the indignity of going into Moloney's backyard and hacking away at the logs he painted with the words 'Mom' and 'Dad'.

Moloney was a warm man, an easy-going Bohemian with ethnographic interests who believed he could give me the unconditional love that he thought I craved and that his version of my mother had denied me. He would often interrupt me to say, 'I love you, goddam it.' His eyes would fill with tears and he'd idly pick at his infected nose, or come at the sore on his forehead from above, fat fingers stretching down, his elbow cocked to the ceiling. But on some days he had to search for my name.

As best I could figure out he'd had a more conventional past, reflected in his first, unimpeachably Freudian book, but now he'd become cracked over the introjected mother and the Okinawan papoose cure. He wore heavy turquoise and silver bracelets, black amulets on his hairy chest, and lived surrounded by bobbing, chiming deities from the Pacific, Asia and Africa (Freud had inaugurated this taste for carved African statues, as photos of his Vienna cabinet revealed).

The other Freudian remnant was the couch. After a few intimidating sessions in a chair I was graduated to the couch, while out of sight behind me, at a desk, Moloney took notes (or wrote something, perhaps one of his pamphlets). I could hear him back there coughing or rummaging around for something or scratching with his pen. More than once I caught him dozing. That he was asleep changed his preceding silence in my eyes from a sharp, therapeutic instrument into an obtuse abnegation. I bored him. This man who claimed to love me was zoning out on me. 'I know what you're thinking!' he shouted. 'You're probably mad as hell. And you have a right to be. You have a right to unqualified love. No time limits, no lapses, eternal, unqualified love. But even Homer nods. The baby squalls, and he's completely in his rights. If I were perfect—and you deserve perfection, it's your birthright—' Here he got confused and ended up scratching his nose.

When Johanna asked me during Christmas vacation how things were going, I said, 'I'm very disappointed. He's a nice man. But he doesn't remember anything about me and each time I mention a friend I have to situate that person all over again.'

'Surely you're exaggerating—'

'Not at all. He's not really interested in the details of my life. Or my life. I don't think he likes men. Or they don't catch his interest. He constantly accuses me of over-intellectualizing, although he's happy enough to exploit my proof-reading skills.'

Over-intellectualizing was considered one of my most serious defences. If I disagreed with one of Moloney's interpretations he'd laugh, show his small white teeth and say, 'If you go on winning every argument this way you'll soon enough lose every chance at happiness. No one around here doubts your intelligence. It's just that I want you to break out of your closed circuit and touch another living human being, goddam it. Come on, take a chance on life—' And here he groped for my name before sketching in a feeble gesture that ended in a shrug. I learned to question all my impulses, to second-guess my motives, to ascribe a devious unconscious purpose to my most unobjectionable actions. If I had a dream about making love to Marilyn Monroe, Moloney would interpret it as a 'flight into health', a ruse I'd invented to throw him off my track by appearing normal, cured. 'In this dream I'm Marilyn Monroe,' he'd say, perfectly seriously. 'Like her I have long hair, a wide mouth, I'm voluptuously put together.'

Now I'd say the worst consequence of my years in psychoanalysis was the way it undermined my instincts. Self-doubt, which is a cousin to self-hatred, became my constant companion. If today I have so few convictions and conceive of myself as merely an anthology of opinions, interchangeable and equally valid, I owe this uncertainty to psychoanalysis. Fiction is my ideal form because a character, even a stand-in for me, occupies a dramatic moment, wants one thing rather than another, serves the master narration. The novel is a contrived simplification of the essay I actually inhabit; it is a story rather than an assertion, a development in time rather than a statement in the eternal present of truth. Fiction suggests that no one is ever disinterested. It does not ask the author to adjudicate among his characters. It is the ultimate arena of situationist ethics.

I saw Moloney three times a week during my last two years at boarding school. I discovered that one of my favourite teachers was also a patient; we met in the waiting room. Though the teacher looked uneasy, as if unmasked, he soon shrugged it off and if one of our appointments happened to coincide with the other he'd drive me in. He was a reserved man, probably not more than six years older than I, twenty-three to my seventeen, but at that age such a gap is unbridgeable. I always wondered what was his 'presenting symptom', but I never found out about anything beyond his inability to 'commit'. He'd broken off several engagements to marry. Problems such as frigidity, however, were never treated as the thing itself; what needed to be treated was some mysterious, underlying neurosis.

I could never get Moloney to concentrate on my homosexuality, for it, too, was just a symptom. 'You'll see, old boy,' he'd assure me, moving heavily but serenely like a shaggy, friendly St Bernard padding in for his daily ration of strokes. 'Once we clear away the psychic underbrush all that will wither away.' He made homosexuality sound like the fate of the state in the Marxist future. He wasn't even very interested in my sexual adventures at school and elsewhere, though he warned me that 'excessive acting out' would make me less sensitive to treatment. Just as the term *over-intellectualizing* called into doubt my mental faculties, so *acting out* suggested that each sexual encounter with another man could be reduced to every other, all of them a childish and annoying, if not very serious, automatism. Nothing could come of acting out beyond a further pointless delay in the treatment process. If I entered into detail about my love for a teacher or my sexual bribery of a football star, he'd wave his hand as if brushing cobwebs out of his face and say, 'Spare me, spare me.' When I asked him if smoking marijuana was dangerous, he assured me it led directly to heroin addiction. He advised me to report a teacher who was turning-on the boys (and who also let me suck his cock). I always regretted squealing on that teacher, though no doubt my penchant toward betraying my sex partners would have sufficed even without Moloney's counsel.

The only moment when Moloney would truly pay attention to me was when I reported a dream to him. To remember a dream I had to write it down right away. On Sundays, when we were allowed to sleep in an extra hour, till eight, I had the greatest likelihood of awakening slowly, not to a bell, and of recalling the last episode or two of a dream.

He was Freudian, I suppose, in believing that a dream was 'the royal road to the unconscious', although he had a different system of interpretation, more Jungian in that it traced the ponderous movements of an endlessly proliferating tribe of archetypes. Now I agree with an Italian doctor friend who ascribes the primacy of dreams in Freud's system to the Viennese habit of eating cheese after dinner. ('Cheese produces excessive neural transmitters; dreams are the downshifting of the brain's gears,' believes my friend the doctor.)

Like Freud, Moloney felt that one of the analyst's main tools is picking through the transference. Freud, however, insists that the patient must know nothing concrete about the analyst, so that it will be clear even to him that he has invented everything and attributed it to the doctor. In the classic Freudian transference, the analysand recreates with his analyst his damaging relationship with his parents; when he recognizes that the doctor has done nothing at all to justify such wrath, resentment or fear, he is forced to admit (and abandon) his habit of endlessly 'projecting' bad motives and harmful feelings on to everyone around him. With Moloney, however, the experiment was compromised because ours wasn't a laboratory-pure isolate. Because he constantly chattered about himself I did know a lot about him, which I had the right to interpret as I saw fit. He might say, 'Stop projecting!' but only his authority lent credibility to such an objection.

He was my first shrink, I had nothing to compare him to and he was my only chance of becoming a heterosexual, of ending the terrible suffering I was enduring as an outcast. He told me so himself; he was certain he was the only qualified doctor around. I contemplated suicide more than once. Never had I met or read anyone who defended homosexuality, although the Kinsey Report had recently done so (I just didn't happen to know anything about it, since copies were kept out of kids' hands).

But even if someone had tried to refute my horror of homosexuality I would have instantly rejected his insinuating proposals, tempting me to settle for second best. I knew that only the most insulting pity and condescension could lead someone to recommend that I surrender to my disease.

Moloney convinced me that I should not go away for school (I had been accepted at Harvard) but should attend a nearby state university so that I could continue my sessions with him. All other psychoanalysts were frauds—money-grubbing impostors or unfeeling, strait-laced Freudians. Only he could help people—that's why he kept taking on more and more patients. He had close to fifty now and was seeing them from six in the morning till midnight, seven days a week. To stay awake he was swallowing handfuls of Dexedrine and then coming down in the evening with constant swigs of bourbon.

I'd drive every week the fifty miles from Ann Arbor into Detroit in a borrowed car. I'd have the eleven p.m. hour, when Moloney was smiley and drunk, then I'd sleep on the analytic couch and awaken him, with great difficulty, for the six a.m. session. I'd have to blast him out of bed by playing his favourite record, 'There Is Nothing Like a Dame.'

His own life was beginning to come apart, he told me. He'd fallen in love with a patient who was seriously ill and he'd left his wife for her. But then, when his wife was diagnosed with a terminal illness, he'd gone back to her. Now his wife was dead and the patient was in a mental hospital.

Moloney seemed more and more disoriented. He was often confused, no longer just the overworked, sometimes indifferent, frequently forgetful doctor but someone obviously lost. He'd aged quickly. He forgot to shave and sometimes he smelled of hangover. His hands trembled and he no longer took notes. His old bravado still hung from him in rags, as if he were a scarecrow in a field the farmer had let go fallow.

I was bitter because I saw I had sacrificed my academic career to him, to the forsaken prospect of being cured. And at the same time I felt a deep affection for him, because he was vulnerable and hurt. I discovered that despite his medical training and his years of psychoanalytic experience, he was sure that there was nothing in a male homosexual that couldn't be straightened out by a good woman—or even just a woman. He introduced me to Suzie, another patient, my first anorexic, a tall redhead who wanted to be a model and who, when periodically hospitalized and force-fed, would run up and down the stairs to wear off the disfiguring ounce she might have regained. She had eyes that crossed interestingly and an overlapping incisor always smeared with lipstick. Her teeth were brown from her obsessional vomiting. She wore such high heels, such chic clothes and so much make-up that she appeared years older—a real lady rather than a companionable girl. Wherever I went with her she threw herself at my male friends; she was what we called a 'nympho'.

During the summer between my freshman and sophomore years at college I saw Johanna. I told her everything. She smiled and said, 'Far be it from me, darling, to criticize someone for being unconventional so long as...' Her voice trailed off strategically.

'As long as he's helping me?' I asked. She bit her lip and nodded sadly, huge eyes trained on mine. 'No, I think it's time I...*terminated.*' I'd found the accurate word.

But when I thought of driving into Birmingham to break off with Moloney, my unconscious invented several excuses. My eyes swelled up—'angio-neurotic oedema' was Moloney's diagnosis over the phone: 'skin rage'. He added, 'The baby is swelling up like a poisonous toad in order to scare off the Good Mother: me, in this case.' My foot became swollen and infected; I was hospitalized in the school infirmary and visited there by the school therapist. I was flunking both chemistry and physics, part of my pre-med preparation, since I'd decided over the summer to become a doctor and eventually a psychoanalyst. The therapist wondered why I'd chosen such a demanding scientific major for which I was so obviously ill suited— and why I was succumbing to so many psychogenic illnesses. I must have revealed that I was disturbed about my sexual orientation, for he said, 'Well, perhaps things like that can't be changed. And perhaps one can learn to live with them quite successfully.'

'I'd never settle for that!' I said angrily. Obviously this guy was homosexual. I wondered if I should seduce him, denounce him or both.

At last I decided I'd never get well until I broke with Moloney. When I limped into his office, I saw that the sore on his nose had become the size of a quarter and he'd let his brows grow so shaggy that they half covered his eyes. Through this white fringe he looked out at me with huge red eyes. For some reason I thought of a white plant feasting on shadow and decay—a mushroom.

'I'm leaving you,' I said, my voice hard and unsteady. 'I can't go on seeing you. It's not working out.' I had prepared many arguments but I didn't need them. Moloney said, 'You're right. I think you're right.'

I was never sure of what became of him. My old teacher, the other patient, said Moloney had given up his practice and moved to Mexico. Suzie, the anorexic, said he'd lost his mind and been confined to an asylum.

After him I had an orthodox Freudian from Vienna who'd renamed herself Alice Chester. At least her name didn't really go with her heavy German accent and her Jewishness; I invented a difficult war for her, possibly a concentration camp. I probably invented her Jewishness as well as her name change. I knew nothing about her except that she was a small, heavy-lidded woman who smiled with an irony that seemed at once exhausted and twinkly, if that's possible. She almost never 'offered an interpretation.' I knew from my reading that a strict Freudian, the sort I'd been longing to see, didn't offer interpretations during the first half-year of treatment. I appreciated her taciturn seriousness as well as her merry little lopsided smile when I cracked a joke.

Although I was analysed by her for two years, she never said much. I longed for a detailed reconstruction of my infancy and childhood, week by week, but she never delivered. Sometimes I feared she didn't really understand English; her constant, ironic smile could just as well have been benign incomprehension or a frightened camouflage of her ignorance. Once, when I was talking about how I 'identified' with Harry Haller, the suicidal hero of Hermann Hesse's *Steppenwolf*, she exhaled smoke, then suddenly lit up with recognition and eagerly exclaimed, *'Ach! Der Steppenwolf!'* She nodded vigorously and smiled hugely. The air was juicy with the explosive German words.

How she must have missed Vienna as she sat there in her tidy little house in the Detroit suburb of Royal Oak, a thousand miles from the nearest cafe. How she must have resented that dim, larval life of Detroit, to which irony or self-consciousness would have seemed as irrelevant and unusable as jalapeños in Krakow. Detroit had known race riots and labour demonstrations and seismic evangelic awakenings but it was hard to picture them while cruising the cold, twilit suburban streets where no one ever walked and the only human contact was the exchange of hostile glances at a stop light on Woodward Avenue; it was a car town. I wondered if Dr Chester knew how to drive.

I sometimes told friends at school that my shrink was a member of 'the original Vienna Circle', as if she'd worked with Freud himself, which was just possible chronologically if she was as old as the century (I had no idea of her age).

Once she said she thought my school friends sounded as if they were self-amused and non-relating—which I instantly repeated with whoops of exaggerated laughter to them. For I'd discovered a few other gay guys in Ann Arbor and I regaled them with stories about my shrink. They'd hold their sides, weep with merriment and shout, *'Ach! Der Steppenwolf!'* We thought we were terminally sophisticated.

The *New Yorker* had made cartoons about shrinks as popular as their cartoons about vagrants. Roland Barthes, I suppose, would have said that the function of such jokes was to domesticate two bits of American weirdness that embarrassed and scared us—an incipient madness, if that meant the inability to live through a contradiction, and extreme poverty, which we preferred to reassign to a kind of droll and desperate dandyism rather than face as proof of that very contradiction, the cruelty of capitalism in a democracy.

Much of the dry-martini gay humour of that period obeyed a similar reflex by laughing at what was most troubling. There was never a gathering that dissolved before one of us felt the other's head for a fever and declared, 'But, my pet, you're not a well woman,' making light of the effeminacy we feared and the mental illness we could not deny. 'We're all sick,' we'd say complacently as we wilted into stylized attitudes of illness. We mocked our low self-esteem without in any way elevating it. If the *New Yorker* never, ever made the slightest allusion to homosexuality, that was because our life was still both invisible and unmentionable or, in any event, too repellent to provide the subject for a cartoon.

W hen I was graduated and moved to New York in 1962 I was too poor to afford a psychoanalyst. I was no longer on my father's payroll. Besides, I was too immersed in Greenwich Village gay life to want to be cured right away. In college I had dated several women but now even that therapeutic measure I put aside...until later. I wanted to sow my wild tares.

Two years later, however, I was back in psychotherapy, this time with Frances Alexander, a PhD psychologist who conducted groups and practised something called 'transactional therapy'. At that time, in 1965, even sophisticates had not yet learned to ridicule 'New Age' or 'California Feel-Good' systems. The Sixties were a magma of political explosion and lifestyle creativity and no one felt obliged to cup such words inside inverted commas. The words didn't feel cheap yet.

I never read the best-selling book on which that system (now forgotten) was based, but apparently it labelled most exchanges between people according to a fairly limited taxonomy of games or transactions. Therapy, as best I could tell from our group sessions, was aimed at unmasking these strategies in order to force the participants to return to (or invent) a sincere, heartfelt communication of feeling. We learned not to play the martyr ('Poor Me!' another client would cry out triumphantly), nor to invoke authority, nor to induce guilt in others, nor to cloak our healthy anger in humble depression ('Let it out, goddam it!'). Freudian psychoanalysis—with its high fees, its glacial slowness, its obsession with childhood sexuality, incest, dreams, the unconscious, the patriarch, the anus, with its arrogant conviction that the patient should be kept ignorant of its methods and theories— was already foundering, challenged by the more democratic group therapy and its principle of every man his own shrink.

And then Stonewall came along, the uprising in Greenwich Village in June 1969, which announced the beginning of gay liberation. The cops raided the bar off Sheridan Square, in the heart of the Village, but for once the gay customers resisted arrest. It was a hot night; Judy Garland had just died and everyone was feeling emotional. With hindsight I can see that everything was in place for just such a revolution in consciousness. Feminism, the sexual revolution and the Vietnam War protests were in full force. It was just a matter of moments before the cards were reshuffled and someone shouted, 'Gay is good,' to make a grand slam with 'Black is beautiful.' Lesbian feminism provided the first and strongest sign of the new homosexual spirit, maybe because every woman could potentially feel the tug of feminism, maybe because women's sexuality was more responsive than men's to politics, the will and the benediction of simple affection.

Not immediately but soon enough Freudian psychology went up in flames and became no more powerful or present than the smell of ashes in a cold fireplace the morning after. Most of the problems Freudianism had addressed were no longer experienced as an individual need to adapt to conventions, but as conventions that needed to adapt to individuals. The various movements of women, blacks and gays redefined personal problems into public campaigns. Everyone asserted his or her rights. In the 1950s people had been ashamed to admit they were inadequate; in the 1960s they became proud to announce they were victims. Psychoanalysis had been addressed to shame culture; identity politics addressed a culture of complaint. Rilke had said, 'You must change yourself!' but now people said, 'Everyone else must change.'

Although a few journalists began to speak of the failure of communism, Marx had won out over Freud—history had replaced nature, the economy, not biology, now appeared to be determinative if not exactly determined, and neuroses pointed to divided class loyalties more often than to a blocked psychosexual development.

In the mid-1970s during an unhappy love affair I sought help from Charles Silverstein, a gay psychotherapist. He was one of the psychologists who'd led the so-called 'nomenclature' battle in the American Psychological Association. A band of gay therapists had convinced the larger organization to reclassify homosexuality as falling within the normal range of behaviour instead of as being an ego disorder. Just by going to him I'd already scrambled all the rules of the game—now I wanted to be a happy gay rather than a rehabilitated homosexual.

Charles was as eccentric as Dr Moloney had been but not at all crazy. Charles was fat and chain-smoked, wore sandals and sloppy clothes—and of course he had the usual carved African deities in his West Side living room. He was pleasant but made no protestations of love. Love was irrelevant, which seemed more honest. I could accept sex for money but not love.

For the first time I'd found a shrink who listened with what I might call a fresh ear. He seemed to have few preconceived ideas. When I complained of low self-esteem, he had me look in a mirror and list all my weak points and strong points; I was shocked to find out the strengths were twice as numerous. Sexual dysfunctions he approached in a straightforward behaviourist fashion—he refused to psychologize them. For the more mysterious regions of the psyche, he traced out surprising new cause-and-effect relationships, tailor-made to me. I'd imagine I'd ended one subject (my father's death) and begun another (writer's block), but he'd show how the first caused the second. He taught me the subtle ways in which internalized homophobia had left its traces all over me, like a lapdog's muddy footprints on clean sheets. He gave a strong impression that he didn't see himself as an authority, much less as a judge, but rather as something like a technician, someone who could put his professional training at my disposal. The possibility of transference was never even discussed.

He was a Gestalt psychologist. I never figured out what that meant except in dream interpretation. Where someone like Alice Chester would interpret the props and personages in a dream as stand-ins for earlier real events and people, Charles Silverstein saw each element in the dream as one part of the personality interacting with every other. He'd invite me to be the sail and the compass, the sun and the shark, and to speak for them. The dialogue felt more complex and representative—even if in the end it was just as arbitrary.

During a weekend group marathon session, Charles asked me to recreate my childhood game of king and slave. I was able to arrange everyone just as I saw fit, bowing as I made my entrance—and then nothing. Nothing. It turned out my fantasy went no further. Once everyone had made an obeisance to me, there was nothing more I required of them. My daydream was incomplete, its gleaming metal cube was empty. Once the combination was entered and the safe opened, there was nothing inside.

Two decades later, in the fall of 1993, I started seeing my last or at least latest shrink. My young French lover, Hubert Sorin, was dying. I found a gay American therapist, Rik Gitlin, who hailed from San Francisco. Although I had been living in Paris for a decade I didn't want a French psychoanalyst. I despised Lacan, a charlatan who counted his money while his patients talked and who invented the twenty-minute 'hour' and felt authorized to reduce it to five minutes if the spirit so moved him, probably so he could cram in an even more lucrative turnover. Lacan had long since been dead but his influence was felt everywhere for typically chauvinistic reasons—he was France's answer to Freud. No matter that he wrote incomprehensible gibberish when he wasn't either spouting dangerous untruths or tricking truisms out in fancy words. (*Entre-deux-morts*, it turns out, is a 'technical term' that refers to the period between someone's death and the extinction of his memory among the living. That's it, folks. *Basta*.)

I wanted to talk to my own kind of funny, disabused American gay man, someone who'd laugh when I laughed and who developed his ideas by moving from anecdote to anecdote, like a long-armed ape brachiating from branch to branch. I knew I'd be going through a lot during and after Hubert's death, and I didn't plan to make the journey alone.

Rik was perfect. He was in his thirties, cute, bright, respectful (I was nearly twice his age). Like me he had a French lover and was willing to compare notes, minor as well as major. He'd come to Paris because he loved a man, not the city, and was far less of an unconditional Francophile than I. He was a compulsive shopper but had a nearly Zen taste for spareness—a paradox that meant he needed lots of storage space. We sat in good chairs and looked at each other; the couch had been relegated to the Freudian attic. He took notes after each session and kept track of my numerous friends, as complicated as those cast lists that used to appear at the beginning of nineteenth-century Russian novels. He was far more a part of fast-lane gay life than Charles had ever been. I may have been a bit past it, but the gay ghetto had been formative for me (its sexual opportunities, shrugging wit, its sketchy history, its alternately glorious and scrappy culture) and I was relieved not to have to explain anything.

Rik was one of the 'What-I'm-hearing-is-a-certain-amount-of-shame' school of therapy in which the psychologist peers through the client's social smiles and ironic demurrals to discern the stark outlines of his real feelings, often the opposite of those he intends to convey. This method depends on sound instincts and nothing else, a nearly canine perception of signals pitched above the ordinary range of human hearing. Rik was gifted with this sort of sensitivity. He was also very companionable.

When I reflect on my life, which has been touched by psychotherapy in every decade, I realize that during my youth Freudianism was my main form of intellectuality, a severe, engrossing discipline too devoid of comforting to serve as a substitute for religion. Freudianism developed in me an interest in the individual and his or her sexual development and a strong sense that the progression from one stage to another could go in only one direction in someone healthy. The 'residue' of this indoctrination was a narrow, normative view of humanity. But when I came to reject Freudianism in my late twenties and thirties, I replaced it with its opposite—an interest in groups rather than individuals, a morality that was situationist rather than absolute, and a rejection of every urge to 'totalize,' if that means to submit experience to one master theory. In my biography of Jean Genet, for instance, I sought to show how he was at once a product of a provincial peasant world—and transcended it. If anyone ever transformed himself radically and repeatedly it was Genet, who went from being a foster kid in a village to criminal to celebrated novelist to avant-garde playwright to political activist on behalf of the Black Panthers and the Palestinians. This career trajectory was paralleled by a psychological evolution nearly as impressive and unpredictable.

Psychoanalysis did leave me with a few beliefs, including the conviction that everyone is worthy of years and years of intense scrutiny—not a bad credo for a novelist. That's it: as a writer I was always competing with Freudianism, and it was no accident that I revered Proust, the supreme psychologist in fiction, someone who was in no way influenced by Freud. I remember that Nabokov (or one of his characters) argues somewhere that Freud thought we admire a woman's hair because we desire her body, whereas the truth is we want to sleep with her because we're so awestruck by her beautiful hair. A novelist can work with Nabokov's insight because it respects the details, the sensuous surface, of experience, but not with Freud's, which is arid and reductive.

I sought out therapy when I was deeply unhappy, driven by desires I wanted to eradicate because I felt they were infantile, grotesque, damaging and isolating. I was never cured, but society changed and redefined homosexuality as an orientation that was acceptable, or nearly so. ☐

THE BIG ISSUE

The new Big Issue

The publishing success of the last decade has entered a new era – The Big Issue has been completely redesigned and is now printed in full colour on glossy paper.

One thing has stayed the same – you'll still find an unrivalled range of campaigning journalism, incisive arts and current affairs coverage and exclusive interviews with celebrities ranging from Naomi Campbell to Mo Mowlam, Reeves and Mortimer to Nicolas Cage. And it's still just £1 – 60 pence of which goes directly to the homeless vendor.

IT DON'T MEAN
A THING
Paul Auster

Antoine de Saint-Exupéry

POPPERFOTO

We used to see him occasionally at the Carlyle Hotel. It would be an exaggeration to call him a friend, but F. was a good acquaintance, and my wife and I always looked forward to his arrival when he called to say that he was coming to town. A daring and prolific French poet, F. was also one of the world's leading authorities on Henri Matisse. So great was his reputation, in fact, that an important French museum asked him to organize a large exhibition of Matisse's work. F. wasn't a professional curator, but he threw himself into the job with enormous energy and skill. The idea was to gather together all of Matisse's paintings from a particular five-year period in the middle of his career. Dozens of canvases were involved, and since they were scattered around in private collections and museums all over the world, it took F. several years to prepare the show. In the end, there was only one work that could not be found—but it was a crucial one, the centrepiece of the entire exhibition. F. had not been able to track down the owner, had no idea where it was, and without that canvas years of travel and meticulous labour would go for nought. For the next six months, he devoted himself exclusively to the search for that one painting, and when he found it, he realized that it had been no more than a few feet away from him the whole time. The owner was a woman who lived in an apartment at the Carlyle Hotel. The Carlyle was F.'s hotel of choice, and he stayed there whenever he was in New York. More than that, the woman's apartment was located directly above the room that F. always reserved for himself—just one floor up. Which meant that every time F. had gone to sleep at the Carlyle Hotel, wondering where the missing painting could be, it had been hanging on a wall directly above his head. Like an image from a dream.

2

I wrote that paragraph last October. A few days later a friend from Boston called to tell me that a poet acquaintance of his was in bad shape. In his mid-sixties now, this man has spent his life in the far reaches of the literary solar system—the single inhabitant of an asteroid that orbits around a tertiary moon of Pluto, visible only through the strongest telescope. I have never met him, but I have read his work, and I have always imagined him living on his small planet like some latter-day Little Prince.

My friend told me that the poet's health was in decline. He was undergoing treatments for his illness, his money was at a low ebb, and he was being threatened with eviction from his apartment. As a way to raise some quick and necessary cash to rescue the poet from his troubles, my friend had come up with the idea of producing a book in his honour. He would solicit contributions from several dozen poets and writers, gather them into an attractive, limited-edition volume, and sell the copies by subscription only. He figured there were enough book collectors in the country to guarantee a handsome profit. Once the money came in, it would all be turned over to the sick and struggling poet.

He asked me if I had a page or two lying around somewhere that I might give him, and I mentioned the little story I had just written about my French friend and the missing painting. I faxed it to him that same morning, and a few hours later he called back to say that he liked the piece and wanted to include it in the book. I was glad to have done my little bit, and then, once the matter had been settled, I promptly forgot all about it.

Two nights ago (January 31, 2000), I was sitting with my twelve-year-old daughter at the dining room table in our house in Brooklyn, helping her with her math homework—a massive list of problems involving negative and positive numbers. My daughter is not terribly interested in math, and once we finished converting the subtractions into additions and the negatives into positives, we started talking about the music recital that had been held at her school several nights before. She had sung 'The First Time Ever I Saw Your Face', the old Roberta Flack number, and now she was longing for another song to begin preparing for the spring recital. After tossing some ideas back and forth, we both decided that she should do something bouncy and uptempo this time, in contrast to the slow and aching ballad she had just performed. Without any warning, she sprang from her chair and began belting out the lyrics of 'It Don't Mean a Thing If It Ain't Got That Swing'. I know that parents tend to exaggerate the talents of their children, but there was no question in my mind that her rendition of that song was remarkable. Dancing and shimmying as the music poured out of her, she took her voice to places it had rarely been before, and because she sensed that herself, could feel the power of her own performance, she immediately launched into it again after she had finished. Then she sang it again. And then again. For fifteen or twenty minutes, the house was filled with increasingly beautiful and ecstatic variations of a single unforgettable phrase: *It don't mean a thing if it ain't got that swing.*

The following afternoon (yesterday), I brought in the mail at around two o'clock. There was a considerable pile of it, the usual mixture of junk and important business. One letter had been sent by a small New York poetry publisher, and I opened that one first. Unexpectedly, it contained the proofs of my contribution to my friend's book. I read through the piece again, making one or two corrections, and then called the copy editor responsible for the production of the book. Her name and number had been provided in a cover letter sent by the publisher, and once we had had our brief chat, I hung up the phone and turned to the rest of my mail. Wedged inside the pages of my daughter's new issue of *Seventeen* magazine, there was a slim white package that had been sent from France. When I turned it over to look at the return address, I saw that it was from F., the same poet whose experience with the missing painting had inspired me to write the short piece I had just read over for the first time since composing it in October. What a coincidence, I thought. My life has been filled with dozens of curious events like this one, and no matter how hard I try, I can't seem to shake free of them. What is it about the world that continues to involve me in such nonsense?

Then I opened the package. There was a thin book of poetry inside—what we would refer to as a chapbook; what the French call a *plaquette*. It was just thirty-two pages long, and it had been printed on fine, elegant paper. As I flipped through it, scanning a phrase here and a phrase there, immediately recognizing the exuberant and frenetic style that characterizes all of F.'s work, a tiny slip of paper fell out of the book and fluttered on to my desk. It was no more than two inches long and half an inch high. I had no idea what it was. I had never encountered a stray slip of paper in a new book before, and unless it was supposed to serve as some kind of rarefied, microscopic bookmark to match the refinement of the book itself, it seemed to have been put in there by mistake. I picked up the errant rectangle from my desk, turned it over, and saw that there was writing on the other side—eleven short words arranged in a single row of type. The poems had been written in French, the book had been printed in France, but the words on the slip of paper that had fallen out of the book were in English. They formed a sentence, and that sentence read: *It don't mean a thing if it ain't got that swing.*

3

Having come this far, I can't resist the temptation to add one more link to this chain of anecdotes. As I was writing the last words of the first paragraph in the second section printed above ('living on his small planet like some latter-day Little Prince'), I was reminded of the fact that *The Little Prince* was written in New York. Few people know this, but after Saint-Exupéry was demobilized following the French defeat in 1940, he came to America, and for a time he lived at 240 Central Park South in Manhattan. It was there that he wrote his celebrated book, the most French of all French children's books. *Le Petit Prince* is required reading for nearly every American high school student of French, and as was the case with so many others before me, it was the first book I happened to read in a language that wasn't English. I went on to read more books in French. Eventually, I translated French books as a way of earning my living as a young man, and at a certain point I lived in France for four years. That was where I first met F. and became familiar with his work. It might be an outlandish statement, but I believe it is safe to say that if I hadn't read *Le Petit Prince* as an adolescent in 1963, I never would have been in a position to receive F.'s book in the mail thirty-seven years later. In saying that, I am also saying that I never would have discovered the mysterious slip of paper bearing the words *It don't mean a thing if it ain't got that swing.*

240 Central Park South is an odd, misshapen building that stands on the corner overlooking Columbus Circle. Construction was completed in 1941, and the first tenants moved in just before Pearl Harbor and America's entrance into the war. I don't know the exact date when Saint-Exupéry took up residence there, but he had to have been among the first people to live in that building. By one of those curious anomalies that mean absolutely nothing, so was my mother. She moved there from Brooklyn with her parents and sister at the age of sixteen, and she did not move out until she married my father five

years later. It was an extraordinary step for the family to take—from Crown Heights to one of the most elegant addresses in Manhattan—and it moves me to think that my mother lived in the same building where Saint-Exupéry wrote *The Little Prince*. If nothing else, I am moved by the fact that she had no idea that the book was being written, no idea who the author was. Nor did she have any knowledge of his death some time later when his plane went down in the last year of the war. Around that same time, my mother fell in love with an aviator. As it happened, he, too, died in that same war.

My grandparents went on living at 240 Central Park South until their deaths (my grandmother in 1968; my grandfather in 1979), and many of my most important childhood memories are situated in their apartment. My mother moved to New Jersey after she married my father, and we changed houses several times during my early years, but the New York apartment was always there, a fixed point in an otherwise unstable universe. It was there that I stood at the window and watched the traffic swirling around the statue of Christopher Columbus. It was there that my grandfather performed his magic tricks for me. It was there that I came to understand that New York was my city.

Just as my mother had done, her sister moved out of the apartment when she married. Not long after that (in the early Fifties), she and her husband moved to Europe, where they lived for the next twelve years. In thinking about the various decisions I have made in my own life, I have no doubt that their example inspired me to move to France when I was in my early twenties. When my aunt and uncle returned to New York, my young cousin was eleven years old. I had met him only once. His parents sent him to school at the French lycée, and because of the incongruities in our respective educations, we wound up reading *Le Petit Prince* at the same time, even though there was a six-year difference in our ages. Back then, neither one of us knew that the book had been written in the same building where our mothers had lived.

After their return from Europe, my cousin and his parents settled into an apartment on the Upper East Side. For the next several years, he had his hair cut every month at the barber shop in the Carlyle Hotel. □

Routledge

castration, carnality, cross-dressing ...
an embarrassment of riches

Carnal Appetites
FoodSexIdentities
Elspeth Probyn

From celebrity chefs to our love/hate relationship with fast food, *Carnal Appetites* charts the explosion of interest in food, shedding light on subjects such as fast food, vegetarianism, food sex, cannibalism, forced feeding and fat politics.

September 2000: 234x156: 176pp
Hb: 0-415-22304-0: **£45.00 US: $75.00**
Pb: 0-415-22305-9: **£12.99 US: $19.99**

Castration
Western Manhood from Jesus to the Posthuman
Gary Taylor

A unique and, er, cutting edge look at the West's fascination with, and misunderstanding of castrated males, taking in the sweep of Western thought on 'the operation'. Essential, if painful, reading.

December 2000: 216x138: 304pp
Hb: 0-415-92785-4: **£15.99 US: $25.00**

Empire of Pleasures
Luxury and Indulgence in the Roman World
Andrew Dalby

Empire of Pleasures presents an evocative and picturesque analysis of the Romans' extraordinary desire for orgies of food and wine and how this quest for the luxurious is woven into the literature, art, language and culture.

September 2000: 234x156: 352pp: 40 b+w photos
Hb: 0-415-18624-2: **£25.00 US: $35.00**

The Changing Room
Sex, Drag and Theatre
Laurence Senelick

The Changing Room traces the origins and variations of theatrical cross-dressing through the ages and across cultures. Lavishly illustrated with unusual and rare pictures, this is the first ever cross-cultural study of theatrical transvestism.

May 2000: 246x189: 560pp: illus. 100 b+w photos
Hb: 0-415-10078-X **£60.00 US: $100.00**
Pb: 0-415-15986-5 **£18.99 US: $29.95**

AVAILABLE FROM ALL GOOD BOOKSHOPS
UK and Europe: to order direct call +44 08700 768853 or email orders@routledge.co.uk
US and Canada: to order direct call 1-800-634-7064 or email cserve@routledge-ny.com
Visit us at www.routledge.com

OBEDIENCE

Ian Parker

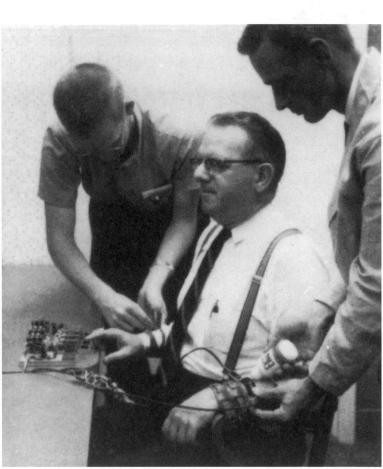

The 'Learner' is strapped into position   STANLEY MILGRAM/PENN STATE

Herbert Winer, who has not tortured anyone for nearly forty years, lives in New Haven, Connecticut, as he did in the early Sixties. He is a likeable, deadpan, Jack Lemmony sort of man of seventy-eight. When we met a little while ago, we took a walk on the Yale campus in New Haven and he led me downstairs into the basement of a neo-Gothic building, Linsly-Chittenden Hall. 'It was cobwebby and dusty then,' he said, 'and it was a real mess, with temporary lights strung up and totally unfinished walls...' We reached the bottom of the stairs and found ourselves in a disappointingly clean, neat, renovated corridor. There was nothing much to see, except a student pinboard carrying notices about eating disorders, God, and rooms to rent. One sheet on the board had a little fringe of tear-off email addresses: PSYCHOLOGY EXPERIMENT, it read; 50 MINUTES ONLY. $8. Mr Winer let out a cry. 'Oh!' he said. 'I don't think that's kept up with inflation. I should call them up and say, "I've been here before—cut it out!"'

Herbert Winer was last in this basement in the summer of 1961, when an observer on the Yale campus might have noticed unusual traffic in and out of Linsly-Chittenden Hall: a stream of New Haven residents, arriving for appointments an hour apart, and leaving, reddened and distraught, their composure lost. The same observer might have heard screams. Here, events were under way that would, in time, acquire a kind of mythical sheen. These screams and troubled looks would claim a place in Holocaust studies, in law and economics journals, in newspaper reports from Rwanda, in late-night debates in pubs and on Internet newsgroups. They would cross into fiction, into pop music and television drama. They would feature on *The Simpsons*. They would get under our skin. Here, a young Yale professor named Stanley Milgram was conducting what would become the most cited, celebrated—and reviled—experiment in the history of social psychology. Here, under the guise of a study into the influence of pain on learning, Professor Milgram was urging volunteers, Herbert Winer included, to give powerful electric shocks to a total stranger, a decent-seeming Irish-American man, who had done them no wrong. And despite the agonized protests of their amiable victim (in fact an actor, who received no electric shocks at all), Milgram's volunteers were doing as they were told. They were

pushing every switch in front of them, right past the one marked
DANGER—SEVERE SHOCK, at which point the screaming man was
falling eerily silent. People were willing to kill their neighbour.
Clearly, then, in that summer nearly forty years ago, in Linsly-
Chittenden Hall, Stanley Milgram was making a profound scientific
discovery; he was unearthing something of lasting, shocking
significance. Either that, or the young Herbert Winer was having his
first experience of performance art.

In the spring of 1961, as Milgram was preparing for the experiment
that would make his name and destroy his reputation, he made the
journey from Yale to New York, met up with a new girlfriend,
Alexandra Menkin, and took a little tour of Greenwich Village art
galleries. 'In one of them,' he wrote to a friend a few days later, in an
unpublished letter held at Yale, 'we met some painters, and we all
decided to applaud people as they passed on the street. It's an
amazingly effective way to draw people into the gallery, for as we
stood there in the doorway applauding various passers-by, they were
impelled to come over and ask why they were the object of so much
enthusiasm. Thereupon we more or less shoved them into the gallery.'

His Greenwich Village girlfriend became his wife, and she now
lives in the same apartment in Riverdale, New York, that she shared
with her husband (who died in 1984), and their two children. There
is a wide view of the Hudson river, and bold modern art bought on
a honeymoon trip to South America. 'He had a lot of energy,'
Alexandra Milgram said. 'A very quick mind, a very good memory.
Go into a museum with him, and you'd think you were just walking
through to get to another part of the building, but he was taking in
everything in the exhibit, every detail, and afterwards he would say,
"Oh, did you notice this, did you notice that?" Where many people
would stay and linger, he very seldom lingered.' Mrs Milgram was
once a dancer, and later trained as a social worker, giving help to
Holocaust survivors. When we met, she had just become a
grandmother for the first time, and she noted approvingly that her
grandson had been given Stanley as a middle name rather than a first
name. 'I think it would be a burden to go around with the name
Stanley Milgram,' she said. 'Too many people know.'

Stanley Milgram was an amateur librettist of musicals, a sketch artist, an amusing and lucid writer, a television producer manqué. He regarded himself as a Renaissance Man. He never closed the door to non-scientific pursuits. Growing up in the Bronx, the son of Jewish immigrants from Eastern Europe, he was active in his high school drama club, but also edited the school science magazine. That set the pattern for life. At university—first at Queens College, New York, then Harvard—he fell away from science to study political science, philosophy, music and art, then turned back again, impatient for 'objective methods'. He finally had a career in a place somewhere between the objective and the subjective, at the ingenious, playful, street-theatre end of social psychology, the place in the American academy most likely to have a call for false beards and hidden microphones. (He was a great admirer of *Candid Camera*, a television show that became a network hit in 1960, around the time he was devising the obedience experiments for Linsly-Chittenden Hall.) He did a kind of science, but on at least one occasion, in Paris, his work—he called it 'experimental invention'—was mistaken for conceptual art. He was perfectly serious, but because in later life he gave close attention to what people do in cities, and what cities do to people, his work sometimes has the flavour of stand-up comedy or *Seinfeld* storylines. (He did research into queue-barging, and how quickly one creates a crowd by pointing into the sky at nothing at all.) He relished scientific stage management—a role that suited a man keen to have an impact on his fellow Americans but not inclined to schmooze. Milgram could be awkward in company—sometimes caustic—but he wanted to be noticed. 'My ideal experiment,' he once wrote, describing work he had done into possible links between television violence and antisocial behaviour, 'would have been to divide the country in half, remove all violence on television west of the Mississippi and include it east of the Mississippi, enforce laws that no one could move from one part of the country to the other, and then see what happens over a five- or ten-year period. It turned out not to be practical, so I had to work with what I had.'

The idea for Milgram's most celebrated experimental invention came to him during the academic year 1959–60. He was at Princeton then, working for his mentor, the psychologist Solomon Asch, whose best-known work, a study of conformity and independence, was first described in 1951 in a paper called 'Effects of Group Pressure upon the Modification and Distortion of Judgments'. In Asch's experiment, a volunteer had been put in a room with people who appeared to be fellow volunteers, but who were in fact Asch's confederates. The group was shown a number of lines drawn on pieces of card and asked to say which two were the same length; the volunteer was asked last. By arrangement, the confederates all gave the wrong answer. Frequently, so did the baffled volunteer. The volunteer gave an answer he could clearly see was wrong.

Milgram once described his revelatory moment to an interviewer from the magazine *Psychology Today*. 'I was trying to think of a way to make Asch's conformity experiment more humanely significant,' he said. 'I was dissatisfied that the test of conformity was judgements about *lines*. I wondered whether groups could pressure a person into performing an act whose human import was more readily apparent, perhaps behaving aggressively toward another person, say by administering increasingly severe shocks to him. But to study the group effect you would also need an experimental control; you'd have to know how the subject performed without any group pressure. At that instant, my thought shifted, zeroing in on this experimental control. Just how far *would* a person go under the experimenter's orders? It was an incandescent moment, the fusion of a general idea on obedience with a specific technical procedure. Within a few minutes, dozens of ideas on relevant variables emerged, and the only problem was to get them all down on paper.'

In the autumn of 1960, Milgram left Princeton to become an assistant professor at Yale, and he took the idea with him. In November of that year, according to papers in the university library, Milgram was claiming on expenses for electrical switches. In the same files there are photocopied passages from *Lord of the Flies*, as well as a note in his handwriting about a railroad accountant he had met called James McDonough: 'This man would be perfect as a victim. He is so mild and submissive.' Also handwritten, there is something that looks like the first draft of a Jerry Lewis script: '75. Ow. 90. Owch. 105. Ow. 110. Ow Hey! This really hurts. 135 OW------150. Ow. That's all!! Get me out of here.'

By the following summer, Milgram was ready to start: he had been awarded a grant of nearly $25,000 from the National Science Foundation, and he had secured the services of a crew-cut first-year graduate student in social psychology called Alan Elms. He had recruited two amateur actors, including the mild and submissive Mr McDonough, and scripts had been written for them. With some flair, Milgram had designed fake electrical equipment, and he had arranged to borrow the sociology department's Interaction Laboratory in Linsly-Chittenden Hall. According to Elms, who now teaches in the psychology department of the University of California, Davis, Milgram also disclosed his intentions to the local police, for fear that someone might tell them about 'this crazy man who was forcing them to do bad things'.

In July 1961 he placed an advertisement in the *New Haven Register*. It read:

> We will pay five hundred New Haven men to help us complete a scientific study of memory and learning...No special training, education, or experience is needed...We want: factory workers, city employees, laborers, barbers, businessmen, clerks, professional people, telephone workers, construction workers, salespeople, white-collar workers, others...All persons must be between the ages of 20 and 50. High school and college students cannot be used... You will be paid $4.00 (plus 50c carfare) as soon as you arrive at the laboratory.

Herbert Winer, then an assistant professor of forestry at Yale, saw the advertisement. 'Four dollars, fifty cents—it attracted me. That's all I can say,' Mr Winer told me on our walk. So he clipped the coupon and was accepted for the experiment, and a few weeks later kept his appointment in the cobwebby basement of Linsly-Chittenden Hall. A young man in a grey laboratory coat, an experimenter, was waiting for him. He checked Mr Winer's name on a list, and shook his hand. 'He was a neutral sort of man,' Winer said. 'He was someone out of a toothpaste ad. You know: "We're just here to keep your teeth clean and free from decay."' Another man, apparently a fellow volunteer, also appeared. He was a big amiable Irish-American man in glasses, eager to please. 'He's smiling. He says, "Hi, good to meet you." He seemed like an ordinary chap like you might encounter on the street.'

Winer saw a big boxy machine on a desk; it had a horizontal line of thirty switches, ranging from fifteen volts to 450 volts. Above the switches was some printed text, reading SLIGHT SHOCK at one end, and DANGER—SEVERE SHOCK towards the other, and beyond that, three crosses, XXX. 'It was a voltage generator,' said Winer. 'Made by this outfit in Waltham, Massachusetts, which was a well-known area of electronics manufacturing. That label was not chosen by accident. It gave verisimilitude to the whole enterprise. You know, if it had been "Little Rock, Arkansas", it wouldn't have had the same weight. But "Waltham, Massachusetts"—that's just where a psychological-shock generator could have been expected to originate.'

Speaking fast, the experimenter told Winer and the other man that they were participating in a study of 'the effects of punishment on learning'. They were asked to choose from two slips of paper, to determine who would play the 'teacher' and who would play the 'learner'. Mr Winer picked 'teacher'. The experimenter then led them into a booth, off the main room, that contained a chair and an electric panel with four buttons. The chair, they were told, was wired to the generator. The 'learner'—willing, smiling—was strapped into the chair, and electrodes were fixed to his wrists, so that he could just reach the line of buttons with his right hand.

The experimenter explained the rules of the experiment. Seated at the generator, in front of a microphone that carried his voice to the man in the booth, Winer was to read a list of word pairs: 'strong arm', 'black curtain' and so on. Then he was to go through the list again, this time giving the learner only the first word from each pair, along with four options to complete the pair: He would say 'strong', and then 'back'; 'arm'; 'branch'; and 'push'. The learner would choose what he thought was the right match by pressing one of the buttons, and Winer would see one of four lights come on in the main room. And now, still using an accelerated, featureless tone, the experimenter explained that if the learner gave a wrong answer, Winer would have to punish him with a jolt of electricity. Starting with fifteen volts, he was to increase the voltage for every mistake. 'The ostensible idea,'

Winer explained, 'was that maybe if he's punished he'll start paying more attention and—damn it—learn better, and stop thinking about next weekend's ball game.' The shocks might be painful, it was explained, but would cause 'no permanent tissue damage'.

Winer was not given a chance to digest what he was hearing. 'At no time during the experiment was there a pause or a break when anything could be raised,' he said. The experimenter led Winer out of the booth back into the main room and they shut the door on the learner. Winer sat in front of the shock generator. The experimenter explained the routine for a wrong answer: the teacher was to say 'wrong', he was to read aloud the voltage about to be given, he was then to administer the punishment and give the correct word pair. 'It is very important,' he said, 'that you follow this procedure exactly.'

The test began, and it was immediately clear that the learner was 'not terribly bright. This guy was a very slow learner.' He made his first error, and Mr Winer gave him fifteen volts.

'Have you ever had a fifteen-volt shock?' Winer asked me. 'You would maybe notice a very mild tingling sensation, but nothing more than that. I've worked with electricity, and I know that fifteen, thirty, sixty volts, you'll notice it, but when you get to over a hundred, it becomes not merely noticeable, but painful.' The learner gave another wrong answer, and another, and Winer gradually began to move from shocks that he knew would cause tingling to those that he knew would cause pain. What, I asked, was he thinking? 'I was just thinking: He didn't get that. So up we go. Hope he does better next time.'

Before long, Winer heard reactions from the learner in the booth, behind the door—first groans, then spoken objections. Winer became uneasy. 'There's such a thing as retrospective wishful thinking,' he told me. 'But I would say it didn't take very many groans and complaints before I started complaining.' But the experimenter dismissed his objections, saying, 'Please continue,' and then, 'The experiment requires that you continue.' Winer was infuriated and his heart began to race, but for the moment he did as he was told.

The voltages increased, and now the learner was crying out in pain and pounding on the walls. At one point, he screamed: 'You know, I've got a bad heart!' And yet the experimental supervisor was unmoved. Winer was faced with a baffling contrast: on one hand, a distraught learner; on the other, an experimenter showing absolute calm. 'There are some details I've forgotten,' Winer told me. 'But I'll never forget that quiet voice: "The conditions of the experiment require that you continue." He was just standing there with his arms folded, so to speak, saying, "I'm sorry, but the conditions of the experiment require that you continue." But the guy's getting hurt! He just kept repeating this mantra about the conditions of the experiment. I think I said, "I've done a few experiments in my day, but this is not fair," something to that effect, but his response was unchanged. Finally I just got wound...like a spring that's wound up to the point where it breaks. My heart rate was way, way up and I was feeling very annoyed and angry. Because I wanted to be obedient. I wanted to be cooperative. I'd forgotten about the four dollars and fifty cents. I knew a little about research and I didn't want to screw things up, but at the same time, neither could I routinely inflict painful punishment... And finally, I just blew up, and said, "I'm sorry, I can't continue."'

The experiment was over. And now came the *Candid Camera* denouement. The learner walked back into the room, smiling, radiating good health and bonhomie, and Winer was told the truth. There had been no electric shocks. The learner had never been hurt; he had been in on the act. Winer learned the details later: the Irish-American man was, in fact, a railroad accountant, earning a dollar-seventy-five an hour to play his slow-witted role. The experimenter was not a lab technician, but a high-school teacher, earning two dollars an hour to wear a grey coat and a blank expression. The word 'teacher' had been written on both slips of paper.

Winer was debriefed, and the emphasis was on soothing words. He was told to have no misgivings about what had just occurred. 'They said, "We appreciate you coming in, here's the four dollars and fifty cents, and we hope that the results of the study will be of interest."' Full disclosure was withheld, for fear of compromising future volunteers. So Winer had to work it out for himself: the experiment, clearly, had not been about 'learning and memory'. It had tested the willingness of one ordinary man to inflict pain on another. It had been an experiment, he realized, about obedience.

Winer cannot remember at which voltage he stopped, and does

not want to remember. 'I've blotted that out of my memory for perfectly good and understandable reasons. If it was a hundred volts, which I kind of doubt, I'd be very gratified. But I suspect it was higher than that. If it was over 150 volts I would be very, very ashamed, and yet it might be.' But he did disobey, eventually, and he has taken quiet strength from the fact for forty years. 'It's not something I pay much attention to. I'm not making big advertising campaigns about my disobedience, but I think it's fair to say that had I not disobeyed I would not have mentioned the subject again.'

His immediate instinct was to confront Stanley Milgram. A few days later, Winer stormed into Milgram's office, and told him—'very plainly'—of his objections. He said he had respect for the ingenuity of the experiment, and he had quickly had a hunch about its political foundations—'Milgram was very Jewish, I was Jewish. We talked about this. There was obviously a motive beyond neutral research'— but he was appalled by Milgram's use of medically unscreened subjects. 'I wasn't shrieking at him, but I was very serious.' Milgram, in reply, said he was sure his subjects would not suffer heart attacks.

Winer's anger was partially fed, he now thinks, by embarrassment that he had been so successfully duped. But he is not surprised by his gullibility. 'Today, people will say, "Surely you weren't foolish enough to get taken in by that?" And the answer to that is, "Go back to the early Sixties, when the credibility index was far higher." I was a credulous naive assistant professor in forestry, and I make no apologies for having been taken in. It's very hard to re-establish the framework of—for want of a better word—innocence which prevailed. This is a psychology experiment! At Yale! My goodness—research! That's very important. Research! That's good with a capital G.'

Today, Winer has respect for the 'dazzling ingenuity' of the experiments, and he keeps up with the Milgram literature, but he is still troubled by the medical risks that he thinks were taken, and by the knowledge that a kind of innocence was lost, a line of trust between academia and the rest of the world. 'There was the time,' Winer told me, 'when Milgram went into a classroom and interrupted it with the news that President Kennedy had just been shot in Dallas. And one of the students stood up and said, "Cut it out, Milgram!" Any other person, he would have got a still, hushed silence.'

Milgram was not fully prepared for his results. In early trial experiments, which he had conducted the previous winter, Yale undergraduates had moved up the shock board with worrying ease, but Milgram thought that the student body must be a skewed sample, and that the clunking prototype 'shock generator' he had used was not fully convincing. He felt sure that, with a broader sampling of subjects drawn from the general New Haven area, and with more sophisticated-looking props, the experiment would show greatly reduced compliance. (When, later, he described his procedure to psychiatrists and asked them to guess at the outcome, they imagined that only a psychopathic fringe would give the highest shock on the shock board.)

Milgram was expecting to have to squeeze compliance out of his subjects. He was then going to take his experiment abroad—to Germany, for example—and make cross-cultural comparisons. But he was overwhelmed by the results in New Haven. Milgram saw compliance, and it was 'terrifying and depressing'. In the standard form of the experiment, where the 'teacher' could hear thumping, but no cries of pain, sixty-five per cent of volunteers continued past the switches on the machine that read DANGER—SEVERE SHOCK. (Beyond this point, the learner made no response at all, as if he had fallen unconscious. Teachers were told to regard no response as a wrong answer, and to continue.) When the experiment was set up so that, like Herbert Winer, the teachers could hear the learners demanding to be set free, sixty-two per cent still obeyed all the way. When the learner was in the same room, forty per cent were still fully compliant.

The assistant in the experiment, Alan Elms, spent much of the summer of 1961 standing behind a one-way mirror with Stanley Milgram, who sometimes brought a film camera. They were, at once, the spectacle's audience and its stage directors. 'It was a combination of keeping an eye on things—we were watching to make sure the experimenter and learner performed their roles right—and at the same time being amazed and at times appalled by a subject's behaviour,' Elms explained when I spoke to him. When the first few subjects went way up the shock board, Elms wondered if they were anomalies. Day after day, others did the same. Many were apparently anguished by their own actions, but they did as they were told. One agitated subject said, as he continued to press the 450 volt switch again and again,

'What if he's dead in there? I don't get no answer, no noise.'

From their hidden vantage point, Elms and Milgram watched with both dismay and amusement. 'We weren't just sitting there and sweating and saying, "Oh my God." We were occasionally laughing at the unexpected behaviour of the subjects, particularly at some of their remarks. There were certainly comments back and forth between us as some subjects went higher and higher on the scale, and at times we were making informal bets as to whether he's going to go all the way.'

Over nine months, Milgram varied the conditions: the learner made more noise or less noise; he had a heart condition or he did not; he was invisible, or visible, to the teacher. At times, other actors became involved, and they urged the teacher on, or urged restraint. The experimenter was put in another room, at the end of a telephone. The two actors, playing victim and experimenter, switched roles, so the victim became a younger, leaner, less lovably Irish figure. After a few months, the experiment changed locations: having started in the grand, Yale-soaked surroundings of the Interaction Laboratory in Linsly-Chittenden Hall, it was forced to move to the under-furnished basement of the same building, where Winer had his appointment (Elms says that Milgram resented the upheaval, but grew to see the experimental advantage of shabbier surroundings). Eventually, the experiment moved to unprepossessing offices above a shop in Bridgeport, close to Yale but with no ostensible connection to the university. Some variations were rejected. According to Elms, Milgram also considered ways to use husband and wife teams as learner and teacher, but knew he might never be forgiven for that.

There were interesting variations in the results. Obedience was lessened by putting teacher and learner close together, and it was lessened—to a modest degree—by non-academic surroundings. The religion and gender of the volunteers seemed insignificant, but the more educated they were, the sooner they disobeyed. And in a curious commentary on the Asch research that had originally inspired Milgram, when a volunteer was placed between two fellow 'teachers' (in fact, actors), he found greater strength to disobey.

But there was nothing encouraging in the experiment's central demonstration. The psychiatrists canvassed by Milgram were entirely wrong: it was not a psychopathic fringe that would push all thirty switches to the end of the board. According to Milgram's experiments, a majority of Americans were willing to do so. In September 1961, just a few months into the experiment, Milgram wrote to his financial backers at the National Science Foundation: 'In a naive moment some time ago,' he told them, 'I once wondered whether in all of the United States a vicious government could find enough moral imbeciles to meet the personnel requirements of a national system of death camps, of the sort that were maintained in Germany. I am now beginning to think that the full complement could be recruited in New Haven.'

Milgram had a world exclusive. He had caught evil on film. He had invented a kind of torture machine. But it was not immediately clear what he should do with his discovery. When he began the study, he had no theory, nor was he planning to test another man's theory. His idea had sprung from contemplation of Solomon Asch, but the 'incandescent' moment at Princeton was a shift away from theory into experimental practice. He had had an idea for an experiment. Now, he was in an odd situation: he had caused something extraordinary to happen, but, technically, his central observation counted for nothing. With no provocation, a New Haven man had hit a fellow citizen with 450 volts. To the general observer, this will come as a surprise, but it is not a social scientific discovery, as Edward E. Jones, the distinguished editor of the *Journal of Personality*, made clear to Milgram when he declined the invitation to publish Milgram's first paper. 'The major problem,' Jones wrote to Milgram, 'is that this is really the report of some pilot research on a method for inducing stress or conflict…your data indicate a kind of triumph of social engineering…we are led to no conclusions about obedience, really, but rather are exhorted to be impressed with the power of your situation as an influence context.' The *Journal of Abnormal and Social Psychology* also rejected the paper on its first submission, calling it a 'demonstration' rather than an experiment.

Milgram had described only one experimental situation. When he resubmitted the paper to the same journal, he now included experimental variables, and it was publishable. In the rewrite, Milgram put the emphasis on the way in which differences in situation had caused differences in degrees of obedience: the closer the learner to the teacher, the greater the disobedience, and so on. These details were later lost as the experiment moved out of social psychology into the larger world. But it could hardly have happened otherwise. The thought that people were zapping each other in a Yale laboratory is bound to be more striking than the thought that zapping occurs a little less often when one is looking one's victim in the eye. The unscientific truth, perhaps, is that the central comparison in Milgram's study is not between any two experimental variables: it is between what happened in the laboratory, and what we thought would happen. The experimental control in Milgram's model is our hopelessly flawed intuition.

'Somehow,' Milgram told a friend in 1962, 'I don't write as fast or as easily as I run experiments. I have done about all the experiments I plan to do on Obedience, am duly impressed with the results, and now find myself acutely constipated.' Milgram found it hard to knock the experiment into social scientific shape. It would be another decade before he incorporated his findings into a serious theory of the sources of human obedience. When he did so, in the otherwise absorbing and beautifully written book *Obedience to Authority* (1974), his thoughts about an 'agentic state'—a psychological zone of abandoned autonomy—were not widely admired or developed by his peers, not least because they were so evidently retrospective. Most readers of *Obedience to Authority* are more likely to take interest in the nods of acknowledgement made to Arthur Koestler's *The Ghost in the Machine*, and to Alex Comfort, the English anarchist poet, novelist, and author of *The Joy of Sex*. Most readers will take more pleasure—and feel Milgram took more pleasure—in the novelistic and strikingly unscientific descriptions of his experimental subjects. ('Mrs Dontz,' he wrote, 'has an unusually casual, slow-paced way of speaking, and her tone expresses constant humility; it is as if every assertion carries the emotional message: "I'm just a very ordinary person, don't expect a lot from me." Physically, she resembles Shirley Booth in the film *Come Back, Little Sheba*.')

But while Milgram was struggling to place his findings in a proper scientific context, they seemed to have found a natural home elsewhere. Stanley Milgram—a young social psychology professor at the start of his career—appeared to be in a position to contribute to one of the late twentieth century's most pressing intellectual activities: making sense of the Holocaust. Milgram always placed the experiments in this context, and the figure of Adolf Eichmann, who was seized in Buenos Aires in the spring of 1960, and whose trial in Jerusalem began a year later, loomed over his proceedings. (In a letter that urged Alan Elms to keep up the supply of experimental volunteers, Milgram noted that this role bore 'some resemblance to Mr Eichmann's position'.) The trial, as Peter Novick has recently written in *The Holocaust in American Life*, marked 'the first time that what we now call the Holocaust was presented to the American public as an entity in its own right, distinct from Nazi barbarism in general'. When Milgram published his first paper on the obedience studies in 1963, Hannah Arendt's articles about the trial had just appeared in the *New Yorker*, and in her book, *Eichmann in Jerusalem*, and they had given widespread currency to her perception about 'the banality of evil'. Milgram put Eichmann's name in the first paragraph of his first obedience paper, and so claimed a place in a pivotal contemporary debate. His argument was this: his study showed how ordinary people are surprisingly prone to destructive obedience; the crimes of the Holocaust had been committed by people obeying orders; those people, therefore, could now be thought ordinary. The argument had its terrifying element and its consoling element: according to Milgram, Americans had to see themselves as potential murderers; at the same time we could understand Nazis to be no more unusual than any New Haven guy in a check shirt.

It may seem bizarre now: Milgram returned to ordinary Nazis their Nuremberg defence, nicely polished in an American laboratory. But the idea struck a chord, and news quickly spread of Milgram's well-meaning, all-American torturers. 'Once the [Holocaust] connection was in place,' said Arthur G. Miller, a leading Milgram scholar, 'then the experiments took on a kind of a larger-than-life quality.' Milgram's work was reported in the *New York Times* (65% IN TEST BLINDLY OBEY ORDER TO INFLICT PAIN), and the story was quickly picked up by *Life*, *Esquire*, ABC television, UPI and the British press. The fame of the experiments spread, and as the Sixties acquired their defining spirit, Holocaust references were joined by thoughts of My Lai; this was a good moment in history to have things to say about taking orders. By the time Milgram had published his book and released a short film of the experiment, his findings had spread into popular culture, and into theological, medical, and legal discussions. Thomas Blass, a social psychologist at the University of Maryland, Baltimore County, who is preparing a Milgram biography, has a large collection of academic references, including a paper in the context of accountancy ethics. (Is it unthinking obedience that causes accountants to act unlawfully on behalf of clients?) Outside the academy, Dannie Abse published an anti-Milgram play, *The Dogs of Pavlov,* in 1973, and two years later, in America, CBS broadcast a television movie, *The Tenth Level,* that made awkward melodrama out of the obedience experiments, and starred William Shatner as a spookily obsessed and romantically disengaged version of Professor Milgram. ('You may know your social psychology, Professor, but you have a lot to learn about the varieties of massage.') Peter Gabriel sang 'We Do What We're Told (Milgram's 37)' in 1986. And there would be more than a whiff of Milgram in the 1990 episode of *The Simpsons,* 'There's No Disgrace Like Home', in which the family members repeatedly electrocute one another until the lights across Springfield flicker and dim. Last year, 'The Stanley Milgram Experiment'—a comedy sketch duo—made its off-off-Broadway debut in New York. Robbie Chafitz, one of the pair, had been startled and amused by the Milgram film as a teenager, and had always vowed to use the name one way or another. Besides, as he told me, 'anything with electricity and people is funny'.

But however celebrated the experiments became, there was a question they could never shake off. It was an ethical issue: had Stanley Milgram mistreated his subjects? Milgram must have seen the storm coming, at least from the moment when Herbert Winer marched into his office, talking of heart attacks. In the summer of 1962, other subjects recorded their feelings about the experiment in response to a questionnaire sent out by Milgram along with a report explaining the true purpose of the experiment. Replies were transferred on to index cards and are now held—unpublished and anonymous—at Yale. 'Since taking part in the experiment,' reads one card, 'I have suffered a mild heart attack. The one thing my doctor tells me that I must avoid is any form of tension.' Another card: 'Right now I'm in group therapy. Would it be OK if I showed this report to [the] group and the doctors at the clinic?'

Since then, the experiment has been widely attacked from within the profession and from outside. To many, Milgram became a social psychological demon; Alan Elms has met people at parties who have recoiled at the news that he was a Milgram lieutenant. The psychologist Bruno Bettelheim described Milgram's work as 'vile' and 'in line with the human experiments of the Nazis'. In his defence, Milgram would always highlight the results of post-experimental psychological studies—which had reported 'no evidence of any traumatic reactions'—and the fact of the debriefings in Linsly-Chittenden Hall, in which care had been taken to give obedient subjects reasons not to feel bad about themselves. They were told to remember, for example, that doctors routinely hurt people in a thoroughly good cause. (Alan Elms wonders if this debriefing was *too* effective, and that subjects should have been obliged to confront their actions more fully.)

But Milgram never quite won the ethical argument. And the controversy was immediately damaging to his career. Someone— perhaps a Yale colleague, according to Thomas Blass—quickly brought the experiment to the attention of the American Psychological Association, and Milgram's application for APA membership was delayed while the case against him was considered. Today, although the APA is happy to include Milgram's shock generator in a travelling psychology exhibition, it is careful to describe the experiments as 'controversial' in its accompanying literature. As the APA points out, modern ethical guidelines (in part inspired by Milgram) would prevent the obedience studies from being repeated today.

The controversy followed him. In 1963 Milgram left Yale for Harvard. He was happy there. This is where his two children were born. And when a tenured job came up, he applied. But he needed the unanimous support of his colleagues, and could not secure it. He was blackballed by enemies of the obedience work. (According to Alexandra Milgram, her husband once devised a board game based on the tenure of university professors.) The late Roger Brown, a prominent Harvard psychologist, told Thomas Blass that there had been those in the department who thought of Milgram as 'sort of manipulative, or the mad doctor. They felt uneasy about him.'

So in 1967 Stanley Milgram left Harvard to become head of the social psychology programme in the psychology department in the Graduate Center of the City University of New York (CUNY). In one sense, it was a promotion; he was a full professor at thirty-three. 'But after Yale and Harvard, it was the pits,' said Milgram's friend and fellow social psychologist, Philip Zimbardo. 'Most people I know who didn't get tenure, it had a permanent effect on their lives. You don't get to Yale or Harvard unless you've been number one from kindergarten on, you've been top—so there's this discontinuity. It's the first time in your life you've failed. You're Stanley Milgram, and people all over the world are talking about your research, and you've failed.' Milgram was the most cited man in social psychology—Roger Brown, for example, considered his research to be of 'profound importance and originality'—yet in later life, he was able to tell Zimbardo that he felt under-appreciated.

The ethical furore preyed on Milgram's mind—in the opinion of Arthur G. Miller, it may have contributed to his premature death—but one of its curious side effects was to reinforce the authenticity of his studies in the world outside psychology departments. Among those with a glancing knowledge of Milgram, mistreatment of experimental subjects became the only Milgram controversy. The studies remained intellectually sound, a minor building block of Western thought, a smart conversational gambit at cocktail parties. 'People identified the problem with Milgram as just a question of ethics,' says Henderikus Stam, of the University of Calgary in Canada, who trained as a social psychologist, but who lost faith and is now a psychological theoretician and historian. 'So in a way people never got beyond that. Whereas there's a deeper epistemological question, which is: what can we actually know when we've done an experiment like that, what are we left with? What have we learned about obedience?'

Within the academy, there was another, quieter, line of criticism against Milgram: this was methodological. In a paper in 1968 the social psychologists Martin Orne and Charles Holland raised the issue of incongruity, pointing out that Milgram's subjects had been given two key pieces of information: a man in apparent danger, and another man—a man in a lab coat—whose lack of evident concern suggested there was no danger. It seemed possible that obedient subjects had believed in the more plausible piece of information (no danger), and thus concluded, at some conscious or semi-conscious level, that the experiment was a fake, and—in a 'pact of ignorance'—been generous enough to role-play for the sake of science. In other words, they were only obeying the demands of amateur dramatics.

Perhaps forgetting that people weep in the theatre, Milgram's response was to argue that the subjects' signs of distress or tension—the twitching and stuttering and racing heartbeats—could be taken as evidence that they had accepted the experiment's reality. He also drew upon the questionnaire he had sent out in 1962, in which his volunteers—now entirely in the know—had been asked to agree with one of five propositions, running from, 'I fully believed the learner was getting painful shocks' to 'I was certain the learner was not getting the shocks'. Milgram was pleased to note that three-quarters of the subjects said they believed the learner was definitely or probably getting the shocks. (He added, reasonably, 'It would have been an easy out at this point to deny that the hoax had been accepted.')

Herbert Winer reports that he was fully duped, and Alan Elms told me that, watching through the mirror during the summer of 1961, he saw very little evidence of widespread disbelief. But it is worth pointing out that Milgram could have reported his questionnaire statistics rather differently. He could have said that only fifty-six per cent accepted his first proposition: 'I fully believed the learner was getting painful shocks'. Forty-four per cent of Milgram's subjects claimed to be at least partially unpersuaded. (Indeed, on his own questionnaire, Winer said he had some doubts.) These people do not have much of a presence in Milgram's writings, but you catch a glimpse of them in the Yale Library index cards. One reads: 'I was quite sure "grunts and screams" were electrically reproduced from a speaker mounted in [the] students' room.' (They were.) 'If [the learner] was making the sounds I should have heard the screams from under the door—which was a poorly fit [sic] thin door. I'm sorry that I didn't have enough something to get up and open this door. Which was not locked. To see if student was still there.' On another card: 'I think that one of the main reasons I continued to the end was that...I just couldn't believe that Yale would concoct anything that would be [as] dangerous as the shocks were supposed to be.' Another subject had noticed how the experimenter was watching him rather than the learner. Another hadn't understood why he was not allowed to volunteer to be the learner. And another wrote, 'I had difficulty describing the experiment to my wife as I was so overcome with laughter—haven't had such a good laugh since the first time I saw the 4 Marx Bros—some 25 years ago.'

For an experiment supposed to involve the undeserved torture of an innocent Irish-American man, there was a lot of laughter in Yale's Interaction Laboratory. Frequently, Milgram's subjects could barely contain themselves as they moved up the shock board ('On one occasion,' Milgram later wrote, 'we observed a seizure so violently convulsive that it was necessary to call a halt to the experiment.') Behind their one-way mirror, Milgram and Elms were at times highly amused. And when students are shown the Milgram film today, there tends to be loud laughter in the room. People laugh, and—despite the alleged revelation of a universal heart of darkness—they go home having lost little faith in their friends and their families.

According to Henderikus Stam, the laughter of the students, and perhaps that of the subjects, is a reasonable response to an absurd situation. It's a reaction to the notion that serious and complex moral issues, and the subtleties of human behaviour, can reasonably be illuminated through play-acting in a university laboratory. The experiment does nothing but illuminate itself. 'What it does is it says, "Aren't we clever?" If you wanted to demonstrate obedience to authority wouldn't you be better showing a film about the Holocaust, or news clips about Kosovo? Why do you need an experiment, that's the question? What does the experiment do? The experiment says that if we really want to know about obedience to authority we need an abstract representation of that obedience, removed from all real forms of the abuse of authority. But what we then do is to use that representation to refer back to the real historical examples.'

What happens when we refer back to historical examples? Readers of *Hitler's Willing Executioners*, Daniel Jonah Goldhagen's study of the complicity of ordinary German citizens in the Holocaust, will learn within one paragraph of a German policeman, Captain Wolfgang Hoffmann, a 'zealous executioner of Jews', who 'once stridently disobeyed a superior order that he deemed morally objectionable'. The order was that he and members of his company should sign a declaration agreeing not to steal from Poles. Hoffmann was affronted that anyone would think the declaration necessary, that anyone would imagine his men capable of stealing. 'I feel injured,' he wrote to his superiors, 'in my sense of honour.' The genocidal killing of thousands of Jews was one thing, but plundering from Poles was another. Here was an order to which he was opposed, and which he felt able to disobey.

Goldhagen is impatient with what he calls 'the paradigm of external compulsion', which sets the actions of the Holocaust's perpetrators in the context of social-psychological or totalitarian state forces. His book aims to show how the crimes of the Holocaust were carried out by people obeying their own consciences, not blindly or fearfully obeying orders. 'If you think that certain people are evil,' he told me, 'and that it's necessary to do away with them—if you hate them—and then someone orders you to kill them, you're not carrying out the deed only because of the order. You're carrying it out because you think it's right. So in all those instances where people are killing people they hate—their enemies or their perceived enemies—then Milgram is just completely inapplicable.'

Goldhagen wonders if the Milgram take on the Holocaust met a particular need, during the Cold War, for America's new German allies 'to be thought well of'. He also wonders if, by robbing people of their agency, 'of the fact that they're moral beings', the experiment tapped into the kind of reductive universalism by which, he says, Americans are easily seduced—the belief that all men are created equal, and in this case equally obedient. Goldhagen has no confidence in the idea that Milgram was measuring obedience at all. The experimental conditions did not properly control for other variables, such as trust, nor did they allow for the way decisions are made in the real world—over time, after consultation. Besides, said Goldhagen, in a tone close to exasperation, 'people disobey all the time! Look around the world. Do people always pay all their taxes? Do what their bosses tell them? Or quietly accept what any government decides? Even with all kinds of sanctions available, one of the greatest problems that institutions face is to get their members to comply with rules and orders.' Milgram's findings, he says, 'are roundly, repeatedly and glaringly falsified by life'.

In the opinion of Professor Stam, this comes close to defining the problems of social psychology itself. It is a discipline, he says, that makes the peculiar claim that 'if you want to ask questions about the social world, you have to turn them into abstract technical questions'. The Milgram experiment, he says, 'has the air of scientificity about it. But it's not scientific, it's...*scientistic.*'

And there is Milgram's problem: he devised an intensely powerful piece of tragicomic laboratory theatre, and then had to smuggle it into the faculty of social science. His most famous work—which had something to say about trust, embarrassment, low-level sadism, willingness to please, exaggerated post-war respect for scientific research, the sleepy, heavy-lidded pleasure of being asked to *take part*, and, perhaps, too, the desire of a rather awkward young academic to secure attention and respect—had to pass itself off as an event with a single, steady meaning. And that disguise has not always been convincing. It's odd to hear Arthur G. Miller—one of the world's leading Milgram scholars—acknowledge that there have been times when he has wondered, just for a moment, if the experiments perhaps mean nothing at all.

But the faculty of social psychology is not ready to let Milgram go. And there may be a new way to rescue the experiments from their ungainly ambiguity. This is the route taken by Professors Lee Ross and Richard E. Nisbett (at Stanford and the University of Michigan respectively), whose recent synthesis of social psychological thinking aims to give the subject new power. According to Professor Ross, the experiments may be 'performance', but they still have social psychological news to deliver. If that is true, then we can do something that the late professor was not always able to do himself: we can make a kind of reconciliation between the artist and the scientist in Stanley Milgram.

Ross and Nisbett find a seat for Stanley Milgram at social

psychology's high table. They do this slyly, by taking the idea of obedience—Milgram's big idea—and putting it quietly to one side. When Ross teaches Milgram at Stanford, he makes a point of giving his students detailed instructions on how to prepare for the classes instructions that he knows will be thoroughly ignored. He is then able to stand in front of his students and examine their disobedience. 'I asked you to do something that's good for you rather than bad for you,' he tells them. 'And I'm a legitimate authority rather than an illegitimate one, and I actually have power that the Milgram experimenter doesn't have. And yet you didn't obey. So the study can't just be about obedience.' What it is primarily about, Ross tells his students—and it may be about other things too—is the extreme power of a situation that has been built without obvious escape routes. (As Herbert Winer said: 'At no time was there a pause or a break when anything could be raised...') 'There was really no exit,' Ross told me, 'there was no channel for disobedience. People who were discomforted, who wanted to disobey, didn't quite know how to do it. They made some timid attempts, and it got them nowhere. In order to disobey they have to step out of the whole situation, and say to the experimenter, "Go to hell! You can't tell me what to do!" As long as they continue to function within that relationship, they're asking the experimenter for permission not to give shocks, and as long as the experimenter denies them that permission, they're stuck. They don't know how to get out of it.' Ross suspects that things would have turned out very differently given one change to the situation. It's a fairly big change: the addition of a prominent red button in the middle of the table, combined with a clearly displayed notice signed by the 'Human Subjects' Committee' explaining that the button could be pressed 'by any subject in any experiment at any time if he or she absolutely refuses to continue'.

According to Ross and Nisbett (who are saying something that Milgram surely knew, but something he allowed to become obscured), the Obedience Experiments point us towards a great social psychological truth, perhaps *the* great truth, which is this: people tend to do things because of where they are, not who they are, and we are slow to see it. We look for character traits to explain a person's actions—he is clever, shy, generous, arrogant—and we stubbornly underestimate the influence of the situation, the way things *happened to be* at that moment. So, if circumstances had been even only subtly different (if she hadn't been running late; if he'd been *told* the film was a comedy), the behaviour might have been radically different. Under certain controlled circumstances, then, people can be induced to behave unkindly: to that extent, Milgram may have something to say about a kind of destructive obedience. But under other circumstances, Professor Ross promised me, the same people would be nice. Given the correct situation, he said, we could be led to do 'terrifically altruistic and self-sacrificing things that we would never have agreed to before we started'.

So the experiment that has troubled us for nearly forty years (that buzzing and howling), and which caused Milgram to have dark thoughts about America's vulnerability to fascism, suddenly has a new complexion. Now, it is about the influence of *any* situation on behaviour, good or bad: 'You stop on the highway to help someone,' Professor Ross said, 'and then the help you try to give doesn't prove to be enough, so you give the person a ride, and then you end up lending them money or letting them stay in your house. It wasn't because that was the person in the world you cared about the most, it was just one thing led to another. Step by step.'

That's the Milgram situation. 'We can take ordinary people,' Ross said, 'and make them show a degree of obedience or conformity—or for that matter altruism or bravery, whatever—to a degree that we would normally assume you would only see in the rare few. And that's relevant to telling us what we're capable of making people do, but it also tells us that when we observe the world, we are often going to be making an attribution error, because lots of times, the situational factors have been opaque to us, and therefore we are making erroneous inferences about people. The South African government says, "Can we deal with this fellow Mandela?" and the answer is, "No, he's a terrorist." But a social psychologist would say, "Mandela, in *one* context, given *one* set of situations, was a terrorist."' According to Ross, that's the key lesson of social psychology; that's how the discipline can be useful in education, the work place, and law. 'Our emphasis,' he says, 'should be on creating situations that promote what we want to promote, rather than searching endlessly for the right person. Don't assume that people who commit atrocities are atrocious people, or people who do heroic things are heroic. Don't get overly carried away; don't think, because you observed someone under one set of discrete situational factors, that you know *what they're like*, and therefore can predict what they would do in a very different set of circumstances.'

It's hard not to think of Stanley Milgram in another set of circumstances—to imagine the careers he did not have in films or in the theatre, and to wonder how things would have turned out if his work had appeared at another time, or had been read a little differently. It may now be possible to place the Obedience Experiments somewhere near the centre of the social psychological project, but that's not how it felt in the last years of Milgram's life. He had failed to secure tenure at Harvard. Disappointed, he moved to New York, assuming he would soon be leaving again, to take up a post at a more glamorous institution. But he was still at CUNY seventeen years later, at the time of his premature death. 'He had hoped it would be just for five years,' Alexandra Milgram told me, 'But things got much more difficult to move on to other places. You were glad to have what you had. And he was happy to do the work that he did. I don't think he was as happy at the university as he was at, say, Harvard, but he was a very independent person: he had his ideas, he had his research.'

The research pushed Milgram into a kind of internal exile. Confirming his reputation as social psychology's renegade, he pursued work that, although often brilliantly conceived and elegantly reported, could look eccentric and old-fashioned to colleagues, and that ran the risk of appearing to place method ahead of meaning. 'It would flash and then burn out,' says Professor Miller, 'and then he'd go on to something else.' He sent his (young, able-bodied) students on to the New York subway to ask people to give up their seats. He co-wrote a paper about *Candid Camera*'s virtues as an archive for students of human behaviour. Pre-empting the play *Six Degrees of Separation*, he studied the 'small world' phenomenon, investigating the chains of acquaintance that link two strangers. He took photographs of rail commuters and showed them to those who travelled on the same route, to explore the notion of the 'familiar stranger'. In an expensive, elaborate, and ultimately inconclusive experiment in 1971, he explored the links between antisocial acts seen on television and similar acts in real life by getting CBS to produce and air two versions of a hit hospital drama, *Medical Center*. He asked students to try to give away money on the street. He tested how easy it was for people to walk between a pavement photographer and his subject. And when he was recuperating from one of a series of heart attacks, he made an informal study of the social psychology of being a hospital patient. He was only fifty-one when he died.

Once, shortly before the Obedience Experiments had begun, Milgram had written from Yale about his fear of having made the wrong career move. 'Of course,' he told a friend, 'I am glad that the present job sometimes engages my genuine interests, or at least, a part of my interests, but there is another part that remains submerged and somehow, perhaps because it is not expressed, seems most important.' He described his routine: pulling himself out of bed, dragging himself to the lecture room 'where I misrepresent myself for two hours as an efficient and persevering man of science... I should not be here, but in Greece shooting films under a Mediterranean sun, hopping about in a small boat from one Aegean isle to the next.' He added, in a spirit of comic self-laceration, 'Fool!'   □

THE WALTER V. SHIPLEY
BEST ESSAY AWARD
SPONSORED BY
CHASE MANHATTAN BANK

$10,000 PRIZE

For a special issue about diversity, Creative Nonfiction magazine is seeking essays that will illuminate the landscape of race, gender, culture and ethnicity.

All writers qualify for the award. Writers at the beginning stages of their careers are encouraged to apply. We are seeking a broad range of voices with a variety of ethnic and cultural orientations.

Contact us for details

CREATIVE NONFICTION

5501 WALNUT STREET, SUITE 202
PITTSBURGH, PA 15232
tel: 412-688-0304   fax: 412-683-9173
e-mail: info@creativenonfiction.org

www.creativenonfiction.org

THE RED CORAL
BRACELET
Judith Hermann

TRANSLATED FROM THE GERMAN
BY MARGOT BETTAUER DEMBO

JULIA MARGARET CAMERON/CORBIS

M y first and only visit to a therapist cost me my red coral
bracelet and my lover.

The red coral bracelet came from Russia. To be precise, it came
from St Petersburg and was more than a hundred years old. My great
grandmother had worn it on her left wrist; it cost my great
grandfather his life. Is that the story I want to tell? I'm not sure. Not
really sure.

M y great grandmother was beautiful. She went to Russia with my
great grandfather because my great grandfather was building
furnaces there for the Russian people. My great grandfather rented a
large apartment for my great grandmother on Vasilevsky Ostrov, one
of the St Petersburg islands. The Greater and the Lesser Neva rivers
lapped at the shores of Vasilevsky Ostrov, and if my great grandmother
had stood on her toes to look out of the window in her apartment on
Maly Prospekt, she would have seen the river and the great Kronstadt
Bay. But my great grandmother did not want to see the river or
Kronstadt Bay or the beautiful tall houses on Maly Prospekt. She did
not want to look out of her window at a foreign land. She drew the
heavy red velvet drapes and shut the doors, the carpets swallowed all
sound, and my great grandmother sat on the sofas, the chairs, or the
four-poster beds, rocking back and forth and feeling homesick for
Germany. The light in the large apartment on Maly Prospekt was dim,
like the light at the bottom of the sea, and my great grandmother may
have thought that this foreign place, that St Petersburg, that all of
Russia was nothing but a deep, twilight dream from which she would
soon awaken.

My great grandfather, though, was travelling all over the country
building furnaces for the Russian people. He built shaft furnaces and
roasting kilns and self-dumping reverberatory furnaces and Livermore
furnaces. He stayed away for a long time. He wrote letters to my
great grandmother, and whenever one of these letters arrived, my
great grandmother would open the heavy red drapes a little and read
by the narrow chink of daylight:

> I would like to explain to you that the Hasenclever furnace we are
> building here consists of muffles which are connected to each other
> by vertical channels and are heated by the flames of a grate-firing

furnace—you remember, don't you, the retort furnace I built in the Blome Wildnis in Holstein and which you liked so much at the time.—Well, in the Hasenclever furnace the ore is also loaded through an opening in the top muffle and...

Reading these letters made my great grandmother very weary. She couldn't remember the retort furnace in the Blome Wildnis any more, but she did remember the Blome Wildnis, the pastures and the flat countryside, the hay bales in the fields and the taste of cold, sweet apple cider in the summer. She let the room subside once more into its twilight and lay down wearily on one of the sofas, repeating, 'Blome Wildnis, Blome Wildnis,' it sounded like a children's song, like a lullaby, it sounded nice.

In those years, in addition to foreign businessmen and their families, many Russian artists and scholars lived in Vasilevsky Ostrov. It was inevitable that they would hear of the German woman, the beautiful pale one with the fair hair who was said to live up on Maly Prospekt, almost always alone and in rooms as dark, soft and cool as the sea. The artists and scholars went to see her. My great grandmother gestured with her small weary hand, asking them to come in. She spoke little, she scarcely understood anything they said, slowly and dreamily she gazed from under heavy eyelids. The artists and scholars sat down on the deep, soft sofas and chairs, sinking into the heavy, dark materials; the maids brought black tea flavoured with cinnamon, and huckleberry and blackberry jam. My great grandmother warmed her cold hands on the samovar and felt much too tired to ask the artists and scholars to leave. And so they stayed. They looked at my great grandmother, and in the dusk my great grandmother merged into something melancholy, beautiful, and foreign. And since melancholy and beauty and foreignness are essential traits of the Russian soul, the artists and scholars fell in love with my great grandmother, and my great grandmother let herself be loved by them.

My great grandfather stayed away for a long time. And so my great grandmother let herself be loved for a long time, she did it carefully and circumspectly, and she made hardly any mistakes. Warming her cold hands on the samovar and her chilled soul on the ardent hearts of her lovers, she learned to distinguish—in their strange, soft language—the words: 'You are the most tender of all birches.' She read the letters about the smelting furnaces, the Deville furnaces, the tube furnaces, in the narrow chink of daylight and burned them all in the fireplace. She allowed herself to be loved; in the evening before falling asleep she sang the song about the Blome Wildnis, sang it to herself, and when her lovers looked at her enquiringly, she smiled and said nothing.

My great grandfather promised to come back soon, to go back to Germany with her soon. But he did not come.

The first, the second, and then the third St Petersburg winter passed, and still my great grandfather was busy building furnaces in the Russian vastness, and my great grandmother was still waiting for the time when she could go back home to Germany. She wrote to him in the deep forests to the north. He wrote back that he would return soon but that he would have to leave again one more time, just one final time—but then, but then, he promised, then they could leave.

The evening of his arrival my great grandmother was sitting in front of the mirror in her bedroom, combing her fair hair. The gifts from her lovers lay in a little jewellery box before the mirror, the brooch from Grigori, the ring from Nikita, the pearls and velvet ribbons from Alexei, the locks of hair from Jemelyan, the medallions, amulets, and silver bracelets from Mikhail and Ilya. The little jewellery box also held the red coral bracelet from Nikolai Sergeyevich. Its 675 little coral beads were strung on to a silken thread, and they glowed as red as rage. My great grandmother put the hairbrush down in her lap. She closed her eyes for a long time. Then she opened her eyes again, took the red coral bracelet from the little box and fastened it around her left wrist. Her skin was very white.

That evening, for the first time in three years, she shared a meal with my great grandfather. My great grandfather spoke Russian and smiled at my great grandmother. My great grandmother folded her hands in her lap and smiled back at him. My great grandfather talked about the steppe, about the wilderness, about the Russian 'white nights', he talked about the furnaces and called them by their German names, and my great grandmother nodded as though she understood. My great grandfather said in Russian that he had to go once more to Vladivostok; he was eating *pelmeni* with his hands while he said it; he wiped the grease from his lips, he said that

Vladivostok was the last stop; then it would be time to return to Germany. Or would she like to stay longer?

My great grandmother did not understand what he said. But she understood the word Vladivostok. And she placed her hands on the table, and on her white wrist the coral bracelet glowed red as rage.

My great grandfather stared at the coral bracelet. He put what was left of his *pelmeni* back on his plate, wiped his hands on the linen napkin, and gestured to the maid to leave the room. In German he said, 'What's that?'

My great grandmother said, 'A bracelet.'

My great grandfather said, 'And where did you get it, if I may ask?'

Very softly and gently my great grandmother said, 'Actually, I was hoping you would. It's a present from Nikolai Sergeyevich.'

My great grandfather called the maid back and sent her to get his friend Isaak Baruw. Isaak Baruw arrived, he was hunchbacked and stooped, and he looked sleepy and confused; it was already late at night and he kept running his fingers through his uncombed hair, embarrassed. My great grandfather and Isaak Baruw walked around the room agitated and arguing; in vain Isaak Baruw spoke calming words, words that reminded my great grandmother of her lovers. Exhausted, my great grandmother sank into one of the soft easy chairs and put her cold hands on the samovar. My great grandfather and Isaak Baruw were speaking Russian, and my great grandmother didn't understand much more than the words 'second' and 'Petrovsky Park'. The maid was handed a letter and sent out into the dark. At dawn my great grandfather and Isaak Baruw left the house. My great grandmother had fallen asleep in the soft easy chair, her small hand and wrist with the red coral bracelet hung limply from the arm of the chair; it was as dark and still in the room as on the bottom of the sea.

Towards noon Isaak Baruw came back and, amidst much bowing and scraping and many condolences, he informed my great grandmother that my great grandfather had died at eight o'clock that morning. On the hill in Petrovsky Park Nikolai Sergeyevich had shot him through the heart.

My great grandmother waited seven months. Then, on 20 January in the year 1905, during the first days of the revolution, she gave birth to my grandmother, packed her suitcases, and returned to Germany. The train she took to Berlin turned out to be the last one to leave St Petersburg before the railroad workers went on strike and all traffic between Russia and the outside world was halted. As the doors of the train closed and the locomotive blew white steam into the winter air, there appeared at the far end of the platform the crooked, hunchbacked form of Isaak Baruw. My great grandmother saw him coming and ordered the conductor to wait, and so at the last second Isaak Baruw climbed aboard the German train. He accompanied my great grandmother on the long journey to Berlin, he carried her suitcases and hatboxes and handbags, and he did not miss a chance to assure her repeatedly of his lifelong gratitude. My great grandmother smiled at him reassuringly but did not speak; she was wearing the red coral bracelet on her left wrist, and even then my tiny grandmother in the willow basket already bore more of a resemblance to Nikolai Sergeyevich than to my great grandfather.

My first and only visit to a therapist cost me the red coral bracelet and my lover.

My lover was ten years older than I, and he looked like a fish. He had fish-grey eyes and fish-grey skin, and he lay, like a dead fish, on his bed all day long, cold and silent; he was in a very bad way, and lying on the bed, if he said anything at all, he said only a single sentence: 'I am not interested in myself.' Is that the story I want to tell?

I don't know. I don't know really.

My lover was Isaak Baruw's great grandson, and in his thin veins ran Russian-German blood. Isaak Baruw had remained true to my great grandmother all his life, but it was her Pomeranian chambermaid that he married. He fathered seven children with her, and these seven children presented him with seven grandchildren, and one of these grandchildren presented him with his only great grandson—my lover. My lover's parents drowned in a lake during a summer storm, and my great grandmother ordered me to go to the funeral—two remnants of her St Petersburg past were being lowered into the soil of Brandenburg and with them the stories which she herself no longer wanted to tell. And so I went to the funeral of Isaak

Baruw's grandson and his wife, and my lover stood at their grave and wept three grey tears. I took his cold hand into mine and when he went home, I went with him; I thought I could console him with the St Petersburg stories; I thought that then he could tell them to me as though they were new.

But my lover did not speak. And he didn't want to listen to anything, and he knew nothing of the winter morning in the year 1905 when my great grandmother kept the train from leaving so that his great grandfather could escape, at the very last moment. My lover just lay on his bed and, when he said anything at all, he spoke just this one sentence: 'I am not interested in myself.' His room was cold and dusty and faced the cemetery; in the cemetery the death bells rang constantly. If I stood on tiptoe and looked out of the window, I could see the freshly dug graves, the bouquets of carnations, and the mourners. I would often sit on the floor in a corner of the room, knees drawn up to my chest, gently blowing the dust balls through the room; I thought it strange for someone not to be interested in himself. I was interested exclusively in myself. I looked at my lover, my lover looked at his body as if it were already dead, sometimes we would make love like enemies, and I would bite his salty mouth. I felt slender and skinny, even though I wasn't; I could act as though I were not myself. The light coming through the trees outside the window was green, it was a watery light, a light one sees near lakes, and fluffs of dust floated through the room like algae and seaweed.

My lover was sad. I asked him sympathetically whether I should tell him a short Russian story, and my lover replied enigmatically that the stories were over, he didn't want to hear them, and anyway I wasn't to confuse my own story with other stories. I asked him, 'And do you have a story of your own?' and my lover said no, he had none. But twice a week he went to a doctor, a therapist. He forbade me to go with him; he refused to tell me anything about the therapist, he said, 'I talk about myself. That's all.' And when I asked him whether he was talking about the fact that he wasn't interested in himself, he looked at me with contempt and said nothing.

So my lover was either silent or he repeated his one sentence, I was silent too and began thinking about the therapist, my face was always as dusty as the soles of my bare feet. I imagined myself sitting in the therapist's office, talking about myself. I had no idea what I should talk about. I hadn't really talked for a long time, for as long as I had been with my lover, I hardly spoke with him, and he practically never talked with me, saying only this one sentence, and there were times when I thought the language consisted solely and exclusively of six words: 'I am not interested in myself.'

I began thinking a lot about the therapist. I thought only of talking to him in an unfamiliar room, and that was pleasant. I was twenty years old, I had nothing to do, on my left wrist I wore the red coral bracelet. I knew the story of my great grandmother, in my mind I could walk through the dark, twilight apartment on Maly Prospekt, I had seen Nikolai Sergeyevich in my grandmother's eyes. The past was so tightly intertwined within me that it sometimes seemed like my own life. The story of my great grandmother was my story. But where was my story without my great grandmother? I didn't know.

The days were silent, as though under water. I sat in my lover's room and the dust wove itself around my ankles, I sat, knees drawn up to my chest, my head on my knees, and with my index finger I would draw symbols on the grey floor; I was lost in thought about I don't know what, it seemed years passed this way, I was just drifting along. Could I talk about it? From time to time my great grandmother came by and with a bony hand knocked on the apartment door, calling for me to come out and go home with her, her voice sounded as if it came from a great distance through the dust spun about the door. I made no move and did not answer her, my lover too just lay on his bed without moving and stared at the ceiling with dead eyes. My great grandmother called to me, luring me with pet names from my childhood—dear heart, little nut tree, precious heart—insistently and doggedly she tapped with her bony hand on the door, and only when I called out triumphantly, 'You sent me to him, now you have to wait until it's over!' did she finally go.

I heard her footsteps on the stairs getting softer and softer; at the door, the dust balls disturbed by her knocking settled down and folded up into a thick mass of fluff. I looked at my lover and said, 'Are you sure you wouldn't like to hear the story about the red coral bracelet?'

Lying on the bed my lover turned towards me with a tortured face. He stretched out his fish-grey hands and slowly spread the fingers, his fish-grey eyes protruded slightly from their sockets. The silence of the room trembled like the surface of a lake into which one has thrown a stone. I showed my lover my arm and the red coral beads on my wrist, my lover said, 'Those are members of the family Coralliidae. They form a little stem that can grow to be three feet tall, and they have a red, horny skeleton of calcium. Calcium.'

My lover spoke with a lisp, he spoke awkwardly and slurred his words as though he were drunk. He said, 'They grow off the coast of Sardinia and Sicily, Tripoli, Tunis and Algeria. There, where the sea is as blue as turquoise, very deep, one can swim and dive, and the water is warm...' He turned away from me again and sighed deeply; twice he kicked the wall and then he lay still.

I said, 'Listen, I want to tell you the stories! The St Petersburg stories, the old stories, I want to tell them so I can get out of them and get away.'

My lover said, 'I don't want to hear them.'

I said, 'Then I'll tell them to your therapist,' and my lover sat up, he took a deep breath so that several fluffs of dust disappeared in a small stream into his gaping mouth, he said, 'You're not going to tell my therapist anything, you can go to anyone else, but not to my therapist,' he coughed and thumped his naked grey chest, I had to laugh because my lover had never before talked so much all at one stretch. He said, 'You're not going to talk about me with someone to whom I talk about myself, that's impossible,' and I said, 'I don't want to talk about you, I want to tell the story, and my story is your story too.' It's true, we were really fighting with each other. My lover threatened to leave me, he grabbed me and pulled my hair, he bit my hand and scratched me, a wind blew through the room, the windows flew open, the death bells in the cemetery rang like crazy, and the dust balls drifted out like soap bubbles. I pushed my lover away and ripped the door open, I really felt thin and skinny; as I was leaving I could hear the dust balls sinking softly down to the floor, my lover with his fish-grey eyes and his fish-grey skin stood silent next to his bed.

The therapist, whose fault it was that I lost my red coral bracelet and my lover, was sitting in a large room behind a desk. The room was really very large, it was almost empty except for this desk, the therapist behind it, and a little chair in front of it. A soft, sea-blue, deep blue carpet lay on the floor of the room. As I entered, the therapist looked at me solemnly, looked me straight in the eye. I walked towards him, I had the sensation of having to walk towards him for a long time before I finally reached the chair in front of his desk. I thought about the fact that my lover usually sat on this chair and spoke about himself—about what?—I felt a tiny sadness. I sat down. The therapist nodded at me, I nodded too and stared at him, I waited for it to begin, for the conversation to start, for his first question. The therapist stared back at me until I lowered my eyes, but he said nothing. He was silent. His silence reminded me of something. It was very quiet. Somewhere a clock I couldn't see was ticking, the wind blew around the tall house, I looked at the sea-blue, deep blue carpet between my feet and pulled nervously and diffidently at the silk thread of my red coral bracelet. The therapist sighed. I raised my head, he tapped the gleaming desktop with the sharp-pointed lead of his pencil, I smiled in embarrassment, he said, 'What is it that's worrying you?'

I took a breath, raised my hands and let them drop again, I wanted to say that I wasn't interested in myself, I thought, that's a lie, I'm interested only in myself, and is that it? That actually there is nothing? Only the weariness and the empty, silent days, a life like that of fish under water and laughter without reason? I wanted to say that I had too many stories inside me, they made my life difficult, I thought, I could just as well have stayed with my lover, I took a breath, and the therapist opened his mouth and his eyes wide, and I tugged at the silken thread of the red coral bracelet and the silk thread tore and the 675 red-as-rage little coral beads burst in glittering splendour from my slender, thin wrist.

Distraught, I stared at my wrist, it was white and naked. I stared at the therapist, the therapist was leaning back in his chair, the pencil now lay in front of him, parallel to the edge of the desk, his hands were folded in his lap. I covered my face with my hands. I slipped off the chair on to the sea-blue, deep blue carpet; the 675 coral beads were scattered over the entire room. They gleamed, more rage-red than ever before, I crawled around on the floor and gathered them up, they were lying under the desk, under the therapist's toes, he pulled his foot back a tiny bit as I touched it, it was dark under the desk, but the red coral beads glowed.

I thought of Nikolai Sergeyevich, I thought, if he hadn't given my great grandmother the red coral beads, he wouldn't have shot my great grandfather in the heart. I thought of the humpbacked, stooped Isaak Baruw; I thought, if my great grandmother hadn't stopped the train for him, he wouldn't have left Russia. I thought of my lover, the fish, I thought, if he hadn't been silent all the time, I wouldn't now have to crawl around under a therapist's desk; I saw the therapist's trouser legs, his folded hands, I could smell him, I bumped my head on the desktop. Once I had collected all the red coral beads under the desk, I crawled back into the light and on through the room, I picked up the coral beads with my right hand and held them in my left, I began to cry. I was kneeling on the soft, sea-blue, deep blue carpet, I looked at the therapist, the therapist looked at me from his chair with his hands folded. My left hand was full of coral beads, but there were more still glowing and blinking all around me, I thought it would take me all my life to pick up all these coral beads, I thought I would never get it done, not my whole life long. I stood up. The therapist leaned forward, picked the pencil up off his desk, and said, 'The session is over for today.'

I poured the red coral beads from my left hand into my right, they made a lovely, tender sound, almost like gentle laughter. I raised my right hand and flung the red coral beads at the therapist. The therapist ducked. The red coral beads rained down on to his desk, and with them all of St Petersburg, the Greater and the Lesser Neva, my great grandmother, Isaak Baruw and Nikolai Sergeyevich, my grandmother in the willow basket and my lover the fish, the Volga, the Luga, the Narva, the Black Sea, the Caspian Sea, and the Aegean Sea, the Gulf of Finland, the Atlantic Ocean.

The waters of the earth's oceans surged in a huge green wave over the therapist's desk and ripped him out of his chair, the water rose rapidly and lifted the desk up with it, once more the therapist's face emerged from the billows and then it disappeared, the water roared, broke, and sang, it swelled and flushed away the stories, the silence, and the coral beads, flushed them back into the seaweed forests, into the shell beds, to the bottom of the sea. I took a deep breath.

I went back one last time to see how my lover was doing. He was drifting—I knew he would be—on his watery bed, pale belly turned to the ceiling. The light was as grey as the light at the bottom of a lake, dust balls were caught in his hair, they trembled softly. I said, 'You know that coral turns black when it lies too long at the bottom of the sea.' I said, 'Was that the story I wanted to tell?' But my lover could no longer hear me.

□

THE FREUD MUSEUM is ...

"a vibrantly living organism ... a fascinating cult site, a place of mythic memory, a shrine, a monument, a haunted house. But it also continues to pulse to a lively current of problems and challenges..." **Marina Warner**

Visit the house where Freud spent the final year of his life, see his study, his amazing collection of antiquities, the couch.

20 Maresfield Gardens, London NW3 5SX (nr. Finchley Rd tube)
Tel: 020 7435 2002 Email: freud@gn.apc.org
Open: Weds. - Sun. 12 - 5pm Admission £4 (Concs. £2)
and visit the virtual museum at: www.freud.org.uk

The Freud Museum has an international reputation for its exhibitions and conferences, but it relies on charity for support. All donations are welcome.

delivering more

pleasure

to more

readers

www.justbooks.co.uk

Europe's leading web site for the purchase and
sale of second-hand, rare and antiquarian books.
email: info@justbooks.co.uk

Just
Books

Second hand. First site.
www.justbooks.co.uk

GORMLEY'S
PEOPLE
Gautier Deblonde

Antony Gormley first became known as a sculptor for his body
casts, moulded on his own body and cast in lead. More recently
his work has become less strictly anatomical. The following
photographs were taken in Antony Gormley's London
studio between 1997 and 2000.

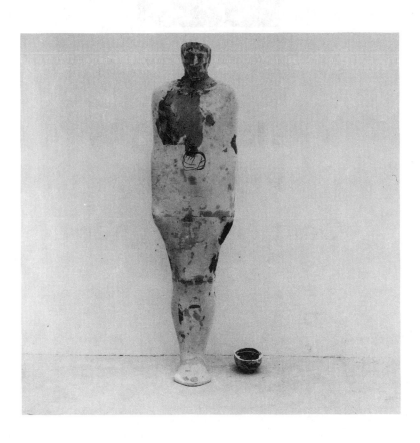

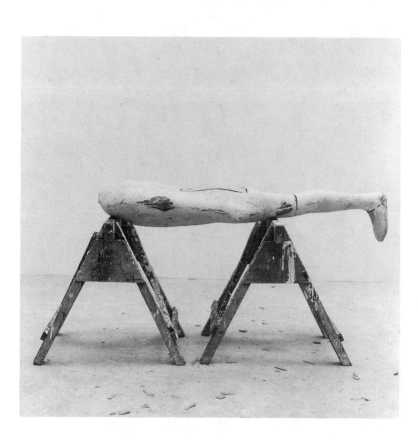

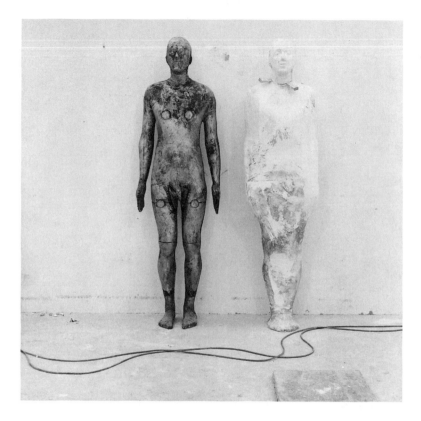

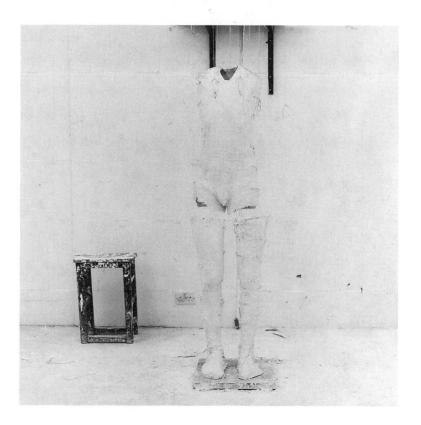

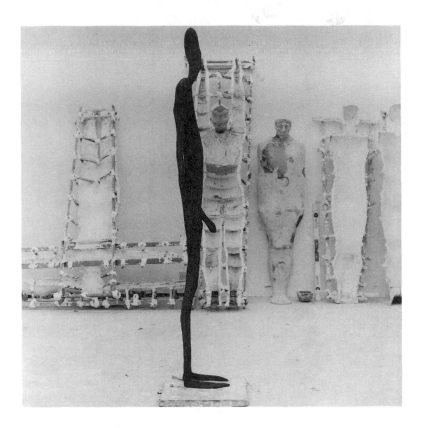

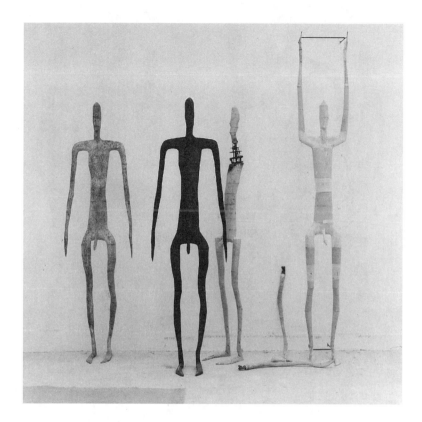

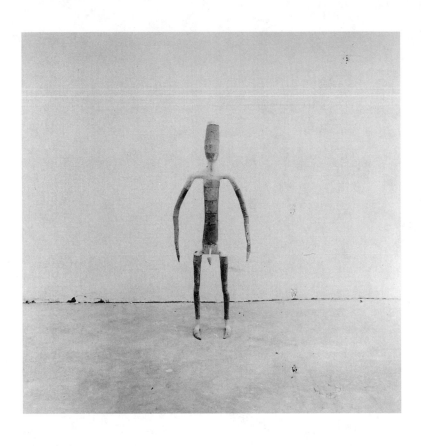

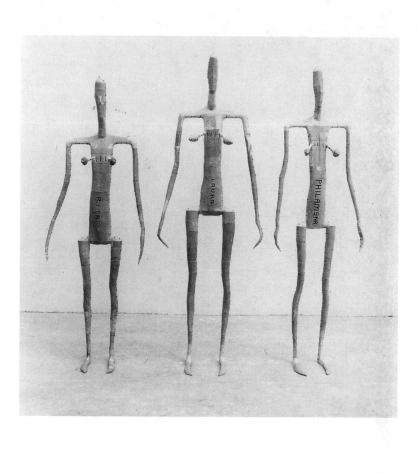

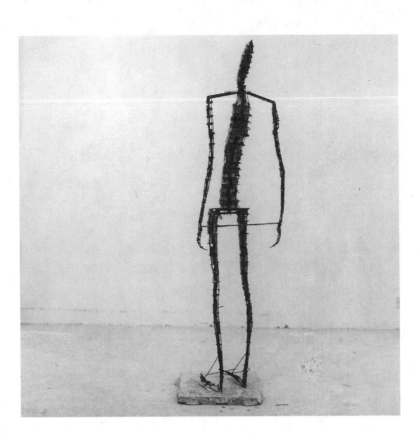

SUBSCRIBE

FICTION MEMOIR REPORTAGE **PHOTOGRAPHY**

There are over 70,000 subscribers to Granta, in every corner of the world.

Why not join them? Or give a subscription as a gift?

You'll save up to £40 on the bookshop price (£8.99 an issue), and get a regular supply of outstanding new writing, delivered to your home.

A one-year subscription (4 issues) is just £24.95. You save £11.
A two-year subscription (8 issues) is just £46.50. You save £25.
A three-year subscription (12 issues) is just £67. You save £40.

'Never take Granta for granted.'
Daily Telegraph

SAVE
as much as
£40

GRANTA

Order form

Subscribe and save:

○ I'd like to subscribe and save:

   ○ 38% with a 3-year subscription (12 issues) for £67.00

   ○ 35% with a 2-year subscription (8 issues) for £46.50

   ○ 30% with a 1-year subscription (4 issues) for £24.95

   Please start the subscription with issue no:_____

My name: _____

Address: _____

Country/postcode: _____

Share and save:

○ I'd like to give a gift subscription, for:

   ○ 3 years (£67) ○ 2 years (£46.50) ○ 1 year (£24.50)

   Please start the subscription with issue no:_____

Recipient's name: _____

Address: _____

Country/postcode: _____

Gift message (optional): _____

Postage The prices above include postage in the UK. For the rest of Europe, please add £8 per year. For the rest of the world, please add £15 per year. (Airspeeded delivery).

Payment Total amount: £_____ by: ○ Cheque (to 'Granta') ○ Visa, Mastercard, AmEx:

Card no / _ / _ / _ / _ / _ / _ / _ / _ / _ / _ / _ / _ / _ / _ / _ / _ /

Expires / _ / _ / _ / Signature _____

Return You can either post ('Freepost' if you live in the UK), using the address label below. Or e-mail, fax or phone your details, if paying by credit card.

In the UK: **FreeCall 0500 004 033** (phone & fax).

Elsewhere: tel: 44 171 704 0470, fax 44 171 704 0470. E-mail: subs@grantamag.co.uk

00JBG710

○ Please tick if you'd prefer not to receive information from compatible organizations.

Granta Magazine

**FREEPOST
2/3 Hanover Yard
Noel Road
London
N1 8BR**

KILLING DRAGONS

THE CONQUEST OF THE ALPS

A funny, wicked and witty history, impossible to put down.

'Fleming has an eye for a ripping yarn and a gift for spinning it.'
Literary Review

'[Fleming] writes in a thoroughly readable style, full of telling anecdotes.'
Nature

Granta Books

Published in October
£20 Hardback
Order now on
www.granta.com or on
Freecall 0500 004 033
to receive a 30% discount

Ways of Life

Gabriel's Fire
A Memoir
Luis Gabriel Aguilera

"[T]he vulnerability and naiveté Aguilera exposes in his youthful persona allow the book to transcend the token Latino narrative and become a touching, informative and often humorous memoir about a boy growing up. . . . As a writer, Aguilera successfully revists that time when the young mind is balanced between sophistication and naiveté, hardness and softness, perspective and self-centeredness."—Kari Lydersen, *Streetwise*
Cloth $22.00

Madumo, a Man Bewitched
Adam Ashforth

"Part ripping adventure tale, part visionary anthropological treatise, Ashforth's gripping memoir of a friendship in a season of crisis offers a startling glimpse into a secret South Africa of today—coming to terms with the challenges of a modern society, while the magic of the ancestors still beckons."—John Phillip Santos, author of *Places Left Unfinished at the Time of Creation*
Cloth $20.00

Stinging Trees and Wait-a-Whiles
Confessions of a Rainforest Biologist
William Laurance

"It is not only the science but the sheer marvel of north Queensland that are captured in Bill Laurance's book. So vivid is his writing that as you read it you can share his delight in every last sight and sound of the forest community. . . . Written by a professional scientist for the popular reader, the book can be recommended for the ecologist and the conservationist alike, plus others concerned—and who cannot be concerned about such a treasure of the Earth?"—Norman Myers, coauthor of *Hotspots: Earth's Biologically Richest and Most Endangered Terrestrial Ecoregions*
Cloth $25.00

Available in bookstores.
The University of Chicago Press
www.press.uchicago.edu

IF I DREAM
I HAVE YOU

Justine Picardie

The savage, it is said, fails to distinguish the visions of sleep from the realities of waking life, and, accordingly, when he has dreamed of his dead friends he necessarily concludes that they have not wholly perished, but that their spirits continue to exist in some place and some form, though in the ordinary course of events they elude the perceptions of his senses.

The Golden Bough Book II, James George Frazer

Justine Picardie and her
sister Ruth, aged six and
four, 1967

Good Friday in the year 2000, Jesus is dead and so is my sister, and I'm running on a treadmill at the gym, watching MTV with no sound on. If my sister were still alive she would be thirty-six in ten days' time. But she died when she was thirty-three, the same age as Jesus. Obviously, I know she wasn't nearly as famous as Jesus was at the age of thirty-three—I'm not *that* crazy, nor even inclined to blasphemy under normal circumstances—but Ruth is a bit famous, because when she was diagnosed with terminal breast cancer in 1997, I asked her to write a column for the London *Observer*'s magazine section, which I was editing at the time. The section was called 'Life' and her column about death came on the final page. She only wrote a handful of columns before she died, but many thousands of readers responded to her pieces, which were later collected, together with her emails and letters, in a book called *Before I Say Goodbye*, published after her death. Thus she has a kind of public afterlife—she rose again, in the best-seller lists at least, which is both a blessing and a curse for those who loved her.

When I think about her now, which is most of the time, it's as if I'm rewinding a silent film in my head. I see the crucial scenes in our lives together: holding her hand while her twins were born in an emergency Caesarean; holding her hand when she kissed them goodbye just before she died two years later. But what I can't hear is her voice in my head, and that silence is driving me crazy. The treadmill is supposed to be good therapy, and sometimes it works, but not today, because Good Friday is the saddest day of the year. I've tried everything since my sister died, in the manner of the sophisticated consumer that I am supposed to be: bereavement counselling, psychotherapy, anti-depressants, Valium, sleeping pills, homeopathic remedies, the gym. Prozac is sufficiently numbing to make the silence matter less, though I'm trying to stop taking it because I've begun to wonder if I've been missing something, whether the impermeable layer it provides is now necessary. But still nothing speaks to me.

I didn't expect silence. We had always talked so much. She was my best friend as well as my sister: a little less than three years younger than me, the child I needed to protect when I was still a child myself (and my parents scarcely grown-ups themselves). When we knew she was going to die, because the tumours had spread to her lungs and liver, we talked about how we would always talk to each other, even after her death. Neither of us had grown up believing in a conventional Christian afterlife (and anyway, I'd given up on that unkind God after his failure to answer my prayers); but even so, it seemed impossible that my sister and I would ever be separated by silence, that our voices were contained only in our flesh and blood.

Yet in the weeks after her death, I heard nothing. At night there were just my own muffled screams in the pillow, or the memory (more difficult to bear) of her agonized breathing on her last night, as she gasped for all that remained of life. I could say nothing to her except 'I love you, I love you, I love you'. 'I love you too,' she whispered, before she disappeared to a place where I could not follow her.

Since then there have been times when I have longed to go after her. But today, after I've finished at the gym, I walk back home and back upstairs to the computer in the attic. I'm almost expecting to find an email from Ruth ('message waiting') but there is nothing, just my half-reflected face on the blank screen. I wonder if she is on the other side, looking back at me looking in. I wonder if I could smash a hole in the screen and put my hand through to reach her. I often dream about being with Ruth in a wood. She is a little girl, lost in the wood, and I am on the other side of a glass screen watching her. In my dream I shatter it with my fists and reach through, cutting my wrists as I do so, on the broken glass. When I was a child I saw a television adaptation of *Wuthering Heights*, and Cathy's ghost came to a dark window; she was on the outside, and she smashed her way in, with bleeding wrists and knuckles. Or maybe—though I can't quite remember, maybe I dreamt this—it was a little girl in the house who closed the window against Cathy's ghost, slamming the window down on her dead fingers as they reached inside.

Do I need a therapist to explain this? No. I need only turn to Iona Opie's very useful *Dictionary of Superstitions*, page 117. 'DEATH: Opening locks/doors and windows frees spirit; 1891 *Church Times* 23 Jan. "Yesterday, at Willey, in Warwickshire, I buried a little boy three years old. It was snowing hard, yet the parents (of the labouring class) would have both front and back doors of their cottage wide open all the time of the funeral."'

So much for communication, then.

When I dream about my sister, which I do almost every night, she doesn't say very much. Just before dawn on Easter Sunday, at about the time that Jesus is doubtless rising again, I dream that I meet Ruth at a party.

'I thought you were dead!' I say.

'No, I just went to America,' she replies, looking evasive.

'But I saw your dead body! I went to the funeral and saw the coffin. You were cremated.'

'Hmm,' she says, infuriatingly.

'And what about the children?' I ask her. 'How could you just go to America and leave Lola and Joe? They've missed you so much! And I've missed you so much! How could you do that?'

She turns away.

'Ruth, listen to me,' I say. 'Your husband's got a girlfriend. They've just moved into a new house together, with the twins. Don't you care? Are you even listening to me?'

She still says nothing. I look at her more closely, at her cropped hair which has been dyed red, and then I realize that it is a stranger, someone pretending to be Ruth.

'You're not my sister,' I say.

'You *bitch*,' she replies, not very originally.

After this dream, I think maybe I need some help. A few months ago, a friend gave me the telephone number for a man—a medium, in fact—called Arthur Molinary, who works at the College of Psychic Studies. I liked his name—it made me smile—and I quite liked the idea of going to the strange-sounding place. But I'd stuffed the number in a drawer. I didn't feel the need to ring him then. Now, though, I couldn't think of what else to do.

Wednesday 26 April I ring the College of Psychic Studies from work. This is a very peculiar phone call to make in an open-plan office, so I try to whisper into the phone.

'I'd like to make an appointment to see Arthur Molinary.'

'Mr Molinary is fully booked until six-fifteen p.m. on the eighth of June,' says a businesslike woman at the other end. 'Would you like to take that appointment?'

'Yes,' I hiss quietly, 'but isn't there anything sooner?'

She pauses for a few seconds, as if she were scanning the appointment book of a popular doctor's surgery. Then: 'You could come in and see our Junior Sensitive on the sixteenth of May at six-thirty. We've been getting very good results from him.'

'I'll take both appointments,' I say, feeling excited, suddenly feeling Ruth. I can see her in my mind's eye, wearing her favourite lavender-coloured skirt from a shop called Ghost.

'See you then,' says the receptionist. 'And we need twenty-four hours' notice if you're going to cancel.'

'I won't cancel,' I say. (Later, when I tell my husband, who is a rationalist, about this conversation, he raises an eyebrow and says, 'You'd think the College of Psychic Studies would *know* if you were going to cancel.')

Monday 1 May It's Ruth's birthday. I've lost my good spirits and sunk back into an angry silence. Both my parents have spent the night at our house (sleeping in separate bedrooms because they are divorced). In the morning we make small talk between slices of toast. I wonder whether to tell them about my appointments at the College of Psychic Studies. My father used to be an Oxford don; my mother is a therapist. I can't see spiritualism going down well with either of them, though as it happens, my paternal grandfather developed an interest in seances after his parents died. This is a rarely spoken of family embarrassment: poor, sad, silly Louis, who was named Lazar (for Lazarus) but changed his name after he was reborn into evangelical Christianity, joined Jews for Jesus, and started listening out for rappings on the table and voices from beyond.

'Dad,' I say. 'Why don't you ever talk about Louis and the spiritualists?'

'Oh, that dreadful *rubbish*,' says my father. 'How absurd, how truly *ridiculous* can you get!'

My father had the first of several nervous breakdowns just after his mother died. I must have been seven or eight when he was taken to a mental hospital near Oxford, where he was given electric shock treatment. Since then, he has had years of therapy and brutal doses of medication that have left him rather frail and shaky. My grandfather's experiences with spiritualism were, possibly, a gentler way of dealing with grief than my father's own psychiatric treatment; but my father would almost certainly disagree with this observation.

As for my mother, she was raised in the rituals of Anglo-Catholicism by her mother, who had been sent away by her parents to a convent boarding school at the age of four. One of her ancestors, Henry Garnett, was a Catholic priest who had been beheaded after the Gunpowder Plot and later canonized by virtue of the image of Christ which was seen in a drop of his blood. As a teenager, my mother had thoughts of becoming a nun, but she decided against it; rather than marrying God, she met my Jewish father and discovered communism and her own cleverness instead. Their marriage failed. My father suffered from depression, and I grew up associating Easter and other holidays with his corresponding bouts of silence and melancholy (cause and effect might be explained by a recent email from him which observed, gnomically: 'There were pogroms in the Tsarist Empire at about Easter time, usually orchestrated by the Russian police themselves and fuelled by the Catholic priests, to blame the Christ-killers who would be accused of murdering Christian children for their blood to make matzos at Passover.') Recently, my father has found some consolation in the rituals of Judaism which he had previously rejected; while my mother returned to the Church with her second husband, who was a doctor—a blood specialist—and also a haemophiliac. When he died from Aids, she discovered a different kind of solace in the apparent science of psychotherapy.

After Ruth's death, I seemed to my mother to be silent and closed; in need of therapy, no doubt. But my own experiences with therapists have not been very successful. The first bereavement counsellor I saw made me irritable, partly because of his twinkly New Age language ('You need a safe place to be held'); and also because he sent me notes on blue paper decorated with pastel bunnies. The second therapist was far better, but we got stuck on my recollection of Ruth's blood phobia (she felt faint—and sometimes fainted, even fitted—at the sight of her own blood). This therapist seemed to suggest that perhaps my sister and I had repressed the memory of our father's suicide attempt: could there have been slit wrists or something? But as I kept telling the therapist, my father had only

Justine Picardie

taken a minor overdose of pills, though during (or maybe because of) this period of therapy, I was haunted by the unasked-for image of him hanging in our living room in Oxford.

This delving into my subconscious soon got to be far too uncomfortable and exhausting. Prozac is so much easier, and anyway, I'm bored of myself; bored of grief; bored of hearing my own voice talking drearily, pointlessly, when what I really want is Ruth's voice.

And if not her voice, then maybe that of a medium who can hear her when I can't? That's what I try to tell my mother on the morning of Ruth's birthday. She looks at me quizzically. Somewhere in her measured response I hear the word 'internalized', but not much else. Then she tells me that she, too, dreams about Ruth.

'Once she was on the other side of a river, waving to me, but I couldn't cross the river,' says my mother. 'Another time, I dreamt I was driving very fast down a motorway, and I saw Ruth flash past in the opposite direction, in another car.'

'But do you ever feel her presence when you're awake?'

'Only in my memory and my sense of loss,' my mother says quietly.

I am silent. She wants me to love her more, but sometimes my love for her is pushed aside by my grief for Ruth. So she leaves without my telling her that I do love her, I do; even though my sister is dead. Then my husband drives my father, me and our two children south across London, over Blackfriars Bridge, the bridge that I crossed so many times, to and from the hospice that housed my sister in her last weeks, to the other side of the Thames. We park at the end of the bridge and walk alongside the grey river, past little bays of rubbish washed up on to the dirty sand. It is May Day. I think that my husband is angry with me for being sad on this spring holiday ('That's pure projection, and you know it,' says the voice of an imaginary therapist, which sometimes comes into my head when I least want to hear it). I walk ahead with the children, who are uncomplicated in their conversation, leaving my husband and my father in our wake.

Finally, we get to the Hayward Gallery, to an exhibition which has been curated by our neighbour, David Toop, whose wife, my friend Kimberley, killed herself five years ago. (Kimberley half believed in spiritualism, and in her despair hoped that death would free her soul

170

from darkness, but that is another story). The exhibition is called 'Sonic Boom', and is about sound, present and absent. I stand in front of a work called *A Procession of Ghosts*, made of graceful wires scratching on a huge, smooth white page. Nothing is there to read, and yet there is the faint sound of something being written. I stare at the blank space and try to imagine Ruth's words on her birthday. But the page stays empty, while the scratching of what might be a pen continues.

Ten days later. I'm sitting in a plane on my way to Hollywood to interview a clutch of film stars for *Vogue*. I look out of the window, in search of Ruth, as ever. The first time I flew after she died, I cried because of the sky's emptiness. This time, it's easier. I think, couldn't she be here in the cabin with me, her spirit flying from her children's pillows at dawn?

'Are you there?' I whisper, mouthing the words.

'I'm here,' says the voice in my head.

I close my eyes and hear her voice as mine.

'Ruth?'

'Yes.'

'I miss you.'

'I miss you, too. But I'm here you know.'

'Can't you just give me a sign?'

'You don't need one.'

'What's heaven?'

'Heaven is a state of mind.'

'And hell?'

'Hell is your unhappiness.'

'What's it like for you now?'

'Blue and fast and silver.'

'So where do you spend your time?'

'With the twins, and you, and by myself.'

'Can you remember the dream I had? The week after you died? We were in the gardens, at night, at the Trinity Hospice, and you were lying on a kind of mat as if you were sleeping. And then you sat up and said to me that you were spending all your time with strangers. I thought of you, like a lost ghost crossing Blackfriars Bridge, to and fro, over and over again.'

'That was before I found myself. I'm better now.'

I open my eyes and I'm crying, 36,000 feet up in the sky, wondering if my dead sister is sitting in the empty seat beside me.

'Of course I am, stupid,' her voice says.

'I *feel* stupid,' I say. 'I'm not as clever as you.'

'Yes you are,' she says to me. 'You are me.'

16 May My appointment with the Junior Sensitive at the College of Psychic Studies. It's a grand building in South Kensington, just around the corner from the Natural History Museum. Beyond the entrance hall is the library that doubles as a waiting room, with faded rows of Victorian books, and a brochure setting out the college's principles. ('Founded in 1884, the College is an educational charity. We seek to promote spiritual values and a greater understanding of the wider areas of human consciousness, welcoming the truths of all spiritual traditions and, equally, each and every individual...'). I wait, browsing through the list of forthcoming lectures. Tomorrow night Dr Edgar Mitchell, who walked on the moon in 1971, will be delivering his thoughts on 'The Quantam Hologram: Nature's Mind', with special reference to 'intuitive, psychic and mystical experiences'. I don't get any further before my name is called.

'Room Four,' says the receptionist. She points up the stairs, past the oil paintings of former presidents and luminaries of the College, past the lecture theatre, to the second floor.

The Junior Sensitive is a middle-aged man, small and balding and nervous in a carefully ironed shirt and respectable trousers.

'Do you mind if I draw the curtains?' he says, in a soft northern accent. 'It's so light outside, it's blinding.'

'Go ahead,' I say, and we both sit down.

He closes his eyes. 'I definitely feel something,' he says. 'I felt it as soon as you came into the room. My nose is itching and my throat, my throat is sore.' He clutches his neck, his eyes still closed.

'There's a very high pollen count outside,' I say, unkindly. 'Maybe you've got hay fever?'

He opens his eyes and looks at me. 'You could be right,' he says. 'It could be hay fever.'

He closes his eyes again and starts waving his hands in the air, paddling them through the twilight in this hot, still room.

'You must remember to breathe deeply,' he says, breathing deeply himself by way of demonstration. 'In, out, in, out. And swim. When you're stressed, go swimming...and you need to drink plenty of water. Lots and lots of water.'

This doesn't seem to me to be particularly helpful advice, nor does it seem to have anything to do with my sister, so I remain silent.

'Clarissa!' he says suddenly. 'Clarissa! Does the name mean anything to you?'

'No,' I reply, wanting to leave now.

'Hmm, well, store that name away for the future.' He breathes deeply again, as if to reassure himself. His brow is furrowed and his nose wrinkles like the White Rabbit in *Alice in Wonderland*.

I gaze at the ceiling, feeling furious and silly and disappointed. What on earth am I doing here? Why would Ruth talk to me in this ridiculous place, through the guise of this peculiar man?

'I see someone who looks like you and talks like you,' he continues, undeterred. 'Do you have someone in your family who has passed on?'

'My sister.' I say this reluctantly.

'She died of cancer,' he says. His hands move to his stomach. 'I can feel her nausea.'

I feel like punching him on the nose, but I'm too polite to leave. I listen to his comments on my dead grandparents. ('They like this time of year. I see them eating ice cream. Did they like ice cream? I'm trying to find some proof for you, here. Did one of them have their tonsils removed, perhaps?')

Finally, I can go.

'Goodbye,' I say. 'Thank you.'

'Goodbye,' he says gently. 'Sometimes the spirits don't tell you what you want to hear.'

I walk down the stairs, past the portraits of Victorian mediums and the posters advertising next weekend's workshop on the path of the soul, and then out of the big front door, where suddenly I find myself laughing, looking up into an early summer sky where the pollen swirls like heaven's dust.

Justine Picardie

The next day I find in the morning post at work a book and a letter written on lavender notepaper. 'Dear Ms Picardie,' it begins,

> I read your article in the *Daily Telegraph*, September 25th 1999, understanding exactly how you feel about your sister Ruth's death two years ago. Your remark about your longing for 'her advice and unique understanding of our shared past' is especially poignant.
>
> Your story struck such a chord with me that I decided to send you my book, *Voices From Paradise*. I feel it can help you not only by expressing shared experience, but in a practical way too.
>
> Please read it and if you feel it adds up, unbelievable though it all may seem at first, perhaps you'll recommend it in whatever way you feel is appropriate.
>
> With kindest regards,
> Judith Chisholm

The subtitle of the book is 'How the Dead Speak To Us', and despite my disappointing experience with the Junior Sensitive, I take it home and read it. It proves so absorbing that I miss *ER*, which is my favourite thing on television (and was also Ruth's: the unreal blood seemed not to disturb her, when we watched it every Wednesday night together before she became ill, and afterwards, and not long before she died, lying side by side on her hospital bed, though by then her brain tumour prevented her from following the dialogue—'What are they talking about?' she complained. 'What are their voices *saying*?').

Judith Chisholm is a former *Sunday Times* journalist (the paper where I learned to be a reporter, though she left years before I arrived), whose son died unexpectedly at the age of thirty-six. The book begins as an account of her grief, moves on to her experiences with mediums and seances, and culminates in a detailed exposition of her belief in what she calls the 'electronic voice phenomenon', or EVP; a means of recording the voices of the dead. In support of this belief she cites Sir Oliver Lodge, the inventor of the spark plug, a former principal of Birmingham University, and president of the Society for Psychical Research from 1901 to 1903. ('The dead live in etheric wavelengths which operate at much higher frequencies than ours,' Lodge wrote in

The Outline of Science. 'Our physical world is working on vibrations that are up to the speed of light. The etheric world operates at frequencies far in excess of the speed of of light.') She also quotes Thomas Edison, who, after inventing the light bulb and the phonograph, wrote at the age of seventy-three that he was 'inclined to believe that our personality hereafter will be able to affect matter' and that 'if we can evolve an instrument so delicate as to be affected or moved or manipulated by our personality as it survives in the next life, such an instrument when made available ought to record something'.

Judith Chisholm's book concludes with instructions on how to record the voices of the dead. 'You need: *a tape recorder* (variable speed is useful as some of the voices are very fast and need slowing down); *a new tape*; *a remote microphone*, if your tape recorder will take one, which should be hung up for maximum efficiency (a remote mike helps cut down background hiss); a quiet room and, very important, *a positive, expectant, cheerful, loving attitude of mind.*' She also recommends recording after sunset on the night of a full moon, preferably during a thunderstorm, because of the increased amounts of electricity and magnetism and what she calls 'gravitational effect'.

Thursday 18 May The children are asleep upstairs. There is a full moon, and a thunderstorm has just passed. 'Have you got a tape recorder and a microphone?' I ask my husband.

'Why?' he says. I don't answer, but he knows what I'm thinking, and looks at me with disbelief and exasperation. But he fetches the tape recorder and the microphone and a blank cassette and sets them up for me on the kitchen table. 'I'm going upstairs,' he says. 'Call me if you need me.'

I light a candle and switch off the lights. I turn on the tape recorder and whisper into it, in case anyone hears me. But then I remember that I want to be heard. I want Ruth to hear me, and Kimberley, and Oscar and Adam and Simon and Jon, all my friends who have died in the last few years. I speak up. 'Um, is anybody there? I would very much like to talk to somebody. I feel like so many people have died recently, it would make more sense to conduct my social life in the spirit world.'

Silence. I leave a gap on the tape, as instructed in the book.

('With the open-mike method, you will not hear any discarnate voices at the time of recording, only on playback. Leave gaps in your own speech for a response on the other side...')

Silence. I believe in this. I do. I have a positive, expectant, cheerful, loving attitude of mind. There is a full moon outside. There has been lightning and therefore masses of electricity. My sister is going to talk to me. She is going to leave me a message on my tape. I know this to be true.

I switch the tape off, rewind it, play it back.

I hear my voice on the tape...and nothing else. But there must be something. I rewind it and play it again. Silence. I consult the book. 'Play your tape back. Listen very carefully. At first it's hard to distinguish anything other than the background hiss of the tape recorder, which you can never completely eliminate, and the sound of your own voice. As the discarnate voices usually imprint at a level below that at which we expect to hear them you have to try to listen to all levels on the tape—listen through it. This is extremely hard at first, but becomes automatic later on. The voices can be whispered. At first they usually are. They are sometimes very fast, often curt, often seemingly banal in their utterances. There is great economy of words yet what is said usually has more than one meaning. Sometimes prepositions and auxiliary verbs are left out. Usually one to three words are imprinted at first. If you hear something that may be an 'extra' voice, run the tape back and listen again—and again.'

I run the tape back. I listen again, and again. Still nothing. I go upstairs and get my husband to listen to the tape. He puts on some headphones and I watch him listening. His eyes fill with tears, but he says nothing.

'Did you hear something?' I ask.

'Only your voice,' he says. 'There's only you. You know that, don't you? It's only you.'

22 **May** I rang Judith Chisholm after the failure of my experiment in EVP and now I am driving through the fading light to her house in east London. 'Are you cracking up?' asks a poster for the Samaritans behind the glass of a bus shelter. No, I'm not cracking up. I feel calm. Judith Chisholm lives in a long, narrow street which ends at the

Hackney Marshes, the kind of place, I think to myself, where ghosts would live, if ghosts were to live anywhere. She lets me in. She is probably the same age as my mother, though my mother's hair is fading to a gentle grey, whereas Judith's is dyed the colour of thick blood. She shows me into her front room. It is painted dark green. There are crucifixes on the wall and containers of home-made wine on a side table. The house smells of damp cats or city roses in the rain. Her youngest son—her surviving son—comes into the room. His name is Vic. He is very thin and very pale. He works as an electrician. He's been expecting me.

'It's so amazing,' he says. 'You lost your younger sister. I lost my older brother. That's not a coincidence. That's a one-in-a-million chance.'

I don't reply. I feel silenced by this house. Judith brings me a cup of tea, and halfway through drinking it I lurch into a question. 'Do you believe in heaven?' I ask her, trying to concentrate on looking at her, rather than Christ hanging on the cross on the opposite wall.

'Spirits go through stages,' she says, not answering the question directly. 'I think some of them go to purgatory. And purgatory is…'

'Like a waiting room,' Vic cuts in. 'Or at least that's what I heard, anyway.'

'Vic, please, go and play with your computer,' his mother says. 'Two people can't do this. We can't both talk to Justine.'

'OK,' Vic says mildly. He looks at me and holds out a hand, which I take, briefly. 'I'm sure we'll meet again.'

Judith tells me about her EVP experiments. She has been engaged in them for seven years, at first in search of her dead son, who said a little, though now he can't get a word in edgeways because the voice that fills her tapes is that of a man called Jack Hallam. She used to work with Jack at *The Sunday Times*. He was the picture editor. He believed in ghosts and wrote books, collecting and editing other people's ghost stories. He died in 1986.

'Time is a curious thing,' Judith says. 'I've heard remarks that suggest that spirits are aware of the passage of time. I heard Jack say "It's a long time since I heard from Chisholm"—that's what he calls me, Chisholm. But I don't think he's aware that fourteen years have passed since his death.'

'Do you think he's in heaven?'

'I think that he's in purgatory. The evidence seems to point to that.'

Her evidence is on her tapes of Jack's voice. She has hours and hours of them, and she has listened to every minute of tape twenty or thirty times over. She says it's exhausting, so exhausting that often her head hurts. Yet now I am here, at last, an independent witness to these endeavours, and she is going to play me some of these tapes; but I will need to read her transcript, too. 'It's not like ordinary speech,' she says. 'You need to accustom your hearing. You may not even hear it. I have an extraordinarily wide range of hearing. I can hear things that other people can't.'

We go upstairs to the first floor, to her study, where she keeps her cassette player and her notes and her Dictaphone: her little door to the other world, where Jack Hallam is always waiting. Once Jack found Judith, it seems he couldn't be silenced.

She plays me the first recording she made of Jack Hallam's voice, on what was then a brand new Dictaphone, which, she tells me, cost eighty-nine pounds, much to her dismay. I hear a whispery, scratchy sound through the speakers—the sound of an empty pen on paper, or shallow gasps, or rats in the attic, a tap at the window; a ghost in the machine.

'Can you hear him?' she says urgently.

'I don't know,' I say.

'Listen,' she says, and rewinds the tape. But I still can't hear the words. So she rewinds it again. This time I ask her to tell me what he is saying. And I think, maybe... I think maybe I hear a voice. I read her transcript while I listen to the tape. It says:

OCTOBER 13TH 1999. KEY: SP = SPIRIT.

Sp: Hallam knows

Me: Having just recently bought this [a new tape recorder]

Sp: Yes

Me: I don't actually like it...

Sp: We do like it

Me: But is it useful to you? Can you come through on this and would you like me to keep it? I'm just going to leave this next bit of tape empty so you can perhaps speak on it

Sp: Now, Hallam's content. Hallam can progress. We need Hallam to know. Hallam needs someone who can help him. Tell him! Go and find Hallam! Go and get Hallam!

She plays me other tapes, and shows me other transcripts. In one, she asks Jack Hallam why he has been sent to communicate with her; could he please explain 'the plan'. 'There is no plan,' he replies. She wonders if she is missing something, because sometimes, despite her experience in these matters, even she finds it hard to understand all the words. And sometimes they frighten her. Her notes of an EVP session that took place on 12 January this year state that she can't tell if the spirit voice is saying 'let's kill her' or 'let's keep her happy' or maybe 'let's keep Hallam' or 'let's kill Hallam'.

She plays the tape to me. 'What can you hear?'

'I don't know,' I say.

She is obviously hoping for a better response from me, but I am unwilling to engage with what is happening here. She scrabbles around her study to find other tapes, searching for them with her glasses perched on the end of her nose like a storybook academic—the Professor Higgins of the psychic world, whose own perfect enunciation contrasts with the mumblings of these recalcitrant ghosts.

But as she plays me snippets of other tapes, I think I can hear the word 'Hallam', though it sounds as if it comes in a dream. Cheered by this, Judith suggests we make a recording together. She turns on the Dictaphone and speaks into it. She gives the date and says she is here with me to make a recording. 'I hope you're not angry with me for...I don't know what for, but I hope you're not angry with me anyway,' she says to Jack. 'Have you got anything you would like to say to us?'

She leaves a gap which is filled by silence. Then she asks me if I would like to say something.

I take a deep breath. 'I wonder if Ruth, my sister, is with you and could...speak to me.'

There is another silence. 'I hesitate to cut in,' Judith says politely. 'I hope I'm not cutting across what's being said, but as we don't really know where you are, Jack, if it is Jack who's speaking, we're not sure whether Ruth is there as well.'

After five minutes or so, she turns the machine off. She rewinds the tape and plays it back. This time I hear the voices. I know I hear them. I can't make out what they are saying, but I hear them, faint, like moths fluttering against a light bulb. I can't hear Ruth's voice, but I do hear a man's voice—Jack Hallam!—saying, hoarsely, 'Ruth!'

Judith is excited. 'That's Jack!' she says. 'It's definitely Jack! I recognize everything about him! He always hogs the recorder! He's so stroppy... But if he's there, they're all there. It stands to reason, doesn't it? It proves that there is life after death.

'You needn't worry about your sister any more,' she continues. 'She's OK. That's an amazing thought, isn't it?'

But I can't hear *her*. I hear Judith but I can't hear Ruth. I suddenly feel dog-tired, as if I'm swimming against the tide. Judith wants to replay the tape, over and over again, but I'm too exhausted to listen. She wants to make a transcript, now, with me, but I say no, it's late, I have to go home. So she makes me a copy of the tape, and we say goodbye.

At home, I take my tape into the kitchen, where Neill is sitting at the table.

'How was it?' he asks.

'Listen to this,' I say, 'just listen to this. I *heard* the voices.'

I play the tape out loud to him. But there is nothing to hear, apart from Judith's voice and mine.

'There's nothing here,' Neill says.

'There is,' I say. 'Well, there was. It must be a bad copy.'

I play it again. I play him the bit where Jack Hallam says 'Ruth!' But it doesn't sound like her name any more. 'That's the sound of a chair moving,' Neill says, 'or the click of the components in the machine, or your breathing. It's just your breathing.'

My face isn't moving but he looks at me as if I'm crying.

'You need to get some sleep,' he says. 'You've got to get some rest now. You'll feel better in the morning.'

1 June I dream that I am cycling over Blackfriars Bridge to visit Ruth's children and her husband and his girlfriend. They have just moved into a new house and it takes me forever to get there, and when I arrive I'm hot and cross. I can't find anywhere to leave my bicycle, and Lola, Ruth's daughter, looks sad and Matt, Ruth's husband, looks anxious and where, exactly, am I supposed to sit? Then, in my dream, I see

Ruth—and for the first time since her death, I see her not as sick Ruth, dying Ruth, but Ruth as full of life as ever. I know that she is dead, that nobody other than me can see her ghost, but she looks happy and spirited, and she flashes her brilliant smile at me and tosses her pre-cancer halo of dark curls. She says nothing, and I am silent too, but it doesn't matter. I have seen my sister. My sister has seen me.

8 June After my dream of Ruth, the date with Arthur Molinary seems less pressing; but now it is here, after all this waiting, and why waste the appointment? This time I feel no excitement as I climb the stairs to the second floor of the College of Psychic Studies. Inside Room Four, Arthur Molinary is waiting for me, a glass of water on the table in front of him, the sun shining through an open window. He gestures me to a chair opposite him, and looks at me through his pebble spectacles, head cocked to one side like a magpie. And then he begins to speak, and at first all I hear is the echoes of other voices in his voice: Yiddish, Italian, Spanish, northern English, merging and separating. I say nothing. He pauses, as if listening to the silence, and then starts talking again. 'You have someone here with you who is very close to you. She's your sister, your best friend, and she loves you very much. She knows that you love her. But she says, why are you unhappy? She is happy now and she wants you to be happy. She comes to you every night when you fall asleep. She is with you...'

'What does she want me to do?'

'She wants you to be happy,' Arthur Molinary says, with a small shrug of his shoulders in his buttercup cotton shirt.

He tells me other things: things I already know ('She had two lumps in her breast, and then her brain was troubled...she was confused and her legs grew weak, she couldn't walk...and when she died, she couldn't breathe, her lungs filled up...she died in the night and in the morning you sat and held her body').

Then he asks me a question. 'Your sister says, why don't you believe in God?'

'Well, *she* never used to,' I say, evasively.

'She does now,' he says, with another slight shrug of his shoulders, a quick blink behind his glasses. This somehow seems to me unlikely, though I do not say so out loud.

And just who *is* talking anyway? Is it Arthur Molinary, or my silent voice, or my sister's that he is listening to? Can he hear my thoughts, or is he stating the obvious here? And does it matter, anyway, because now I realize that I am her, and she is me, and my sister lives on inside my head and courses through my blood like life itself.

At home that night, I listen to the tape that Arthur Molinary made for me of our session. A lot of it is quite wonderfully true of Ruth, and some of it just as wonderfully banal. (My grandmother on the other side wants me to eat more Marmite, for the vitamins.)

Mostly, though, he is sensitive. He is a very senior sensitive, after all. As I listen to the tape, my faith in what he's telling me ebbs and flows. But I love my sister. And my sister loved me. And now I know, that after all this, in the end there is a beginning, there is life after death, because I am still living... Or that is what I seem to know, and I tell that to my husband as we lie in bed at the end of the long day.

He listens to me and then says, 'Have I ever told you about my friend, Tony King, who killed himself? He walked into the River Thames and drowned. It was after the death of his mother, but also he heard voices in his head. He was schizophrenic.'

'Well, I'm not mad,' I say, 'if that's what you're suggesting.'

'I'm not suggesting anything,' he says evenly. 'I'm just telling you about Tony... I'm sure I've told you this before—his mother died of a bee sting, and on my mother's birthday, he gave her a glass jar with three Roman nails in it that he had found on the shore of the Thames. He loved the river.'

'How did he know they were Roman nails?' I sound as if we're in court, not bed. 'That's too symbolic, like they were the ones used to nail Christ to the cross or something.'

'I don't know if they actually were Roman,' Neill says, 'but that's what he believed them to be. Anyhow, a couple of years after he died you and I played on a Ouija board one night with some friends.'

'That doesn't sound like you,' I say, 'the great sceptic, and I can't remember anything like that.'

'It was our first New Year's Eve together,' he says—and then I do recall the scene, but only that: no words, no story.

'I still felt guilty about Tony, I suppose, and I missed him.

Anyway, I asked him where he was, and the board spelled "home".
I said, "Where's home?" And he said, "The sea".'

'So you do believe in something,' I say, point scoring while
missing the point, trying to keep a small triumph out of my voice.

'I don't believe in one thing or the other,' he says. 'It made me
feel better, that's all.'

'I'm feeling better now,' I say.

'I know,' he says. 'I'm glad.'

11 **June** Pentecostal Sunday in the year 2000. The voice on the radio
at breakfast this morning tells me that this is the day of the coming
of Jesus's spirit: fifty days after he ascended to heaven, his spirit
returned to his disciples on earth, just in the nick of time, just as they
were sinking into despair as they waited for a sign in an upstairs room.

In my own upstairs an email has arrived from my father. He
composed it yesterday as an early birthday present for me; a
reconsideration of his father, written at my request. 'Your grandfather
Louis was evangelized into an inspirational form of Christianity by a
highly unorthodox class teacher when he was about nine or ten,' my
father has written. 'He wept at the account of the crucifixion...He was
soft and sentimental, easily moved to tears...Later, people pitied me
for having such a naive father and didn't blame me as much as him
for my "meshugassen"—madnesses...As well as going to seances he
went in for aura-seeing, through violet-tinted motorcycle glasses,' my
father continues crossly, though maybe he was smiling, as I do now,
grateful for these fragile threads of memory that bind us together. 'I
was shown the invisible aura of myself and others at the age of about
eleven, and I knew from then on that my father belonged to the world
of strange cults which gave him the sense of belonging...Of course he
despised Freudian insights into his very evident mechanisms of denial
and projection of his deep cultural unease.'

There is more, but it's enough for now—I don't want to stay in
with God on the radio or Christ on the computer (or Freud, which
is where I know my father's birthday message is heading). So I send
him a quick email back, telling him that I love him. Then we go out
into the park, my husband and my children and some neighbours.
The boys play football together, while I go for a walk with my dead

friend Kimberley's daughter, Juliette, who is my elder son's best friend. The local churches have congregated on the dried grass of the old bowling green for a Pentecostal celebration; Juliette and I stay on the outskirts of the crowd, unwilling, or maybe just unable to join in the hymns because we don't know the words.

A woman walks towards us, smiling. She hands me a hymn sheet and the order of service. HOLY SPIRIT WHO ARE YOU? is printed at the top of the page, and then the words to the hymn 'Shine, Jesus, Shine'. I can see the choir and the congregation singing, but their voices are lost in the open air. I can't hear the words so I read them instead. 'Lord, I come to Your awesome presence/from the shadows into Your radiance/by the blood may I enter Your brightness...' But God doesn't speak to me, again, and all I feel is slightly embarrassed, as if I'm intruding. I look down at Juliette, though she's not looking at me, she's looking at all the people around us, watching quietly without saying a word.

'Shall we go?' I ask her.

'I don't mind,' she says, and then meets my eyes and smiles. We walk away, across the park, while the voices of the congregation drift into nothing behind us, into the wide, empty sky, where the silence reaches to the end of everything, where the dead wait, and speak in the beat of our hearts.

So, if I dream I have you, I have you,
For all our joys are but fantastical.
'Elegy 10: The Dream', John Donne
□

PAOLO
Tim Parks

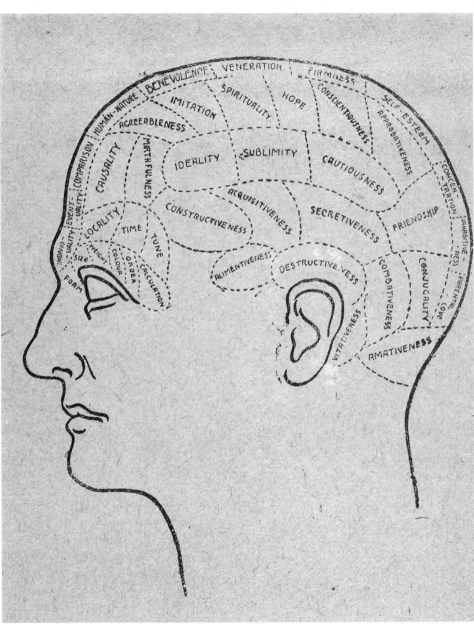

A late nineteenth-century phrenological head

MARY EVANS

'*Pronto?*' I lift the phone in our bedroom.

'My name is Paolo Baldassarre and I wish to speak to the writer Mr Timothy Parks.'

It's a breathless, urgent, demanding voice that drags me back ten years and more.

'Paolo!'

I knew they'd recently allowed him access to a phone, so I should have been ready for a call.

'I'll get Rita,' I tell him; his younger sister, my wife.

But he insists he wants to speak to me.

'Next week we'll be seeing each other,' he says.

'That's right. I'm looking forward to it.'

'I want you to know I've changed. I'm very sorry about what happened.'

My last glimpse of Paolo was on the platform at Verona station when I pointed him out to the police. He had announced he was coming to Verona, where I live, to kill me. Shabby, frantic, and obese, he waved three or four bunches of keys as they took him away; he had slipped one round each finger to form a sort of gothic knuckleduster. Shortly afterwards we received a visit from the Digos, Italy's elite anti-terrorist police. At first I thought they were Jehovah's Witnesses, but then two men in plain clothes showed me their IDs and guns. Paolo had written to tell them I was working with Mossad to eliminate Palestinians in Italy. Now, a decade on, I assure him there are no hard feelings. I knew he was going through a bad patch.

'I'd like you to help get the Anglo-American sanctions against me lifted,' he says. 'In time for my release, the year after next.'

He begins to explain that he needs to purchase an academic book called *Symbolic Logic*. He has to read it at once. Only the American publisher is demanding £600 for a hardback edition. This is because of the sanctions against him. He can pay, of course, but would like me to negotiate the deal for him and bring the book personally, otherwise it will be confiscated by the post office. He must complete his education before leaving the institute. That is imperative. 'As you know my father never let me study,' he announces. 'He poisoned my orange juice.'

I mildly suggest that all this is bullshit. 'I bet I can get you a hefty discount on that book, Paolo.' From the other end of the line comes a nervous chuckle, the same one my son uses when he's been caught out telling a tall story. Except that my son is fourteen and Paolo forty-seven. Daunted by my bluntness, he changes tack. He begins to ask entirely sensible questions about our new house, the children, what we're doing for our holidays and so on. For five minutes we enjoy a completely normal brother-in-law conversation. 'A presto,' I sign off.

Paolo was diagnosed as a paranoid schizophrenic some twenty-five years ago when both he and Rita were studying in the States, she at UMass Amherst, he at the University of Albany. The previous semester Paolo had written home asking if his mother would come to live with him. Then at a certain point he had stopped responding to either letters or phone calls. This had gone on for months. Finally Rita took the bus to Albany. She found her brother barricaded in his room in a supposedly supervised dorm, ankle-deep in filth, delirious and hallucinating. Nobody had noticed anything.

It is a curiosity of schizophrenia that while psychiatrists seem able to recognize and diagnose the condition with a certain rapidity (often a single interview is considered sufficient) it nevertheless remains extremely difficult to define or even describe. DSM-IV, the manual of diagnostic criteria prepared in 1994 by the American Psychiatric Association, is able to offer only a loose set of guidelines which at first glance seems to encompass an enormous range of possible disorders. Basically, for a diagnosis of schizophrenia, the manual demands that the patient exhibit at least two of the following symptoms: delusions, hallucinations, disorganized speech, grossly disorganized or catatonic behaviour, a 'flattening' of emotive responses, a loss of volition. These must be present for at least one month, although, somewhat enigmatically, 'continual signs of the disturbance' must be present for at least six months. In what way present, one wonders, if the 'symptoms' need be there only for a month?

When it comes to functional criteria, the manual becomes even vaguer, requiring that there be a noticeable impairment in the patient's ability to function in at least one of the following areas: work, personal relationships and self-care, and this 'for a significant portion of time since the onset of the disturbance'. What is 'a significant portion of time'? Aren't these areas in which many people, in certain periods of their lives, find it difficult to function?

But it is in its so-called 'exclusion criteria' that the manual is revealing of the psychiatric profession's embarrassment with this most perplexing of conditions. For although most psychiatrists are convinced that the cause of schizophrenia is in some way biological— not that it is the result of stress or particular social conditions—all the same DSM-IV explicitly rules out a diagnosis of schizophrenia in the event of a patient's problems being attributable to the physiological effects of a specific medical problem. The reason for this exclusion criterion, no doubt, is that over the last century all attempts to demonstrate a direct causative link between a biological malfunction and the disorder have proved vain. More mysterious than either cancer or Aids, schizophrenia becomes that organic illness for which, by definition of the psychiatric profession's diagnostic manual, there can be no organic cause.

Despite these problems of description, to read a series of case histories, or to talk with schizophrenics themselves, is to sense at once that the syndrome does have a character all its own, even if it's hard to pin it down to any one symptom. My brother-in-law Paolo's case is typical. Sent back from Albany to his family, then living in Ecuador, he began a long series of fruitless, short-lived therapies in Quito, Rome, Khartoum, Algiers and finally, when his father retired, Italy again. He seemed abnormally attached to and at the same time extremely antagonistic towards his parents. Incapable of forming relationships with girls he mailed pornography to his sister and myself. From time to time he disappeared and lived as a bum, practised various kinds of self-mutilation, attempted to buy an Algerian prostitute as a bride, 'ran rings', as he boasts, round a number of analysts, and read some of the most advanced books on quantum physics ever published. Or at least, those books were purchased for him, often at considerable expense.

In this way he was for many years a considerable financial burden, emotional strain and even potential physical danger to his parents. When violent he could be forced to stay in hospital and take the neuroleptic drugs that calmed him down. But then the law required he be released and being well aware of the long-term negative side effects of the drugs (drowsiness, obesity and, ultimately, impaired movement) he stopped taking them. Very soon the paranoid delusions and agitation would begin again. In the end it was only after he had committed a serious crime that he could be imprisoned and forced to take a sophisticated cocktail of medicine on a regular basis for a long period of time.

This happened seven years ago. Paolo held his mother at knifepoint, then smashed up the family home with a sledgehammer. Since then his parents have visited him fortnightly, first in high-security jails, then in the less restrictive mental institutions. We were told he didn't want to see other members of the family and so lost touch. But on New Year's Day 1999 my father-in-law died. Now his wife—we both call her Mamma—who never learned to drive, needs someone else to take her to where Paolo is presently based, way up in the rugged highlands between Genoa and Savona, a place apparently unreachable by public transport.

My mother-in-law arrives in Verona on the train from the family home in Pescara some 300 miles to the south on the Adriatic coast. Going to bed at nine she tells us we must be up at the crack of dawn to set off on the drive west to Genoa. She is irritated when Rita and I refuse to start before seven-thirty. Next morning, no sooner are we on the turnpike than we run into a big tailback. There's been an accident. 'Setting off early, Adelmo and I never had these problems,' Mamma announces.

In the car there's my mother-in-law, my wife, myself and Lucia, our five-year-old daughter. But the presence of little children was never an obstacle to adult conversation in the Baldassarre family. As we sit and simmer, waiting for the turnpike to clear, the old lady begins to talk about her husband's bones. Adelmo was buried in the earth, but in Italy the authorities remove the remains after fifteen years in order to recycle the space. 'Under no circumstances,' Mamma says heatedly, 'are those bones ever to be moved into my family tomb. Do you understand that, Rita? I will not have that whoremonger's bones in my family tomb.'

My father-in-law, I reflect, may have been willing to start early for every trip, but he had few other virtues in his wife's vision of things. Theirs was an embattled marriage. Towards the end they lived in separate apartments on the same decaying family property. Struck by a massive heart attack, having no phone in his apartment, Adelmo staggered over to knock on her windows in the middle of the night. She called an ambulance and went back to bed, believing he had overeaten again. In hospital he didn't wish to see her and she made no attempt to visit. Three days later he was dead.

My wife objects that Babbo—Dad—didn't want to be put in Mamma's family tomb, otherwise he wouldn't have insisted on being buried in the earth, would he? Being buried in the earth is often considered a little low-class in Italy. 'He'll be happy with the common ossuary,' Rita says. Then she steers the conversation to Mamma's favourite subject: the possibility that now, after seven years' imprisonment, Paolo will be allowed out of the institution for a week in order to come down to visit her in Pescara. 'Roberto can drive him down,' Mamma decides. Roberto is one of Rita's two younger brothers. Paolo was the firstborn. 'We can all be together for a week!' For some time she becomes extremely cheerful and excited thinking about this, as if such a visit could somehow cancel out all the terrible things that have happened. There is even a catch in her voice, as of someone looking forward to a week's pure evasion, with a lover perhaps, in any event a bliss beyond which life need never resume again.

A round one o'clock, an hour behind schedule, we finally get off the turnpike south of Alessandria and Mamma instructs me to take a first right up into the hills. But the map shows that there's a much shorter route starting from further down the valley. 'It'll be quicker,' I tell her. Mamma gets anxious. 'Adelmo always said there was only one road. It takes about an hour and a half.' After a brisk argument, I get my way and we reach our destination in just thirty-five minutes. Yet my father-in-law was no fool, I reflect. He must have known about this other road. And as I drive I realize that, either to spite Mamma, or because he was in no hurry to see his schizophrenic son, Babbo deliberately took the longer route. My father-in-law was a man who would always have chosen not to arrive at his destination if he could avoid it. He frequently said the happiest times with Mamma were in the car, he driving while she slept, his most enjoyable meals in the restaurants of turnpike service stations.

Three thousand feet above sea level, the mental institute is housed in a converted hotel. This is a region of thickly wooded but not dramatic or especially beautiful hills. Once travel became easier, people from the nearby towns who had used the area as a holiday destination started to go further afield for their fresh air. So amid the general atmosphere of decay and lost enterprise that characterizes the tiny villages along the way, it does not seem inappropriate that an erstwhile hotel should now house forty or so men and women who seem emblematic of all that is run-down and futureless, shuffling vacantly from room to room or standing catatonic in corners, trapped in a vacation that will never end. 'Then if they try to escape,' Mamma says, gesturing to the uninhabited landscape, 'it's easy for the police to find them before they reach the nearest town.'

In the porch, by the reception desk, an unshaven man standing in the attitude of one who has shat in his pants asks all and sundry for cigarettes. The receptionist gets on the phone to track down Paolo and after a few minutes he appears. To my immense relief, apart from the hollow, hunted eyes, the hunched shoulders, and the fact that on a hot day he is wearing at least five layers of shirts, jumpers and jackets, he seems pretty normal. We exchange friendly greetings and even a hug. The truth is, I had not fully understood, despite my wife's warnings, that the difficult person to deal with during this encounter would not be Paolo, but Mamma. 'Look at the make-up she's put on for him,' Rita had whispered that morning, but I'd thought nothing of it.

Immediately Mamma is kissing her son, almost on the lips. She disengages, but only to throw out her arms and embrace him again, kiss again. Seconds later she's adjusting the collar of one of his shirts. It's not straight. It's not clean. And his hair's too long. He hasn't been eating enough. Has he eaten? She apologizes that we didn't arrive at ten, as she promised. I had no idea she had promised such an impossible thing. 'There was a four-hour tailback,' she announces, exaggerating wildly. 'A terrible accident! Horrendous! We would have been here hours ago.' Paolo merely nods amiably, informing us that he's already had his lunch, but that he'll be happy to sit beside us while we eat at our hotel. So we climb back in the car and drive a further half mile to the place where we are to spend the night.

Some thirty years ago, in the crazy Sixties, a group of psychotherapists added to the confusion of those heady times by concluding that many mental disorders, including schizophrenia, might in some way be related to the family relationships surrounding the sufferers. In part the movement can be seen as a backlash against traditional psychiatry and its failure, as some perceived it, to go beyond the development of more and more sophisticated tranquillizers. In part, it came out of a frustration with Freudian psychoanalysis. In any event, a form of therapy was developed which involved getting the whole family together and trying to change the way people behaved with each other. Some successes were scored, particularly with anorexia, but any number of sensibilities were offended too. Who wants to hear that they are even indirectly responsible for anything? The feminists ran to the defence of the mothers who were being made scapegoats. Parents' associations complained about public money being spent on such mad ideas. Add to all this that with schizophrenia, particularly chronic schizophrenia, the results of this kind of therapy were disappointing, and it's hardly surprising that by the mid-Eighties the game was up. The medical profession settled back into its traditional vision that schizophrenia is basically the result of a biological disorder.

So today, if you consult the latest literature, you'll be told that the disorder is partly genetic (though how big a part they can't say), or that it may be due to an abnormally large right brain hemisphere (though many schizophrenics don't have this and many who aren't do), or that it's the result of an unidentified virus contracted in the mother's womb but mysteriously clicking in not, as you'd think, when they're cutting the umbilical cord, but twenty years later when most of us have our scissors out to deal with the apron strings.

Observe us, then, as we sit down to lunch, a perfectly 'normal' family except that twenty-five years ago one member sadly succumbed to this hypothetical organic anomaly, or gene defect, or virus...

The hotel restaurant is empty but the pleasant proprietress offers to rustle up what is the standard fare of Italian holiday hotels: tagliatelle and ragout followed by a steak. I had been warned that on a previous such visit Paolo drank two litres of Coke and suffered an attack of diarrhoea in the car afterwards, but so far his behaviour is exemplary. For some years now he has been receiving all the state-of-the-art neuroleptic tranquillizers, and one has to admit they are having a positive effect. Of course they are not designed to deal with the cause of this disease. They are not curing him. He is still completely crazy, already bothering Rita with the story of the hugely expensive *Symbolic Logic*, plus various other books he must order and read before his fantasized release in two years' time, not to mention the international sanctions against him that have still to be lifted. But he is calm and pleasant. 'No, no tagliatelle for me,' he tells the waitress cheerfully. 'I've already had an excellent lunch, thanks.'

'Bring a plate for him as well,' his mother says.

'Mamma,' Rita protests. 'He says he's eaten! Just the steak for me,' she tells the waitress. 'No pasta, thanks.'

'Bring a plate for my son,' the old lady orders.

'Mamma, no, I've had enough.'

'You're thin,' she accuses.

Proudly, Paolo begins to explain that over the last two months he's managed to lose ten pounds. The waitress is hovering.

'Bring tagliatelle for him as well!'

'Mamma, for Christ's sake!' I wade in. 'The guy's an adult. He knows whether he wants to eat or not!'

'You understand nothing!' she yells at me. 'Nothing! He's starving himself.'

'You're hopeless,' Rita tells her mother.

But exactly as we gang up against Mamma, Paolo turns his head to the waitress and says, 'Yes, do bring me a plate. I'll be happy to have the tagliatelle.' Then immediately he embraces his mother. He begins to caress her wrists and neck and face. One hand has slipped inside the arm of her short-sleeved dress. She is kissing him.

'*Mammina*,' he says. '*Mammina*. You're all I have left now. There's only us two. Just a few years together,' he whimpers. '*Povero, povero*,' she says with immense satisfaction at our expense. But as he pulls away from her, he demands: 'So, have you brought the money? I want my money.'

One of the purposes of these trips is to bring Paolo his monthly spending money.

'We'll have to talk about that later,' Mamma says.

'But you can't not give me my money,' he whines. He uses the diminutive word, '*soldini*'—which is to say, small change, or pocket money. But there's a threat in his voice. In fact what we are talking about is the equivalent of £150 for his regular allowance plus £200 he has somehow managed to run up in debts since the last visit.

'We'll talk later,' Mamma says, patting his hand, and then the tagliatelle arrive in a great heap on a long metal dish. And she begins to serve.

Photos of Rita around the age of eleven or twelve show a pretty girl who is distinctly overweight. It wasn't until fifteen or sixteen that she got control over her own food intake. Now there is no question of anybody insisting that she touch the tagliatelle, while Paolo, who has already eaten, faces a considerable pile. When Mamma begins to insist on seconds, I ape her gestures of maternal insistence with Lucia. '*Povera cara ciccia*,' I wheedle, 'you really do need a secondy helpingy, don't you? You can't say no!'

Lucy laughs, belches and pushes her plate away. She doesn't want. Paolo breaks out into a huge grin. He understands perfectly. All the same the whole miserable rigmarole of his being persuaded to eat is repeated when the steaks arrive. First he surreptitiously slips his meat on to Rita's plate. Complicitous with his rebellion, she starts to eat it. But as soon as Mamma sees what's happened, she raises her hand in the air. 'Waitress! Waitress! Another steak!' Instinctively, Rita and I protest. Immediately, and one feels with deliberate perversity, Paolo capitulates, then turns to embrace her. '*Mammina, Mammina!*' Then: 'You will give me the *soldini*,' he demands.

Watching mother and son, I see with belated insight that the odd dynamic between them, something they are both equally involved in and responsible for, is forcing me to take on the role of my dead father-in-law. Except that this was probably the moment when the old man gave Paolo a soda or promised him money to counter these disturbing embraces and reassert his role as head of the house. Babbo always held all the purse strings. 'I understand money,' I remember him telling me once, 'but not women.'

Babbo, however, is no longer with us. This gambit in the family repertoire can no longer be played. Perhaps that explains the extreme anxiety now apparent on Paolo's face as he demands his cash. He's not quite sure he's going to get it. After all, one of the jollier talking points in the Baldassarre family is Mamma's extraordinary parsimoniousness, to the extent of using the same bowl of water for the dishes breakfast, lunch and dinner and then emptying it on the vegetable garden. And the bidet water too! Babbo, as Paolo well understood and learned to exploit, threw money around to annoy her.

After lunch there's a break while Paolo returns to the institute for his 'therapy'. We hang about in the lounge where there are ping-pong and pool tables, but the few inmates present are all smoking in front of the TV.

'Tell me about the therapy,' I ask when we're back in the car. It seems the ritual of these visits is to drive down to the nearest town thirty tortuous miles away, spend half an hour there, then drive back. This will exhaust the rest of the day.

'Just pills,' he says. He names an impressive list of drugs, mostly dopamine-blockers. He clearly relishes his expertise in this field. 'We're all schizophrenics,' he says candidly, 'all nuts, so we need these things, otherwise we'd smash the place up. Sometimes people do smash the place up, then they get a big injection right off.'

Sitting next to him now, in the front of the car, with the opportunity to talk quietly between ourselves, I begin to notice that Paolo's conversation is mostly normal so long as you don't touch on two key subjects: the reasons for his illness or 'failure in life', and the possibilities for his future. If this is the effect of a virus, it sure is an odd one.

Driving along he gives excellent directions, warns me of tough hairpins, gives information on the countryside, on some Roman ruins.

He tells me how useless the dance therapy classes are, though the teacher is attractive, explains that cigarettes can be had extremely cheaply from a machine in the institute—'Yes, about sixty per cent off the regular price! They hope we'll die of cancer.' He laughs. He's one of the very few who don't smoke. Mamma is proud of his not smoking. Sometimes an inmate wants a prostitute and smashes up his room when he can't get one. 'Basically people deal with each other through threats, violence and wheedling,' he explains. This seems all too recognizable a scenario.

But then I ask him if they ever try to reduce the amount of drugs they're giving him, to see if he still needs them. He says yes. 'And how is it?' 'Fine.' 'So why don't they reduce them some more?' 'They can't,' he says, 'because the levels were stipulated in the sentence that condemned me to my imprisonment.' 'I bet that's not true,' I tell him. 'They don't stipulate drug levels in court rulings.' He mutters something under his breath. 'What?' He grins. 'Come on, Paolo, what did you say?' 'I'm a *migliorillo*,' he laughs.

How can I translate this word? He's invented it. It must mean something like, 'I'm a bettersome boy'. 'I try to get better,' he says, 'so that I'll be ready to come out in two years' time.' I say nothing, because we all know that there is no limit to the ruling that forced him to live in an institute. He can only come out when a psychiatrist decides he's well enough.

We drive on. I find myself going very slowly, as if in memory of my father-in-law, one of the world's slowest drivers. And as I speak to Paolo, I can't help but feel he's engaging me in a sort of teasing game, inviting me to discuss serious questions, then suddenly retreating into fantasy when I poke my nose where I shouldn't. In each case these fantasies have to do with things that blocked him in the past or are preventing him from having any future now. In the past there was his father's perfidy, ordering that he couldn't study, couldn't marry and putting poison in his food. Now there is the court ruling about his level of drug treatment and the Anglo-American conspiracy to stop him reading by denying him books, or demanding he pay thousands of dollars for them.

'I used to shout a lot when I was in the States,' he says. 'That's why they threw me out. The acoustic insulation in the dorm was very poor. People heard me shouting. It's better nowadays.' He begins to discuss the technicalities of modern insulation about which he is surprisingly well informed.

'So if they'd had better insulation back in the Seventies, none of this would have happened and they wouldn't be trying to stop you from reading American books?'

He nods, faintly smiling.

'But Rita tells me you used to have a copy of this book *Symbolic Logic*. So they did let you have it for a while.'

'That's right.' Paolo admits that he himself tore the book up. One day he walked into his room and a voice from outside screamed, 'ZEOAM!'

'Which means?'

'Down with the Americans!' So he tore up all his American books. 'I only study in English. The Americans are a great nation.' He then begins a perfectly sane account of how one goes about destroying a book, first removing the cover from the pages, then separating out sections of pages thin enough to be reduced to shreds.

I interrupt. 'So it's not a conspiracy stopping you reading, but yourself. Something to do with being sent to America to study, maybe. After all, Babbo did pay for you to go to university.'

'Bullets,' he says.

'What?'

'You're preparing bullets for the lethal blow.'

'Only a suggestion,' I say.

'You shouldn't prepare bullets.'

'Just having a chat, it's been so many years.'

Under his breath, he mutters, 'Rita, Francesca Valentina.'

'I beg your pardon?'

He repeats, grinning. 'Rita, Francesca Valentina.'

'And what does that mean?'

'It means Rita has two degrees, one in French, Francesca, one in English, Valentina. But I don't have any.'

'But how could I have understood that?'

'*Francesca*, French, is easy. *Valentina* from *"valore"* [value] and *"ina" inglese*—English.'

'I could never have guessed that.'

He agrees, laughing. Despite the bullets, he seems to be enjoying himself. It's as if he'd found a willing sparring partner at a satisfactorily inferior level.

'So how can you expect people to understand you when you speak in code? Or would it help if we read *Symbolic Logic*?'

He pauses. Solemnly he announces: 'Everybody understands me according to his or her own ability.' He repeats. 'Each according to his ability.'

'And Mamma, how much does Mamma understand you?'

He turns brusquely in his seat. '*Mammina, Mammina*. You're the only one who cares for me.'

Mamma smiles and begins to talk about his possible visit to Pescara. Roberto will drive him down. 'That would be wonderful,' he agrees. 'So nice. I can see my old room. You will give me the money, won't you, *Mammina*?'

The following morning, waking in the early hours from a weird dream, some strange business where an old school friend was giving a lecture on how to keep the minutes of legal hearings while I was in a panic about the eyebrows sprouting over my nose, it occurs to me that yesterday's conversation with Paolo had a dreamlike process about it. There was the same bizarre meandering, the same explosion of odd images when something important seemed to be at stake. Perhaps the difference between those who believe schizophrenia is a disorder that at least partly comes out of the structural trauma of family relationships, and those who believe it is entirely organic, is not unlike the difference between those who believe that dreams have meaning, if only you could decode them, and those who are convinced they are completely random.

The plan is that we stay the morning with Paolo, see his doctor, lunch together, then drive Mamma directly down to Pescara where we can spend a few days by the sea. So immediately after breakfast we hurry over to the institute again, where two big surprises are in store...

The first is a bus stopping right outside. People get on and off. And where does that bus come from? From Savona. So it would be possible, after all, for Mamma to take the train to Savona and then the bus to the institute! It would be a tough journey for an old lady, but in the end no tougher than first coming up to Verona and then crossing Italy in the car.

'So you see, you can visit him when we're away in August,' Rita tells her mother.

Waiting for our interview with his psychiatrist, we discuss the situation. Paolo is extremely sensible. 'Why on earth come so often, Mamma?' he asks, 'especially when it's so hot. Wait till October.'

But Mamma has always insisted that she must visit him once a month if possible, once every two months at least, even though a number of doctors have suggested that these visits have a negative effect on Paolo.

'You can send the money by post,' he suggests.

She says she'll think about it. But as soon as Paolo goes off to the bathroom for a moment, she hisses, 'What on earth am I supposed to do with him if I come without a car? What am I going to say to him all day?'

Briefly I imagine lovers who don't share the same language and who have been forbidden to embrace. What can they do but, as we did yesterday, drive around all day while others do the talking? That is why Rita and I are here, not because Mamma needed transport. We are chaperones to their mad mismatch.

When Paolo returns Mamma is very businesslike and says it's time to sort out the money. Reluctantly, she gives him what he wants.

The second surprise comes when the psychiatrist finally ushers us into his office, forty minutes late for our appointment. I'd thought Mamma was going to ask whether Paolo could be granted leave to go down to Pescara. Instead she starts complaining about some detail related to her son's disabled person's pension, something that clearly has to do with an administrator not a psychiatrist. She rails about the tangles of Italian bureaucracy. The doctor agrees and in a matter of seconds seems to think the interview is over.

'But what about the visit to Pescara?' I ask. Mamma leans over to whisper, 'He'll never grant it. I asked last time.' She gets up to go. But I feel that if we don't ask about this visit, the interview will have been wasted.

'We've been wondering,' I say, 'if Paolo is well enough to spend a few days with the family in Pescara.'

Just as I speak the phone rings. With astonishing rudeness, the doctor becomes engaged in ten minutes of very jocular conversation about some barbecue he is planning. When finally he puts down the receiver I have to remind him of the question.

'What do you think, Paolo?' he asks.

Paolo is clearly unhappy to be exposed like this.

'I'd like to go,' he hesitates, 'so long as no one touches my room here. I'm very happy here.'

'Of course nobody will touch it,' the doctor says. 'That's fine then. Let's say, in three or four months' time, shall we? In the autumn.'

Suddenly I see that the doctor knows perfectly well that this visit will never happen because neither Mamma nor Paolo wants it. When autumn comes round no one will mention it. So his words are completely empty. Vaguely he grants what they vaguely ask. He isn't interested in discussing the contradiction of their dreaming about something they don't, when it comes to it, really want. Thus he integrates himself perfectly in the way they operate together. They can fantasize about it, without needing to clinch anything. In any event, the interview is over now. The doctor offers a limp hand over his handsome desk.

As soon as we're out Mamma is again very businesslike. No mention is made of the Pescara trip. 'You've got to have a haircut,' she tells Paolo. 'I don't want one,' he says. Mamma turns to us. 'You must drive him to the nearest village to get a haircut.' 'Paolo?' Rita asks. 'I don't want one,' he says. I say, 'But the moment we attack Mamma you'll start hugging her, right?' He grins.

So the haircut it is.

Then over our farewell lunch, Rita asks: 'Paolo, did they ever suggest you have some therapy with the family?'

Actually, I know she knows the answer to this. We discussed it with her father once.

Paolo nods. He's very matter-of-fact. He did two sessions with Babbo, he says, but Mamma wouldn't come.

'That's not true,' she exclaims.

'Yes it is,' Paolo is mild and matter-of-fact, completely convincing, 'I remember you said you didn't want to come.'

Mamma is furious. 'Do you think I wouldn't have come if it could have been useful for you? I can't believe this!'

Immediately he withdraws and we're back to the *Mammina* routine. Apparently it is impossible for him to comment openly on his mother's contradictory behaviour, her strange mixture of love and recalcitrance. Or could it be that he actually wants things this way, encourages this behaviour? Certainly there's no question here of any one person's being solely to blame, it's more the way each person's behaviour complements the other's that seems so unhealthy.

As we prepare to say goodbye, Paolo and I are left alone a moment while the others are in the bathroom. Standing outside the hotel, he suddenly stumbles rather strangely and bangs his nose on the top of the car.

'Paolo, what happened?'

'Some people produce a strong neuroperfume,' he explains, wiping away a bead of blood. 'It makes me fall over.'

I can only presume the 'some people' is myself. But then he hugs me. 'It's been lovely to see each other again.' 'Next time we'll come on our own,' I tell him. 'Mamma and Babbo had told us you didn't want to see us.' 'Not at all,' he says. 'Not at all.'

The drive down to Pescara is a long one. Seven hours. We start talking about the building work that must be done on the family property. But this only leads Mamma to attack Babbo again. He deliberately kept it in a poor state of maintenance to spite her because it was originally her family's not his. He always spited her. She starts to get wound up, once again rehearsing the tension and betrayals of fifty years of marriage. It's a litany we're all too familiar with, if only because the policy of both parents was to tell you unpleasant stories about their partner, only to side with each other if you ever said anything openly to their faces.

'So why did your father marry me?' Mamma suddenly demands, 'if all he wanted was his whores and sluts?' Fortunately little Lucia is asleep. 'Why? We were engaged for years, the whole war, he had time to say no. Then the very day after the wedding, the very day, I knew it was a mistake! I knew he didn't love me!'

'Why didn't you leave him then?' Rita rehearses. It's an ancient conversation. Once it gets going, no one seems able to stop it.

'Well, why didn't he leave me, if he didn't want me? If he'd just said, "I don't want you," do you think I would have stayed? Anyway,' she suddenly reflects, 'I couldn't upset my parents, could I? It would have been the death of them if our marriage had failed, just like that. They couldn't have borne it.' On other occasions, however, Mamma will tell you almost proudly that her father also had endless 'little sluts', only he was sufficiently respectful to do it far from home. 'Your father never respected me,' she insists to Rita.

'It's true he was always making promises he never kept,' my wife acknowledges. But this only introduces another area of family myth: how Babbo was always just about to visit, or to treat, or to take his children on a trip, but never quite got round to it. As always, various incidents are remembered, half with amusement, half in pain. 'There was the time,' Rita laughs, 'when not turning up from Algeria he sent a telegram that simply said: LETTER FOLLOWING. Which of course it never did.'

'Well, anyway, thank God both your old folks died without having to think you'd separated,' I remark.

Mamma sees no irony in what I've said. *'Grazie al cielo,'* she says. 'It would have been the death of them.'

As evening draws on, speeding along this turnpike that my parents-in-law drove up and down so many times, it comes to me that in this family to talk about anything always means to talk about everything, because nothing has ever been resolved between them. The whole family is somehow marooned in the ambiguous behaviour of my father-in-law exactly fifty years ago when he married a woman without apparently wanting to, yet at the same time forever promising that one day everything would sort itself out, one day there would be the dreamt-of resolution, the whole family together and happy by the sea in Pescara.

It's a mentality that fits perfectly with the contemporary and strictly organic approach to schizophrenia. For the time being the patient can be tranquillized on what are truly very sophisticated drugs. If one has to be marooned somewhere, it's as well to keep the anguish levels low. Anyhow, nothing else can be done and it's certainly no one's fault—unless, that is, we're going to be so primitive as to believe that people can really drive each other mad. In the twenty-five years of Paolo's illness no one has suggested to Mamma that she might look for different ways of behaving with her son. No one has suggested that her weirdly intense relationship with him might have anything to do with the unhappy prevarications of her husband. But then, why bother? In the future, when medical research finally gets there, the whole disorder will be cleared up with an appropriate medicine and everybody can go on behaving exactly as they please. □

REAL TIME
Amit Chaudhuri

On their way to the house, Mr Mitra said he didn't know if they should buy flowers. They were very near Jogu Bazaar; and Mr Mitra suddenly raised one hand and said: 'Abdul, slowly!'

The driver eased the pressure on the accelerator, and almost brought the Ambassador to a standstill. Not looking into the rearview mirror, he studied two boys with baskets playing on the pavement on his left.

'Well, what should we do?' Mr Mitra's face, as he turned to look at his wife, was pained, as if he were annoyed she hadn't immediately come up with the answer.

'Do what you want to do quickly,' she said, dabbing her cheek with her sari. 'We're already late,' she said, looking at the small dial of her watch. He sighed; his wife never satisfied him when he needed her most; and quite probably it was the same story the other way round. Abdul, who, by sitting on the front seat, claimed to be removed to a sphere too distant for the words at the back to be audible, continued to stare at the children while keeping the engine running.

'But I'm not sure,' said the husband, like a distraught child, 'given the circumstances.' She spoke then in a voice of sanity she chose to speak in only occasionally.

'Do what you'd do in a normal case of bereavement,' she said. 'This is no different.' He was relieved at her answer, but regretted that he had to go out of the car into the market. He was wearing a white cotton shirt and terry cotton trousers because of the heat, and shoes; he now regretted the shoes. He remembered he hadn't been able to find his sandals in the cupboard. His feet, swathed in socks, were perspiring.

He came back after about ten minutes, holding half-a-dozen tuberoses against his chest, cradling them with one arm; a boy was running after him. 'Babu, should I wipe the car, should I wipe the car...' he was saying, and Mr Mitra looked intent, like a man who has an appointment. He didn't acknowledge the boy; inside the car, Mrs Mitra, who was used to these inescapable periods of waiting, moved a little. He placed the tuberoses in the front, next to Abdul, where they smeared the seat with their moisture. Mr Mitra had wasted some time bargaining, bringing down the price from sixteen to fourteen rupees, after which the vendor had expertly tied a thread round the lower half of the flowers.

'Why did she do it?' he asked in an offhand way, as the car proceeded once more on its way. Going down Ashutosh Mukherjee Road, they turned left into Southern Avenue.

Naturally, they didn't have the answer. They passed an apartment building they knew, Shanti Nivas, its windows open but dark and remote. Probably they'd been a little harsh with her, her parents. Her marriage, sixteen years ago, had been seen to be appropriate. Usually, it's said, Lakshmi, the goddess of wealth, and Saraswati, of learning, two sisters, don't bless the same house; but certainly that wasn't true of the Poddars, who had two bars-at-law in the generation preceding this one, and a social reformer in the lineage, and also a white four-storeyed mansion on a property near Salt Lake where they used to have garden parties. Anjali had married Gautam Poddar very soon after taking her MA in History from Calcutta University.

As they passed a petrol pump, Mr Mitra wondered what view traditional theology took of this matter, and how the rites accommodated an event such as this—she had jumped from a third-floor balcony—which couldn't, after all, be altogether uncommon. Perhaps there was no ceremony. In his mind's eye, when he tried to imagine the priest, or the long rows of tables at which people were fed, he saw a blank. But Abdul couldn't identify the lane.

'Bhai, is this Rai Bahadur R. C. Mullick Road?' he asked a loiterer somewhat contemptuously.

The man leaned into a window and looked with interest at the couple at the back, as if unwilling to forgo this opportunity to view Mr and Mrs Mitra. Then, examining the driver's face again, he pointed to a lane before them going off to the right, next to a sari shop that was closed.

'That one there.' They went down for about five minutes past two-storeyed houses with small but spacious courtyards, each quite unlike the other, till they had to stop again and ask an adolescent standing by a gate where Nishant Apartments was. The boy scratched his arm and claimed there was no such place over here. As they looked at him disbelievingly, he said, 'It may be on that side,' pointing to the direction they'd just come from.

'That side?' Mr Mitra looked helpless; he'd given up trying to arrive in time. What preoccupied him now was not getting there, but the negotiations involved in how to get there.

It turned out that what the boy was suggesting was simple. The main road, Lansdowne Road, divided the two halves of Rai Bahadur Mullick Road; one half of Mullick Road went left, the other right.

'Don't you know where they live?' asked Mr Mitra as Abdul reversed and turned the car around. The over-sweet, reminiscent smell of the tuberoses arose in the front of the car with a breeze that had come unexpectedly through the window.

'But I've only been there three or four times—and the last time, two years ago!' she complained. 'I find these lanes so confusing.' The lanes were confusing; there were at least two, one after another, that looked exactly the same, with their clothes lines, grilles and courtyards.

About ten or eleven days ago, they'd noticed a small item in the newspaper, and were shocked to recognize who it was. Then an obituary appeared, and Mr Mitra had called his daughter in Delhi, who remembered Anjali from visits made in childhood. Last week, another insertion had told them that 'Observances will be made in memory of Mrs Anjali Poddar, who passed away on the 23rd of February, at 11 a.m. at 49 Nishant Apartments, Rai Bahadur R. C. Mullick Road. All are welcome.'

They didn't expect it would be a proper *shraddha* ceremony; they didn't think people would be fed. So Mrs Mitra had told the boy at home, firmly so as to impress her words upon him, 'We'll be back by one o' clock! Cook the rice and keep the dhal and fish ready!' Without mentioning it clearly, they'd decided they must go to the club afterwards to get some cookies for tea, and stop at New Market on the way back. So they must leave the place soon after twelve; it was already ten past eleven.

The first to be fed was usually a crow, for whom a small ball of kneaded *aata* was kept on the balcony for it to pick up; the crow was supposed to be the soul come back—such absurd make-believe! Yet everyone did it, as if it were some sort of nursery game. Mr Mitra, looking out through the windscreen, past the steering wheel and Abdul's shoulder, speculated if such practices might be all right in this case. Here the soul had made its own exit, and it was difficult to imagine why it would want to come back to the third-floor balcony of Nishant Apartments.

'Ask him!' said Mrs Mitra, prodding her husband's arm with a finger. She nodded towards a watchman standing in front of what looked like a bungalow. 'Ask him!'

'Nishant?' said the thin, moustached chowkidar, refusing to get up from his stool. Behind him was an incongruously large bungalow, belonging to a businessman, hidden by an imposing white gate and a wall. He barely allowed himself a smile. 'But there it is.' Two houses away, on the left.

It was clear from the size of the cramped compound, with the ceiling overhanging the porch only a few feet away from the adjoining wall, that Nishant had been erected where some older house once was, which had been sold off to property developers and contractors. It must be twelve or thirteen years old. An Ambassador and two Marutis were parked outside by the pavement. Mr Mitra, holding the tuberoses under his right arm, glanced at his watch as he entered the porch, then got into the lift, which had a collapsible gate, hesitantly. He waited for his wife, looked at himself quickly in the mirror, and pressed a button. Mrs Mitra smoothed her hair and looked at the floors changing through the collapsible gate.

A narrow, tiled, clean corridor, going past forty-six and forty-seven, led to the main door to forty-nine, which was open. Faint music emanated to the corridor; and a few people could be seen moving about in the hall. There was a jumble of slippers and sandals and shoes by the door, promiscuously heaped on each other. Mr Mitra took off his with an impatient movement; Mrs Mitra descended delicately from hers—they had small, two-inch-high heels.

Mr Talukdar, who was standing in a white shirt and trousers talking to another couple and a man, excused himself from their company and came to the newly arrived couple. 'Come in, come in,' he said to Mrs Mitra. To Mr Mitra he said nothing, but accepted the tuberoses that were now transferred to his arms. 'Nilima's there,' he said, indicating a woman who was sitting at the far side of the sitting room upon a mattress on the floor, an old woman near her. So saying, he went off slowly with the tuberoses in another direction.

A small crystal chandelier hung from the ceiling, gleaming in daylight. Near where Nilima, Anjali's mother, sat, a ceiling fan turned slowly. Some of the furniture had been cleared away for mats to be laid out on the floor, but some, including two armchairs and a divan, had been left where it was. On the sideboard was a Mickey Mouse-shaped pencil box, next to a few photographs and curios. A clock upon one of the shelves said it was eleven twenty-five.

Mr Talukdar was a tallish man, heavy, fair, clean-shaven. Most of his hair was grey, and thinning slightly. He'd held some sort of important position in an old British industrial company that had turned into a large public sector concern a decade after independence: British Steel, renamed National Steel. He was now standing next to a television set, whose convex screen was dusty, and talking to someone.

Mr Mitra seemed to remember that he had two sons in America, and that the sons had children. But Anjali had had no children, and that might have made things worse for her. He looked at a man singing a Brahmo *sangeet* on a harmonium in the middle of the room, attended only by a few listeners, and saw that it was someone he knew, an engineer at Larsen and Toubro.

The song stopped, and the sound of groups of people talking became more audible. The hubbub common to *shraddha* ceremonies was absent; people welcoming others as they came in, even the sense, and the conciliatory looks, of bereavement. Instead there was a sort of pointlessness, as people refused to acknowledge what did not quite have a definition. Mr Mitra's stomach growled.

He looked at his wife in the distance, the bun of hair prominent at the back of her head; she bent and said something to Nilima, Anjali's mother. Suddenly, there was a soft, whining sound that repeated itself, low but audible; it was the cordless phone. Mr Talukdar stooped to pick it up from a chair, and, distractedly looking out of the window, said 'Hello' into the receiver, and then more words, nodding his head vigorously once, and gesturing with his hand. He walked a few steps with the cordless against his ear, gravitating towards a different group of people. Mr Mitra realised that the tuberoses he'd brought had been placed on that side of the room, beside three or four other bouquets.

He felt bored; and he noticed a few others too, some of whom he knew, looking out of place. *Shraddha* ceremonies weren't right without their mixture of convivial pleasure and grief; and he couldn't feel anything as complete as grief. He'd known Anjali slightly; how well do you know your wife's distant relations, after all? He'd known more about her academic record, one or two charming anecdotes to do with her success at school, her decent first class degree, and about her husband Sumit Poddar diversifying into new areas of business than about her.

'Saab?'

Thank God! A man was standing before him with a platter of *sandesh*—he picked up one; it was small and soft; he took a tiny bite. It must be from Banchharam or Nepal Sweets; it had that texture. There was another man a little further away, with a tray of Fanta and Coca-Cola. Mr Mitra hesitated for a second and then walked towards the man. He groped for a bottle that was less cold than the others; he had a sore throat developing.

'Mr Mitra!'

There was a man smiling widely at him, a half-empty Coke bottle with a straw in one hand.

'I hope you remember me; or do I need to introduce myself?'

'No, I don't remember you; but I spoke to someone at the club just the other day who looks very like you, a Mr Amiya Sarbadhikari,' said Mr Mitra jovially, taking a sip of faintly chilled Fanta. A large painting of a middle-aged woman holding flowers faced them.

They talked equably of recent changes in their companies, catching up from where they'd left it in their last exchange; then to their children, and a brief disagreement about whether civil engineering today had a future as a career.

'Oh I think so,' said Mr Sarbadhikari, 'certainly in the developing world, in the Middle East, if not in the West.' His Coke bottle was now almost empty; he held it symbolically, putting off finishing the dregs. There was an uneasiness in their conversation, though, as if they were avoiding something; it was their being here they were avoiding. Of course, people never remembered the dead at *shraddha* ceremonies; they talked about other things; but that forgetfulness occurred effortlessly. In this case, the avoidance was strategic and self-conscious; the conversation tripped from subject to subject.

'Mr Mitra, all this Coke has swollen my bladder,' said Sarbadhikari suddenly, 'and, actually, from the moment I stepped in...'

From his manner it looked like he was familiar with Talukdar's flat. Gathering the folds of his dhoti in one hand, he turned histrionically and padded off in the direction of a bathroom door. A child, the only one among the people who'd come, ran from one end of the hall to the other. There were a few people on the balcony; Mr Mitra decided to join them.

'I told them,' a woman was saying to a companion, 'this is no way to run a shop, if you don't exchange a purchase, say so, but don't sell damaged goods.' He quietly put down the bottle of Fanta on the floor. There wasn't much of a view; there was the wall, which ran towards the street you couldn't see, and another five-storeyed building, with little, pretty balconies. Below him was the porch to the left, and the driveway, which seemed quite close. A young woman, clearly not a maidservant, was hanging towels from the railing in one of the balconies opposite.

Did it happen here? He watched the woman attach clips to another towel. Apparently those who always threaten to, don't. Anjali had been living with her parents for a month after leaving her husband. She'd left him before, but this time she'd said her intentions were clear and final. There was a rumour that her parents had not been altogether sympathetic, and had been somewhat obtuse; but it's easy to be lucid with hindsight. He was still hungry, and he looked back into the hall to see if he could spot the man with the *sandesh*. But he had temporarily disappeared. As he moved about exploratorily, he caught his wife's eye and nodded at her, as if to say, Yes, I'm coming, and, Yes, it's been a waste of time.

Cautiously, he tried to trace, from memory, the route that he'd seen Sarbadhikari take about ten minutes ago. He found himself in a bedroom where the double bed had been covered neatly with a pink bed cover; he coughed loudly. He opened a door to what might be the bathroom, and, once inside, closed it behind him again. As he urinated into the commode, he studied a box, printed with flowers, of Odomos room freshener kept above it; then he shivered involuntarily, and shrugged his shoulders. He had a vaguely unsatisfying feeling, as if the last half-hour had lacked definition.

Once inside the car, he said to his wife, 'I don't know about you, but I'm quite ravenous.' □

THE ODDITY
OF HEIGHT
Fergus Fleming

Mont Blanc

JOHN NOBLE/WILDERNESS

In 1541 the Swiss naturalist Conrad Gesner made an extraordinary decision. 'I am resolved,' he wrote to a friend, 'that as long as God grants me life, I will each year climb some mountains, or at least one, at the season when the flowers are in bloom, in order that I may examine these, and provide noble exercise for my body at the same time as enjoyment for my soul.'

Gesner's decision was unusual for several reasons. In the short, uncertain and uncomfortable lifespans of the time, most people did not seek extra toil; climbing a mountain even once, let alone every year, was an unnecessary and profitless burden. Then there was the very fact of mountains; they were steep, nasty, cold, frightening and potentially hazardous. They were also high, and height was anathema. What could one do with height? Nothing. One could not till its thin soil. One could trade only with difficulty over its rocky passes. One could hardly even invade one's own neighbour if height intervened. It was a worthless and obstructive thing. All these factors made Gesner's decision unusual. But what made it extraordinary was his decision to climb not just mountains but the Alps.

The Alps were—and are—Europe's most majestic mountain range. Springing in the west from the Tenda Pass above Nice, the main chain of summits runs in a 700-mile arc to the south-west of Vienna. Lesser offshoots poke southwards to the Adriatic and the Balkans, but in the sixteenth century it was the main chain, and in particular the western part of the main chain, that first sprang to mind when anybody mentioned Alps.

Lying at the cultural crossroads of Europe, where French, German and Italian influences met, the western Alps should theoretically have been a vibrant, cosmopolitan area. And to an extent they were: the Romans had marched over them, as had Hannibal and his Carthaginians; since the second century AD Christian missionaries had proselytized in the valleys; pilgrims from as far away as Iceland had crossed the Great St Bernard Pass and other of the twenty-three major passes which led to Rome. For a brief period they were controlled by Saracen bandits. Every conceivable nationality had either passed over the Alps or settled below them. One region was proud of its Scandinavian heritage, another of its Prussian; one area venerated an Irish monk; in others the place names were clearly Arabic in origin; neighbouring valleys spoke different languages, held different political allegiances and embraced different religious beliefs. Yet for all this diversity, for all this coming and going, the Alps were a blank on the map. Apart from a few pockets of civilization such as Geneva and Bern and other cities which prospered in the mountains' shadow, and apart from the well-trodden passes (which had once been well maintained but since the fall of Rome had become increasingly ruined), nobody cared about the rest. Scattered agricultural communities, inbred and disease-ridden, grazed livestock on the upper pastures. And that was all people knew or wanted to know about the place. The culprit was height.

The Alps were, indeed, tremendously high. Within the central range, which was in places 120 miles wide, there were hundreds of peaks higher than 10,000 feet, dozens higher than 13,000 feet and one, Mont Blanc, which at 15,771 feet was the highest in Europe. So high were the mountains that they formed one of the continent's great climatic barriers, wringing the moisture from prevailing winds to divide Europe into cold, wet north and warm, dry south.

The Alps were more feared than any other area in Europe. Early pilgrims wrote gruesome accounts of avalanches and rockfalls which swept them away or imprisoned them in lonely hospices for days on end. They feared the cold, the altitude, the views and the wildness. Alpine villagers were no less frightened: they never knew when the mountains might fall on their heads, or whether the serpentine glaciers would advance, covering their orchards with ice, or retreat, leaving piles of stone in their wake.

Such was the ignorance surrounding the mountains that most of them had no names—if they did, they were called things like Accursed or Unapproachable—and the very term 'alp' was itself a misnomer: when early geographers had pointed at the peaks and asked what they were called, locals had replied *alpes*. But this referred only to the high-level meadows on which they grazed their stock; they had no word for the mountains themselves. Thus the name which appeared in world atlases became an unwitting reminder of just how little Europeans knew of the wilderness in their midst.

By Gesner's time the Alps were a source of terror and superstition. Plains-dwellers still shuddered at the thought of

Hannibal's march in 218 BC. On the whole, the Alps were as distant from the normal world as was the moon. Anything could happen in this icy semicircle of teeth that bit off Italy from the outer world. When people approached them, it was only to scuttle over their passes as speedily as they could, alert for impending danger. Many travellers were carried blindfold lest they be overwhelmed by the awfulness of the scenery. The idea that anyone might actually want to climb one of these mountains was inconceivable. Gesner's decision, therefore, was radical to say the least. For several generations his example was studiously ignored.

Bit by bit, however, the terror waned and by the late eighteenth century it had been replaced by curiosity. What secrets did the Alps hide? Was it true that dragons and alien races dwelled on the peaks? Exactly what went on up there? These questions had to be answered, and there was no better place to answer them than on Europe's highest mountain, Mont Blanc.

In August 1786 a Swiss farmer named Jacques Balmat became the first person in history to climb Mont Blanc. Balmat's interest in the Alps—unlike Gesner's—was a far from solitary passion; by the mid-eighteenth century certain circles had become positively infatuated with the idea of height. Two centuries after Gesner first expressed his unusual interest in the mountains, Alpine enthusiasts such as Marc-Théodore Bourrit, the Precentor of Geneva Cathedral and self-styled 'Historian of the Alps', and his rival, Horace Benédict de Saussure, Professor of Natural History at the Geneva Academy, were competing to be first to the top of Mont Blanc. Saussure and Bourrit in particular had created an Alpine industry through their copious writings and researches. Both men had also made failed attempts upon the summit, and in 1760 Saussure had even offered a reward—the precise sum is not known—to the first person to climb Mont Blanc. In 1786 the reward remained unclaimed. Balmat decided it should be his.

Jacques Balmat was in many ways a late entrant to the race. He may not have had much in the way of mountain expertise, but he was supremely fit. As he reminisced in old age, 'I had a famous calf and a stomach like cast iron, and I could walk three days consecutively without eating, a fact I found useful to me when lost on the nearby

Buet. I munched a little snow—nothing more. Every now and then I cast a sidelong look at Mont Blanc and said to myself, "My fine fellow, whatever you may say or whatever you may do, I shall get to the top of you one day."'

Balmat trained for every possible difficulty to such a degree that he dreamed of nothing else. 'I would plant my feet on pieces of rock and feel them shake like loose teeth,' he wrote, 'and the sweat would fall from me in great drops...Never mind, keep going! I was like a lizard on a wall. I saw the earth sinking away beneath me. It was all the same, I only looked at the sky. All I cared for was to reach the top...At that moment I was awakened by a vigorous box to the ear by my wife, and, would you believe it, I had caught hold of her ear and was tugging it as if it were India rubber.'

Finally, on 5 June 1786, he put his dreams and his plans to the test. He told his wife that he was going after crystals and would be back within two days. Climbing via the village of La Côte, through the Taconnaz glacier, he reached the series of rocky outcrops called the Grands Mulets, near the Dôme du Goûter, without mishap. The summit of Mont Blanc lay to the east, but Balmat was prevented from spying the ground ahead thanks to a cloud that enveloped both the peak and himself. Undeterred, Balmat then did the unheard of: he decided to spend the night where he was. Lacking as he did a tent, and provisioned with only a loaf of bread and a bottle of brandy, he would be considered foolhardy by any standards. By those of the time his decision was unimaginable folly. Nobody had ever spent a night in the open at such a high altitude. It was widely believed that any who did so would die.

Balmat's chosen resting place was a little perch of hard snow about six feet long surrounded by rocks. A few feet away yawned an 800-foot drop. For fear of rolling down the cliff in his sleep, Balmat remained awake, seated on his knapsack, beating his hands and feet together to combat the cold. Shortly before midnight the mist turned to snow. 'My breath was frozen,' he recalled, 'and my clothes were soaked...soon I felt as if I was stark naked. I moved my hands and feet faster, and began to sing to drive away the thoughts that were seething in my brain.' His voice died away in the whiteness. There was no echo. 'Everything was dead in this ice-bound world and the sound of my voice almost terrified me. I became silent and afraid.'

At two a.m. the sky grew lighter and by four Balmat was confident that he had survived. He spent another day and yet another numbing night on the mountain before deciding to go back. On the way down, however, he was horrified to meet a party of three guides coming up. Ostensibly they were looking for lost goats; but Balmat suspected they were actually planning an attempt on the summit. If they were successful they would gain the reward. When they asked him what conditions were like higher up, his suspicions were confirmed. By now, Balmat had been climbing more or less continually for two days, but the prospect of being outstripped by the fresher men was more than he could bear. When they asked him to join them he accepted immediately. There was one problem: Balmat had promised his wife he would be back within two days. In an extraordinary display of vigour he therefore ran down to Chamonix, told his wife that he was back and then, having grabbed some food and a change of socks, told her he was off again.

He left his home at eleven p.m. and two hours later had caught up with the others. By three a.m. the whole party was standing on the Dôme du Goûter from where, in the early dawn, they could see the summit. Here the throng was swelled by another pair of guides. Their excuse that they had decided to climb to the Dôme for a wager was more than Balmat could stomach. Appalled at the prospect of having to share the reward with so many, he set out on his own and within a few hours was sitting astride a narrow ridge or arête leading to the summit. It 'seemed a path fit only for a rope dancer' and was interrupted by an ugly clump of rocks but, looking down, Balmat thought he could discern a route over the glacier below—the so-called Grand Plateau. Unfortunately, he was in no position to make the journey. He was starved of sleep, he had run out of provisions, and the weather was deteriorating. He had no choice but to retreat.

On reaching the Dôme he discovered that the others, too, had given up. They had gone home, expecting Balmat to follow. Rather than do so, however, he spent the rest of the day criss-crossing the Grand Plateau. That night he again slept uneasily on the mountain side. Thousands of feet below him, he could see the lights of Chamonix being extinguished one by one. It did little to raise his spirits. 'No man is made of iron,' he admitted, 'and I felt far from cheerful. During the short intervals between the crash of avalanches I heard distinctly the barking of a dog at Courmayeur [on the Italian side of Mont Blanc] though it was more than a league and a half to that village from the spot where I was lying. The noise served to distract my thoughts, for it was the only earthly sound that reached me. At about midnight the barking ceased, and nothing remained but the deathly silence of the grave.'

At two a.m. he awoke and began his descent. He reached home six hours later, badly sunburned and utterly exhausted. Rejecting his bedroom—'I was afraid of being tormented by the flies'—he went into the barn and stretched out on a pile of hay where he slept for twenty-four hours. In all, his odyssey had taken the better part of five days during which he had slept, fitfully, for only two nights. He had covered incredible vertical distances at an astonishing rate—his second ascent must have been made at a run, even allowing for an exaggeration of his times. He had proved that it was possible to survive a night in the open at a very high altitude and, above all, he had found a route to the summit. It was a great achievement and if it yielded no immediate profit Balmat did not care. 'I was despondent but not disheartened by these two vain attempts,' he recorded. 'I felt quite certain I should be more fortunate a third time.'

For three weeks Mont Blanc was shrouded in cloud. This was no use to Balmat. The clouds which looked so innocuous from below contained driving snow and sleet which even his constitution could not endure for long. Equally important, they meant that observers would be unable to see people on the summit. It was all very well to reach the top, but it would be pointless to do so unless the conquest could be verified by telescope from below. And there was another thing: Balmat had to find a respectable person to climb with. Even if he reached the summit and turned somersaults in the full view of a thousand spectators, it would be considered valueless without a man of science to hand with his barometer. Where could one find such a man in Chamonix? At the door of Michel-Gabriel Paccard, the town's twenty-six-year-old doctor.

Paccard had been peering vainly at Mont Blanc through his telescope for more than three years in search of a route to the summit.

When Jacques Balmat approached him with the news of his discovery—also for advice about his sunburn—and the offer of making a joint attempt, Paccard did not hesitate. They agreed to start as soon as the weather cleared. The clouds dissipated in the early hours of 8 August 1786, leaving Mont Blanc outlined in all its unconquered glory. Balmat was at Paccard's house before dawn.

In 1832 the novelist Alexandre Dumas was to visit Balmat and persuade him to give his version of what happened next. The resulting narrative owed much to Balmat's sense of self-importance, a great deal to Dumas's journalistic skills, and even more to his interviewing technique—he paid for, and Balmat consumed, three bottles of wine—but even so it is worth repeating because it remains the only detailed description of the historic climb. 'I went to Paccard,' related Balmat, 'and said, "Well, Doctor, are you determined? Are you afraid of the cold or the snow or the precipices? Speak out like a man." "With you I fear nothing," was his reply. "Well then, the time has come to climb this molehill."'

They set off at five o'clock in the evening, taking separate routes so as to avoid drawing attention to themselves, and met up again at the village of La Côte. 'The same evening we slept on the top of La Côte, between the glaciers of Bossons and Taconnaz. I carried a rug and used it to muffle the Doctor up like a baby. Thanks to this precaution he passed a tolerable night. As for me I slept soundly until half-past one. At two the white line appeared, and soon the sun rose without a cloud, brilliant and beautiful, a promise of a glorious day! I awoke the Doctor and we began our day's march.'

After a quarter of an hour they were crossing the Taconnaz glacier, surmounting crevasses 'whose depth could not be measured by the eye' and snow bridges that 'gave way under our feet'. 'The Doctor's first steps were halting and uncertain,' Balmat recorded, 'but the sight of my alertness gave him confidence, and we went on safe and sound.' Up they went to the Grands Mulets where once again Paccard's confidence waned as Balmat showed him where he had spent the night. 'He made an expressive grimace, and kept silent for ten minutes; then, stopping suddenly, said, "Balmat, do you really think we shall get to the top of Mont Blanc today?" I saw how his thoughts were drifting and answered him laughingly.' At the projecting rocks known as the Petits Mulets the wind rose and Paccard's hat was snatched off his head. 'I turned on hearing his cry, and saw the felt hat careering over the mountain to Courmayeur…"We must go into mourning for it," I said, "you will never see it again for it has gone to Piedmont, and good luck be with it." It seemed my little joke had given offence to the wind, for my mouth had scarcely closed when a more violent gust obliged us to lie down on our stomachs to prevent our following the hat. The wind lashed the mountain sides and passed whistling over our heads, driving great balls of snow almost as big as houses before it. The Doctor was dismayed…At the first respite I rose, but the Doctor could only continue on all fours.'

At the Dôme du Goûter, Balmat took out his telescope and looked back at the town below. He had arranged with a shop woman to look out for them at this point and, sure enough, there she was with fifty others. Balmat waved his hat and the villagers waved back. But the hatless Paccard, who had finally stood up thanks to 'considerations of self-respect', could only be distinguished by his big coat. At this point Paccard's nerve seems to have gone altogether, if Balmat is to be believed. 'Having used up all his strength in getting on his feet, neither the encouragement from below, nor my earnest entreaties could induce him to continue the ascent. My eloquence exhausted, I told him to keep moving so as not to get benumbed. He listened, without seeming to understand, and replied, "All right." I saw that he was suffering from the cold, while I also was nearly frozen. Leaving him a bottle [of brandy], I went on alone, saying that I should very soon come back to find him. He answered, "Yes! Yes!" and telling him again to be sure not to stand still, I went off…From that time onward the route presented no very great difficulty, but as I rose higher the air became much less easy to breathe, and I had to stop almost every ten steps and wheeze like one with consumption. I felt as if my lungs had gone, and my chest was quite empty. I folded my handkerchief over my mouth, which made me a little more comfortable as I breathed through it. I kept walking upward, with my head bent down, but finding I was on a peak which was new to me, I lifted my head and saw that at last I had reached the summit of Mont Blanc!

'I had no longer any strength to go higher; the muscles of my legs seemed only held together by my trousers. But behold I was at the end of my journey...I had come alone with no help but my own will and my own strength. Everything around belonged to me! I was the monarch of Mont Blanc! I was the statue on this unique pedestal!'

Then Balmat remembered Paccard. He shouted for him but received no answer. Alarmed, he retraced his steps and found Paccard rolled up in a ball, 'just like a cat when she makes herself into a muff'. Even the news that Balmat had reached the peak had no effect on him. All he said was 'Where can I lie down and go to sleep?' Balmat hoisted him to his feet and when he complained that his hands were cold gave him one of his hareskin mittens—'I would not have parted with both of them even to my brother'—before shoving him up to the summit which they reached shortly after six p.m.

The sun shone brilliantly and stars could be seen in the deep blue sky. Balmat, who had completely recovered from his previous fatigue, marvelled at the view.

They stayed there for an hour. Paccard brought out his thermometer and barometer—despite a temperature of 6°F below freezing, which caused his ink to freeze as he tried to put down the results. Then at seven p.m., with only two and a half hours of daylight remaining, Balmat gave one last wave of his hat to the villagers below and, holding Paccard under the arms, began the descent. The doctor was 'like a child, no energy or will. I guided him along the good places and pushed, or carried him, along the bad'. Every few minutes Paccard would stop, saying he could go no further, and had to be pushed on by brute force. When they crossed the snowline at eleven p.m. Paccard announced that he could no longer feel his hands:

'I took off his gloves and found that his hands were dead white, and my hand also from which I had taken the glove was quite numb. I said, "Well, we have three frost-bitten hands between us." He did not mind but only wanted to lie down and sleep. He told me, however, to rub them with snow, and that was easily done. I began by rubbing his hands and finished by rubbing my own. Soon sensation returned, but accompanied by pains as if every vein had been pricked by needles. I rolled my baby up in his rug and put him to bed under the shelter of a rock; we ate and drank a little; pressed as close to one another as possible, and fell fast asleep.'

The following morning Paccard was completely snow-blind. 'It is funny, Balmat,' he said, 'I can hear the birds singing but can see no daylight.' He wondered whether it was because he could not open his eyes. Yet, according to Balmat, they were 'glaring like those of a horned owl'. Paccard followed Balmat downhill, holding on to his knapsack until they reached La Côte, where Balmat hurried home, leaving the doctor to feel his way back with a stick.

When Balmat looked in a mirror he was horrified. 'I was quite unrecognizable. My eyes were red, my face black and my lips blue. Every time I laughed or yawned the blood spouted out from my lips and cheeks, and in addition I was half-blind.' Within a week, however, he was fit enough to travel to Geneva to claim Saussure's prize. And a month later the story of his ascent was published by the Historian of the Alps himself, the indefatigable Bourrit.

Bourrit's account of Balmat's climb broadly accords with that of Dumas fifty-six years later. Not everything was the same: Balmat was seventy when he spoke to Dumas and was confused by old age as well as an obvious animosity towards Paccard. The humiliating scene on the Dôme du Goûter, for example, was a complete fabrication. They never went there, but ascended instead via the Grand Plateau which lies beneath it. Equally, Balmat's claim that he struggled alone to the summit while Paccard sank into hypothermic slumber is open to doubt: Paccard would have frozen to death in the estimated hour and a half it must have taken Balmat, after leaving him, to reach the summit and then rejoin him; and if not dead, Paccard would have been in no condition to record the temperature let alone make observations with his barometer, which he undeniably did. Such details aside, however, the two stories are very similar. According to Bourrit, who published his findings in a public letter on 20 September 1786, Balmat was the hero and Paccard a feeble tagger-on. Not only had Balmat reached the top before Paccard but he had had to drag the doctor after him. In every respect Balmat had breathed life into the enterprise while Paccard had to be coaxed, shoved and bullied to the summit. It is a masterful and engaging story culminating with a typical flourish: 'Chamonix contemplated them, strangers from below saw them through their glasses; they had followed them on their march with inquietude and they rejoiced at the sight of the two little beings upon so lofty a pinnacle of the globe.'

It was very impressive. But nothing that Bourrit said agreed in the slightest with Paccard's version of events. Having got wind of Bourrit's machinations Paccard produced a detailed certificate describing the climb. It was signed by Balmat and stated unequivocally that Paccard had proposed the route, had led the ascent, had encouraged Balmat when he was flagging and had helped him with his baggage, and that when he had reached the summit Balmat 'was obliged to run to be nearly as soon as he was on the aforesaid spot'. Balmat stated outright that 'Paccard called me and I followed.' His signature was witnessed by two of his fellow guides. Paccard was perhaps going a little far here, but he gave a more restrained account to Saussure, who stated in his diary that as they neared the summit 'they endured great fatigue from the fact that the surface was covered with a thin crust which alternately bore them and gave way under their steps. The guide told him he could not persevere unless he (Paccard) was prepared to take the lead from time to time and to break the snow and he did this all the way to the top.' A brace of German barons, who had been advised by Saussure to watch the climb from a nearby hill, had seen the two men waving from the summit. And every subsequent report from Saussure and others attributed the climb if not solely to Paccard then certainly to both men.

Tempers in Chamonix ran high. When Balmat accused Paccard of forging the certificate the doctor knocked him to the ground. Eventually, Saussure had to intervene, forcing Bourrit to reword his letter in less antagonistic terms. Bourrit made a number of pale excuses: Paccard hadn't actually reached the summit; his narrative was badly written; it contained information damaging to Saussure's reputation; if he, Bourrit, did not believe what he had written then he would have published it anonymously; and so on. In the end Bourrit made a few reluctant amendments, but even the revised document was damaging. One of Paccard's relatives was imprisoned for a day for using foul language about its author.

Paccard fought back as best he could. He sent two letters to the *Journal de Lausanne* correcting Bourrit's assertions and issued a prospectus inviting people to subscribe to his own forthcoming narrative. His manuscript, which he foolishly gave to Bourrit's editor Bérenger, was never published—or if it was, it was circulated privately; at any rate, no copy of it has ever been found—and in the absence of any solid opposition Bourrit's version therefore became accepted as the true one. After all, was he not the Historian of the Alps? Balmat was accepted as the conqueror of Mont Blanc and Paccard as his accomplice. Balmat received Saussure's reward—Paccard, unwisely, made no claim; he had no need of the money, as Bourrit had pointed out, but it would have strengthened his position—on top of which Balmat was given a gift of fifty Piedmontese pistoles by the King of Sardinia, who also granted him the title 'Balmat dit Mont-Blanc'. A public subscription was opened for his benefit, managed rather inefficiently by Bourrit who was suspected for a while of siphoning some of the money into his own pocket, and on the proceeds Balmat built a handsome house for himself. Plaques and statues were erected in his honour, roads were named after him. He was worshipped in Chamonix and became the most sought after guide in the valley.

From this distance it is impossible to judge fairly who was the first to climb Mont Blanc. Essentially the controversy revolved around Bourrit's jealousy and Balmat's desire to get his hands on Saussure's money. The argument sputtered into the twentieth century when, on the emergence of clarifying documents, and amid a wholesale weariness, Balmat and Paccard were each given a share of the credit. But by then the question had become almost incidental. Following their example, Victorian climbers swarmed through the Alps ticking off peaks like partners on a dance card. To these explorers Mont Blanc was as nothing. They sought to conquer the entire Alpine chain. Gesner's message had at last got through. Height was not horrible—it was sublime. □

Modern Painters
Modern Painters
Modern Painters

AMERICAN ISSUE: ON SALE 14 SEPTEMBER

AMERICAN ISSUE: ON SALE 14 SEPTEMBER

AMERICAN ISSUE: ON SALE 14 SEPTEMBER

AMERICAN ISSUE: ON SALE 14 SEPTEMBER

AMERICAN ISSUE: ON SALE 14 SEPTEMBER

Through a twist of fate that the author of *Labyrinths* himself would have relished, these lost lectures given in English at Harvard in 1967–1968 by Jorge Luis Borges return to us now, a recovered tale of a life-long love affair with literature and the English language. Transcribed from tapes only recently discovered, *This Craft of Verse* captures the cadences, candor, wit, and remarkable erudition of one of the most extraordinary and enduring literary voices of the twentieth century.
Charles Eliot Norton Lectures
new in cloth

this craft of verse
JORGE LUIS BORGES
EDITED BY CĂLIN-ANDREI MIHĂLESCU

other traditions
JOHN ASHBERY

One of the greatest living poets in English here explores the work of six writers he often finds himself reading "in order to get started" when writing. Among those whom John Ashbery reads at such times are John Clare, Thomas Lovell Beddoes, Raymond Roussel, John Wheelwright, Laura Riding, and David Schubert. Less familiar than some, under Ashbery's scrutiny these poets emerge as the powerful but private and some-what wild voices whose eccentricity has kept them from the mainstream—and whose vision merits Ashbery's efforts, and our own, to read them well.
new in cloth

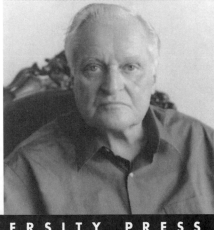

HARVARD UNIVERSITY PRESS
US: 800 448 2242 • UK: 020 7306 0603 • www.hup.harvard.edu

IN SEARCH OF
THE THIRD WAY
Roy Hattersley

The waiter told us 'sit wherever you like'—which could only mean that no other customers were expected that evening. So, hunger dampened by agoraphobia, I chose a corner table and asked for the wine list with stuttering shame. I was taking Pat Moynihan to dinner and I could not imagine that at any stage of his glittering career— Ambassador, Special Counsel to the President, and Senator—he had ever been asked to eat in a restaurant which so recklessly proclaimed its unpopularity. Moynihan himself seemed not to notice our isolation. He had begun to perform the last rites of social democracy in the Strangers' bar of the House of Commons and after two hours of continuous obsequies, he still had earth to throw on the coffin. Nothing was going to distract him from completing his threnody for Roosevelt's New Deal, which had inspired his youth, and Kennedy's New Frontier of which he had been part. As we sat down, he shouted above the noise of the table legs scraping over the tiled floor, 'All over! Over!' I think that he said 'over' seven times, before he added, 'Finished!'

In 1962, when Moynihan was John F. Kennedy's Assistant Secretary of Labor, he launched so many federal government initiatives that *Time* magazine had featured his smiling picture on its cover under the splash headline PAT ANSWERS. So I asked him what had happened to the young man who, full of Keynesian fervour, had asked the President of the United States to double the number of daily postal deliveries—not to improve the performance of the United States post office but in order to create half a million new jobs for black Americans. Moynihan stood up and, flinging his arms in the air, addressed a print of Canaletto's Grand Canal on the distant wall. 'He was wrong,' he said. 'That young man was wrong. Wrong! Wrong!' It was when he had shouted 'wrong' for the seventh time that eating in a deserted restaurant seemed not such a bad idea.

No doubt I looked as despondent as I felt. But, whatever the reason, Moynihan decided to lift my spirits by anticipating the new dawn of radical politics which would end the long night of Reaganism in America and Thatcherism in Great Britain. 'Somebody will come up with a new idea. Not the pretence that the market solves our problems or the hope that government can, itself, put everything right. Sooner or later, we'll find a third way.' At the time, I thought

PETER MARLOW/MAGNUM PHOTOS

of the phrase as no more than politicians' shorthand—smart talk rather than any kind of answer to the question which was already beginning to haunt progressive politics. So I made a joke about it. If he would begin the search for the missing philosophy, I would be Doctor Watson to his Sherlock Holmes.

Now, I am not sure if the image was completely appropriate. Perhaps I should have offered to be Sancho Panza to Moynihan's Don Quixote, riding out on their quest for a great cause to defend; or Petty Officer Evans to his Captain Scott, setting off on a doomed voyage of discovery. If the Antarctic provided the best analogy, I should have thought of myself as Captain Oates. For, even then, I did not feel happy inside the big tent.

Looking back on the long search, the analogy which comes to mind is the attempt to produce helium—the gas which scientists knew to exist in the solar system but for some time could not create on earth. In 1993, Hillary Clinton sounded like such a scientist; perhaps alchemist is nearer the mark. She confided in the *New York Times* her determination to develop a theory of government which would 'marry conservatism with liberalism, capitalism and statism and together produce practically everything'. The new philosophy would unite 'the way we are and the way we were, the faults of man and the word of God, the end of Communism and the beginning of the new millennium' and it would provide an antidote to 'crime on the streets and on Wall Street, teenage mothers and foul-mouthed children and frightening drunks in the park, the cynicism of the press and the corrupting role of television, the breakdown in civility and the lack of community'. What Mrs Clinton called 'a unified theory of life' made up in scope what it lacked in precision. But in America it needed a name with which to catch the public's imagination. Her husband provided one in his 1998 State of the Union message when he declared 'an end to the sterile debate between those who say that government is the enemy and those who say government is the answer', and announced, 'We have found the Third Way.'

At the time of President Clinton's Third Way declaration I had just left the House of Commons after thirty years' continuous service in the Labour cause, and had completed the transition which was recorded in successive volumes of *Who's Who*—'politician' in 1964, 'politician and writer' in 1979, 'writer and politician' in 1992 and (with immense relief) 'writer' five years later. But for a time I saw myself as a private detective, examining every piece of evidence through my metaphorical magnifying glass and at that stage of the investigation the forensic technique produced rewarding results. The crucial clue—which revealed what Clinton hoped for the third way—lay not in the two words of his title but the way in which the initial letters of those words were capitalized in the official text of his speech, making clear that it was not simply an alternative route towards an established goal or a different technique for achieving recognized ends. Clinton's Third Way was a distinct political philosophy.

Back in 1989 Will Hutton (then the *Guardian's* economics editor) made a film about German politics. It described the resurgent Social Democrats—who rejected both the free markets which had produced West Germany's *Wirtschaftswunder* and the command economy of the Communists' Democratic Republic in the East—as campaigning for a third way. It was, not surprisingly, social democracy. The Social Democrats did not claim to have found anything which was new. They simply wanted to emphasize that democratic socialism was a distinct philosophy of government. And their vision of a better society differed from Clinton's in a second and more fundamental way. Social Democrats had a unifying ideology to guide them along the path which their third way took. There was no need for them to search for a 'big idea'. They already had one. President Clinton did not. His view of the Third Way has exactly the same intellectual force as Herbert Morrison's insistence that socialism was whatever the Labour Party was doing at the time. To Clinton the Third Way is whatever policies are introduced by the Democratic President of the United States.

Perhaps it was unreasonable to look for the answer to a philosophical conundrum in the United States, the home of unideological politics. But President Clinton's active participation in the construction of a Third Way is in itself a defining feature of the process. I began to feel like Sherlock Holmes again—or even Doctor Watson. For it required only the most elementary deduction to confirm that, since President Clinton would not support anything that resembled socialism, the Third Way (which he supports) cannot be socialism, defined either as the active promotion of greater equality or as the extensions of common ownership and government intervention in the working of the market. Yet European party leaders who call (or have called) themselves socialists happily participate in discussions about its creation. I began to examine the proceedings of their Third Way seminars in the hope that, as well as discovering their conclusions, I would learn their reasons for taking part in an exercise which required the abandonment of long-held beliefs.

The question is easily answered in Tony Blair's case. For him the construction of a coherent and consistent Third Way is an emotional necessity. That is the only possible explanation for his announcement that he was a devout believer in the new philosophy and was therefore calling a meeting of political scientists and intellectuals from related disciplines to work out what it was. Politicians are usually conversant with the basic tenets of their philosophy before they announce their commitment to it. And prime ministers usually enter office with a long-held principle (called a prejudice by their opponents) which they hope to turn into practice by the implementation of ill-defined and badly prepared policies. Tony Blair stood the rule on its head. Nobody doubts that, when he was elected, he had a precise programme which he was determined to carry out. But he lacked—and clearly felt he needed—an idea which would pull the disparate policies together.

According to detective fiction, the police always lose their tempers when they discover that less sophisticated investigators have complicated their work by disturbing the evidence. Searching for the Third Way I understood how they feel. The Prime Minister, hoping to find a friendly philosophy, trampled vital clues into the ground. Initially he followed what, for him, was a false trail and believed that his search was over when he found 'stakeholding', an idea set out most recently and with greatest clarity by Will Hutton, who after his stint at the *Guardian* became, briefly, the editor of the London *Observer*. Hutton published *The State We're In* (his prescription for creating 'the good society') in June 1995 and the book was a best-seller by the end of August—thus demonstrating that its main idea had some appeal to the public imagination. Hutton was invited to the Leader of the Opposition's house shortly after the summer sales figures were announced. Author and politician spent more than two hours together and Hutton was flattered by the belief that the next prime minister had read his book. The two men parted with a handshake and what Hutton, reasonably enough, believed to be an endorsement. 'I am,' said Tony Blair, holding a copy of *The State We're In*, 'broadly for it.'

The Labour leader was better than his word. In Singapore during January 1996 he made a speech which was an explicit endorsement of 'stakeholding'. In consequence, it contained genuinely radical sentiments.

> It is surely time to assess how we shift the emphasis in corporate ethos from a company being a mere vehicle for the capital market to be traded, bought and sold as a commodity, towards a company as a community or partnership in which each employee has a stake and where a company's responsibilities are more carefully delineated.

Newspapers which had written admiring reviews of Hutton's book began to recognize what John Pender of the *Financial Times* described as the author's 'instinctive suspicion of the free market, his unreconstructed enthusiasm for public spending and his unrestrained assault on the City of London'. What had been interesting as an exercise in utopian whimsy became a threat when it was adopted by a practising politician. Blair was accused of endorsing every proposal which it contained. Hutton now believes that the Prime Minister came late to the discovery that stakeholding required a regulation of the free market. Whatever his reason, Tony Blair began to back away from the ideas he had set out in Singapore. A new idea was needed and a new search began. It was then that he announced his commitment to the Third Way.

Arthur Conan Doyle and Agatha Christie always pretend that gifted amateurs are more likely to solve mysteries than trained professionals. In the real world, the opposite rule applies. So, when the Prime Minister began his Downing Street investigation, it was reasonable to believe that it would come to a speedy conclusion and a definitive answer. He assembled—some as witnesses, some as interrogators, some as both—a starry cast of distinguished political scientists and policy analysts. Most notable amongst them were

Anthony Giddens, Director of the London School of Economics and Professor the Lord Plant, then Master of Saint Catherine's College, Oxford. It was generally agreed in the Prime Minister's political office that if those men did not know what the Third Way was, nobody did. Recklessly, they did not even consider that possibility. Evidence about the afternoon's discussion was easy to come by. Several participants were anxious to explain what a crucial part they had played in the deliberations. Despite the disagreements over fact and emphasis, it was clear that the star of the Downing Street conference was none of the established academics but Charles Leadbeater, who describes himself as 'independent writer, research associate and consultant to leading companies'. He had been a journalist and, in one of his many manifestations, worked with Helen Fielding on 'Bridget Jones's Diary' in its first humble days as a newspaper column. Mr Leadbeater has a New Labour mindset; a belief in market research. He followed his exposition on the fugitive idea with the distribution of a scorecard which was headed THE THIRD WAY LITMUS TEST. To help with the adjudication, the paper asked eleven questions, each of which encapsulated an essential element of Leadbeater's exposition. They included 'What are the cultural politics of the Third Way?' and 'Is it a political philosophy, a fully engineered ideology or a political project to command hegemony?' The crucial criterion, against which above all else the Third Way was to be judged, came last. 'Can it inspire people? What is the bottom line: ideals or ideology?' His audience was invited to evaluate each aspect of his theory by giving each question marks out of ten.

The silence which followed the distribution of the questionnaire had two distinct causes. First, the more literate members of the seminar were considering how to answer, in numbers, questions to which an intelligent reply could only be given in words. Second, the participants were deciding, before they gave their fearlessly objective judgements, what the Prime Minister would like those judgements to be. Mercifully Tony Blair ended the anguish by specifically commending Leadbeater's formula for change—though he did not say whether the rigorous test showed the litmus paper to turn blue or remain red. He said that he was 'broadly for it'. Unfortunately Will Hutton was not at the Downing Street brainstorm. So there was no one there to warn Leadbeater about the danger of reading too much into that form of words. There was, however, within the general admiring gathering one dissenting voice. It came from Wilfred Stevenson, the Director of the Smith Institute. He scored every question zero—an evaluation for which the Prime Minister thanked him with a brevity that suggested, at least to some of those present, that his gratitude was not genuine.

The Smith Institute—not to be confused with the Adam Smith Institute which shares the Labour Government's passion for the free market and private enterprise—was named after John Smith, the Labour leader who succeeded Neil Kinnock in 1992 but died two years later. Smith was what has come to be called (often contemptuously) 'Old Labour'. So an institute founded in his memory had at least a nominal connection with the Labour Party which existed before Blair won the leadership in 1994. But Stevenson's objection to Leadbeater's analysis had less to do with nostalgia for the newly unfashionable principles of democratic socialism than with the belief that the questionnaire confirmed that some of the Downing Street encyclopedists were neither seeking to dump an old philosophy nor hoping to find a new one but indulging the Prime Minister. However, Stevenson's views interested the Downing Street political office far less than his associations. The Smith Institute serves as a platform for Gordon Brown, the Chancellor of the Exchequer. Every one of the Chancellor's statements is regarded by the paranoids of Downing Street as part of his unflagging campaign to succeed (and possibly subvert) the Prime Minister. Because of the close connection, it was assumed at the Downing Street seminar that, if Wilfred Stevenson did not believe in the Third Way, the Chancellor of the Exchequer did not believe in it either and that he would use his scepticism to outsmart Tony Blair in some way. Careful research, predicated on the premise that everything the Chancellor does is meant as a preparation for his eventual premiership, revealed that he had only once spoken of the Third Way in public. And that was only a passing reference. What he said about it in private remained a mystery; as, unfortunately, did the meaning of the Third Way. For within months of seeming its most popular exponent, Charles Leadbeater disavowed the whole idea.

Leadbeater's attitude, which seemed plain enough in Downing Street, became first more ambiguous and then, if his published work is to be relied on, positively antagonistic. By the spring of 1999 he had little time for the idea about which he had spoken with such enthusiasm a year before. That, in itself, does not provide much evidence about where the Third Way leads. But it does confirm one of the characteristics of those who follow it. They are ideologically foot-loose—some people would say philosophically promiscuous. The idea to which Leadbeater moved on was the overriding importance of 'the knowledge economy'—the exploitation (in that word's nicest sense) of the revolution in information technology as a means of creating a new prosperity. In his book, *Living on Thin Air*, Leadbeater certainly endorsed some of the priorities which had been discussed at the Downing Street seminar—the investment in social capital as distinct from social spending and the related imperative of concentrating more resources on education. But he was explicitly critical of the Third Way as a discrete ethical system. 'The emergence of the Third Way and its continual variants marked the end of free market dominance. But the way ahead is not to navigate a middle course between the old left and the new right. The way ahead is to adopt a different destination altogether.' Although *Living on Thin Air* does not provide much help in determining the content of the Third Way, it expresses a firm opinion about the reasons for its creation. The Third Way, according to Leadbeater, is not simply located between the left and right poles of political thought. It is an attempt to reconcile, perhaps even marry, the two extremes. As a result, he scored most of his own 'litmus test' questions zero. The Third Way, at least according to the man who helped to confirm the Prime Minister's belief in it, is not 'a political philosophy or a fully engineered ideology'. In consequence it is unlikely 'to inspire people'. The Prime Minister's endorsement of *Living on Thin Air* ('an essential feature of any map of the new political landscape') was not as fulsome as some of his previous commendations ('extraordinarily interesting...critical questions...will be widely read'). But Peter Mandelson, Tony Blair's closest confidant, described it as 'setting out the agenda for the next Blair revolution'.

Leadbeater's shift—from open advocate to implied critic—is not quite the apostasy that it first seems. Although the Clintons claim that the Third Way is something intellectually discrete and ideologically distinctive, its practitioners in Europe always defend it as a pragmatic necessity which they employ in response to changing times. They are without exception the leaders of socialist and social democratic parties who constantly tell their members of the need for reform. The old nostrums are, they say, not only inappropriate to the new millennium, they are impossible to apply in new circumstances. The new circumstances are the global market and the rise of the Web and the Internet to which *Living on Thin Air* was a response.

A strategy which aims to meet a global challenge needs a global dimension of its own. It was necessary to sanctify Clinton's declaration and the Downing Street seminar with an international conference. It was held in New York in September 1998. I was in New York the month before the world leaders came together and, over lunch with Pat Moynihan, I asked him for his latest view on the Third Way. He was, unsurprisingly, preoccupied less with the President's philosophy than with the President's future—the Monica Lewinsky tapes had just been published. When I told him that I was going to see Kenneth Galbraith the next day, he suggested that I pursue my enquiries with him. 'Got an idea about everything,' Moynihan said. 'President Kennedy made him Ambassador to India to stop him bombarding the White House with his theories.' I took Galbraith to lunch in Cambridge, near his home in Massachussetts, and he entertained the whole restaurant with high decibel stories about the great men he had known. 'Adlai Stevenson? I keep his collected speeches on the shelf reserved for my complete works... Lyndon Johnson? Great command of metaphors. Normally based on bodily functions.' He then said that meeting John Maynard Keynes was the most exciting moment of his life—a suggestion to which his wife took instant exception. I later discovered that our meeting had been arranged on the couple's fiftieth wedding anniversary—a date which Galbraith had forgotten. After lunch we returned to the house he has occupied for almost as long as he has been married—a great gloomy barn which Roy Jenkins believes should be moved to the Smithsonian Museum and labelled 'habitat American academic, circa 1950'. I told him that Moynihan had suggested that he might help me to find the

Roy Hattersley

Third Way. 'Do you know,' Galbraith asked, 'that Nixon made him Ambassador to India to stop him bombarding the White House with his theories?' Then he told me, 'The Third Way is purely a political concept. The increase in numbers and the power of the middle-income groups means that governments choose to meet their needs first. The Third Way is the justification of that necessity.'

That was not the principle on which the New York seminar was convened. To contribute to the impression of serious ideological discussion, Tony Blair anticipated the meeting with the publication of a Fabian Society pamphlet which, had the search for the Third Way been a murder hunt, would have been regarded as the suspect's attempt to confuse his pursuers. For as well as insisting that 'policies flow from values and not vice versa' it went on to describe the Third Way as 'work in progress'. The two statements cannot be reconciled. If the Prime Minister is still working on the definition of his values, the policies which he has already implemented cannot be based upon the eternal veritas of which he is still uncertain. However, *New Politics for a New Century* did contain one important statement of Third Way fact, as Tony Blair saw it. 'With the right policies, market mechanisms are critical to meeting social objectives, entrepreneurial zeal can promote social justice.' That is a view of economics with which few serious politicians, outside North Korea, would disagree. But the fact that Tony Blair chose to make his respect for markets an early canon of the nascent philosophy gives that aspect of the Third Way a special significance.

Socialists and social democrats have always believed that 'the right policies', which balance competitive capitalism and a proper distribution of power and wealth, include government intervention in the market. But now that the market has become global the ability of national governments to intervene has been severely limited. It is impossible to control capital movements between one country and another, fix exchange rates or determine levels of taxation and worker protection without at least considering the possibility of investment moving to more 'business friendly' nations. Parties of the left exist to influence events. The reduction in their power to regulate demand and (as some of them believe) either to set minimum levels of welfare or redistribute wealth, had a traumatic effect on some party leaders. They concluded that socialism was over. For Tony Blair personally, it never really began. So he was happy enough to play his part in finding the alternative. Once again the evidence suggests that the Third Way is a reactive rather than a creative force, a response rather than an original idea.

The British Prime Minister, it must be said, is not so much reconciled to the primacy of the market as positively enthusiastic about it. Other social democrats—notably Lionel Jospin of France—remain heroically optimistic about man's power to control his economic environment. The French Prime Minister persists in the belief that 'we are the protagonists, we can lead and not submit... We are the masters of our collective destiny on earth.' That view reflects exactly the socialist paradox—the simultaneous belief both that man is shaped by his environment and that he can reshape the environment around him. But Tony Blair—who has explicitly rejected what he calls 'Marxist determinism'—stands on some of these issues to the right of Jospin's opponents—as illustrated by a conversation with Jacques Chirac before the 1997 General Election.

The French President had found consolation in the thought that the defeat of the Tories (sister party to his neo-Gaullist RPR, *Rassemblement pour la République*) would at least result in a more Euro-friendly British government sending its representatives to the Council of Ministers. Tony Blair gave him a polite warning. He should not assume that Labour would fully implement the whole Social Chapter in the Maastricht Treaty. The New Labour government would not risk the loss of efficiency at home and sales abroad which would naturally follow inflexible labour markets. The President responded that his economists believed that the costs of the social chapter—ranging from paternity leave to job-loss compensation—were low on the list of industrial detriments. Indeed they probably paid for themselves by stimulating the efficiency which follows commitment. Tony Blair disagreed. His economists had no doubt about the need for labour market flexibility. The argument went on until Chirac tapped Blair on the knee and asked him, 'Am I right in thinking that you are the leader of the British left and that I lead the French right, or is it the other way round?' Tony Blair had the grace to grin.

French scepticism about the Third Way was confirmed in the

lecture which Lionel Jospin gave on 23 July 1998 to inaugurate the Foreign Policy Centre—an institution invented by Robin Cook (the British Foreign Secretary) and supported (both morally and financially) by the Government. The formal presentation over, Jospin agreed to answer questions. The first was a request for his opinion of Blair's new theory. The French Prime Minister put on an impressive display of Gallic embarrassment. He walked from side to side of the stage, beat his hand against his brow, counterfeited a stutter and completed the theatrical business by throwing up his arms in despair. Then, smiling broadly in order to ensure that even the less perceptive members of his audience identified his subtext, he announced, 'It would be wrong of me to comment on the domestic policies of a friendly government.'

Lingering doubts about Jospin's attitude were removed when, in November 1999, he, in his turn, published a Fabian pamphlet. He was majestically dismissive about one definition of the Third Way. 'If,' he wrote, 'it lies between communism and capitalism, it is merely a new name for democratic socialism'. In a subsequent article he rejected the alternative definition out of hand. 'If the Third Way means to find an intermediary position between social democracy and neo-liberalism, this is not my way.' Conscious of his obligations to a friendly government he went on to express the hope that it was no more than the British contribution to the 'effort to reform theory and politics...which all European political parties of socialist or social democratic inspiration are engaged in'. His own contribution to updating all philosophies had been made clear in the Fabian pamphlet. He believed in the pursuit of a more comprehensive assault on inequality—one 'which goes beyond the traditional reliance on redistribution alone. Taxation and the welfare state are means of striving towards greater equality after the event [but] we need to act before the event to prevent the greater accumulation of inequalities.' He also wrote of the need to 'reconcile the middle and working classes, though their interests may differ and sometimes diverge'. Those divergences are what Karl Marx believed to be the causes of what, in his rhetorical way, he called 'the class war'. Unlike Tony Blair, Lionel Jospin does not believe it to be over. He wants a negotiated peace.

Despite his scepticism, Lionel Jospin took part in the Third Way conference which was convened in Florence's Palazzo Vecchio on 21 November 1999. There, hard by the bridge on which Dante first saw Beatrice, William Jefferson Clinton, Gerhard Schröder of Germany, Massimo D'Alema of Italy and Fernando Henrique Cardoso of Brazil met with Lionel Jospin and Tony Blair. Each party leader brought with him a full supporting cast of philosophers, economists and sycophants. The first category within the British delegation was filled by Anthony Giddens, who by then had published a best-selling book on the subject. Giddens's academic discipline was sociology. His influence on the Third Way debate was proving crucial—not so much because of the intellectual merits of his little book as because of the time and effort which he devoted to the subject. His 'sociological' approach—seeing the Third Way as the product of the society in which it developed rather than the expression of an independent ethical imperative—confirmed the Third Way, at least in Britain, as an attempt to face the reality of contemporary life. Before he wrote *The Third Way* he had already argued that 'Keynesianism became ineffective as a result of the twin and interconnected influences of intensified globalization and the transformation of everyday life'— thus setting out the perceived need for a new philosophy without trying to describe what it might be. According to one participant, the Florence Seminar did nothing to fill the vacuum.

Polly Toynbee of the *Guardian* had been a passionate enthusiast for David Owen's Social Democratic Party and had remained loyal to the cause long after other converts had judged that they had nothing to gain by remaining on the middle ground of politics. She seemed ideally suited to the Third Way. But on her return from Florence she wrote of both the proceedings and the participants with something that approached contempt. 'Nothing much has been achieved yet and they are all too slow, too prudent, too idle and too cowardly...As yet, there has been no seismic leftward shift to drag conservatism along in its wake the way Thatcher and Reagan altered the political landscape for ever.' So, if the Toynbee analysis is to be believed, nothing very positive came out of Florence—at least recently, in terms of the Third Way.

But although Ms Toynbee found little substance in the Third Way her report from Florence identified another element in the urge to create a new political philosophy. The left had been hypnotized by the way in which 'Thatcher and Reagan altered the political landscape' and intimidated by the achievements of their neo-liberal philosophy. As Ms Toynbee put it—expanding on Giddens's bold assertion— 'globalization has created some ineluctable universal economic rules by which countries now abide or die—stability, low debt, low inflation. The aim of social democrats is to prove the iron will of the market does not rule alone and it is compatible with social justice.' In their different ways, Giddens and Toynbee helped to identify why they too search for a Third Way. But they did little or nothing to help any of us find it. Neo-liberalism, they both believe, has combined with the global market to make socialism untenable and market capitalism irresistible. Intellectual strength has joined economic force to make the shibboleths of free enterprise universally accepted. It therefore became necessary to find the compromise which Jospin rejected, Leadbeater despised and Clinton pretended was not the object of the Third Way enterprise. Unfortunately none of the 'official' investigations—London, Washington or Florence—made any progress in determining how that compromise should be constructed. At the end of 1999 Tony Blair described the position exactly. Work, he said, was still in progress.

It was about ten o'clock on the evening of 3 December 1999 when I decided to attempt to achieve on my own what the progressive leaders of the free world had been unable to accomplish together. I was, at the time, in the senior common room of Saint Catherine's College, Oxford, and concentrating so hard on peeling an apple with a knife and fork that at first I did not hear the Master say that he had a small gift for me.

I had known Raymond Plant for twenty years and, thanks to me, he had chaired the Labour Party inquiry into electoral reform— a task which he had performed with such intellectual honesty that, during the long weeks of discussion, he had converted himself from a believer in 'first past the post' (the reason I appointed him) to a devotee of proportional representation. He had been appointed Master of Saint Catherine's in 1994 after warning the Fellows that, if he was their choice, they would have to put up with him for life. But, an academic at heart, he had grown tired of university administration and resigned to reclaim his old chair and devote his life to scholarship. He had decided to leave the Master's lodgings during a meeting at which he had been required to adjudicate in a dispute between Fellows over the kind of marmalade which should be available for breakfast. He presided over his last formal dinner without any obvious signs of regret.

During the first part of the meal, I had sat next to Dr Barry Juniper, a botanist who had traced the genetic origins of a strain of supposedly English apple to the steppes of Siberia. So by the time that we all changed places for dessert, my mind was already focused on the pursuit of unlikely information. When Lord Plant told me that his gift was a monograph on the Third Way which he had written for the European Policy Forum, I immediately wondered if he had solved the mystery which had defeated so many prime ministers and presidents. Recalling his change of views on the subject of electoral systems, I asked him if he was for, against or dangerously open-minded. He told me that his paper described his approach as 'constructive but not uncritical'. Depressed by that admirably balanced response, I tried to provoke him into a more positive reaction by reporting that another political scientist, Professor Bernard Crick, had called it a 'chimera'. Acoustics were bad in the common room and another diner passed Plant the port as we spoke. 'A what?' he asked. A zoologist further down the table, thinking that we were arguing about the meaning of the word, suggested 'An organism containing genetically different distinct tissue formed by mutation or grafting'. His neighbour, a classicist, added 'A fire-breathing monster with lion's head, goat's body and serpent's tail'. For the first time I felt that I was making progress in my search for the Third Way.

Plant, as one would expect, set out what he saw as the new idea's genesis with firm clarity. 'Many of those who have been most involved in talking about the project have seen it as a third way either beyond or between free market, and unlimited economic liberalism on the one hand and social democracy committed to state intervention, social justice and greater equality of outcome on the other.' I was hoping to discover what the Third Way stood for, yet once again I was merely being given the map reference of its political location. But Plant went on to say that he did not suggest that it 'only exists in relation to its contrast with these other views and has no positive content of its own'. Was this, I wondered, the big breakthrough? Plant leaned over the table and, telling the lady on his left, 'We've both written about this,' by way of apology for our dialogue, revealed to me what he clearly thought to be the Third Way's inherent contradiction and thereby raised doubts about his own insistence that it has an independent existence. The neo-liberals do not simply argue for the market economy. They claim that social justice is a meaningless idea and that any attempt to impose it on a free society is immoral as well as economically damaging. Those two ideas—one holding social justice to be the moral imperative of civilized government and the other regarding social justice as an excuse for theft by taxation of the rich—cannot be reconciled.

It was Plant who, long ago, pointed me in the direction of Friedrich von Hayek's *Law, Legislation and Liberty*, a far more revealing work than *The Road to Serfdom* which Margaret Thatcher once regarded as her political route map. That work confirms that neo-liberals believe in something called 'market justice'. As Hayek wrote:

> It has, of course, to be admitted that the manner in which the benefits and burdens are apportioned by the market mechanism would, in many instances, have to be regarded as very unjust if it were the result of a deliberate allocation to particular people. But this is not the case. These shares are the outcome of a process, the effects of which on particular people are neither intended nor foreseen. To demand justice from such a process is clearly absurd and to single out some people in such a society as entitled to a particular share is evidently unjust.

The search for social justice gets even shorter shrift in Hayek's *New Studies*. Only the market distributes goods and services in a way which can be morally defended. 'Agreements by the majority on sharing the booty gained by overwhelming a minority of fellow citizens or deciding how much to be taken from them is not democracy. At least it is not the ideal democracy which has any moral justification.' It is hard to imagine how that view of ethics can be amalgamated or even reconciled with anything like social justice. Yet, for two solid years, Anthony Giddens had tried his best to prove that new liberalism and social democracy meet rather than collide somewhere along the third way.

I am not sure why it took me so long to approach Anthony Giddens, the author of *The Third Way* and therefore an authority on the subject. Perhaps it was because I was overawed by his progress up the academic ladder. Giddens, like me, is a graduate of Hull—a most unfashionable university. Yet he rose to be Professor of Sociology at Cambridge and a Fellow of King's. As he said to me when we eventually met for lunch, 'That doesn't happen to many Hull students.'

In the end, the meeting was his idea not mine. I met him after a lecture given by Harold Evans at the London School of Economics. Evans, formerly editor of *The Sunday Times* and *The Times*, is an old friend and (or though) a distant supporter of New Labour from his home in New York. The lecture was an essentially New Labour, if not a Third Way, event; on the platform, both Giddens and Evans took off their jackets—Evans's red braces probably won him the points. At the dinner which followed Giddens, to my surprise, asked me if I would join a panel of critics and commentators who were to be assembled to discuss his second book on the new philosophy— *The Third Way and its Critics*. It was not natural modesty which prompted my surprise but memories of the excoriating review which I had written of Giddens's first volume in the series, *The Third Way*.

In that review, I had congratulated Giddens on correctly identifying the chief characteristic of neo-liberalism—'antagonism to the welfare state'. But it seemed to me that the 154 pages had been thrown together at a speed which was inconsistent with the intellectual rigour that the reader had a right to expect from the director of the LSE and therefore a lineal descendant of Sidney Webb, William Beveridge and Lionel Robbins. The book failed to develop a coherent and continuous idea. And I was offended by its platitudes: 'Strong family ties can be an effective source of social cohesion only if they look outwards as well as inwards...family relations are part of the wider fabric of social life.' Still, Giddens invited me to take part in the discussion, which was also to take place at the London School of Economics, and (since it was some weeks away) I accepted.

The LSE discussion was—naturally enough—held on the day that

The Third Way and its Critics was published. I am irrevocably opposed to serious authors printing pre-publication commendations on their back covers. *The Third Way and its Critics* seemed to me to have taken that undesirable practice to unreasonable extremes. Tony Blair called it 'an important contribution to the debate'. Romano Prodi (Prime Minister of Italy when he attended Third Way seminars, then elevated to the Presidency of the European Commission) wrote of Giddens providing 'vital clues about how to achieve...new thinking about democracy and economic development'. The President of Brazil, Fernando Henrique Cardoso, supplied an even more comprehensive encomium, describing the little book as 'marking a major further development in the evolution of the Left'.

The temptation to inquire about how these champions of the Third Way put their principles into practice was irresistible. Being of an emollient turn of mind, I quoted a passage from *The Third Way and its Critics*, which seemed to me self-evidently true but was too often denied by Third Way enthusiasts. 'Conservative writers are fond of arguing that "poverty is not an excuse" for those who do not fare well, since some exceptional individuals from even the most deprived backgrounds do achieve personal successes. But they succeed precisely because they are exceptional...' Did this not, I asked, reveal a fundamental disagreement between Giddens and the Government? Had not the Prime Minister actually said that poverty is no excuse for the failure—as defined by examination results—of some inner-city schools? Surely Tony Blair's endorsement of a book which took up so contrary a position to his, made the idea of the Third Way as a consistent philosophy absolutely meaningless. The tent had become so big that men and women with precise views would feel lost inside it.

Giddens was outraged that he should be used as a surrogate by those who wanted to attack politicians of whom they disapproved. Perhaps I should have explained that once Blair endorsed his idea, Giddens became responsible for the policies which that idea engendered. But, instead of pursuing that polemic argument, I confined my further remarks to the text—an approach, I assumed, that a scholar would welcome.

In *The Third Way and its Critics* Giddens cannot make up his mind whether he believes in equality of outcome or equality of opportunity. In a single paragraph he supported and rejected both aspirations. 'Social diversity is not compatible with a strongly defined equality of outcome.' That piece of nonsense was reinforced by the sentence which followed: 'Third Way politics looks instead to maximize equality of opportunity.' But that assertion of what Third Way politics stands for—a happy contrast to the usual explanation of what they are against—was then qualified out of existence. 'However, this [sic] has to preserve a concern with limiting inequality of outcome too' because 'equality of opportunity can generate inequalities of wealth and income'. I asked him if he believed in equality of outcome or of opportunity. He was outraged once again. The answer to my question was, he said, clear to anyone who had read and understood the book. In any case there was no real difference between equality of outcome and equality of opportunity. A gasp of incredulity echoed round the audience.

A couple of weeks later (perhaps to make amends for leading the LSE chorus of derision as much as to pursue my enquiries) I invited Giddens to lunch. We ate (only I drank) at the Garrick Club. Giddens was engagingly frank about what he believed to be my wilful failure to understand the importance of his work—a contribution, he insisted, to the intellectual revival of radical politics. He feared that I had placed too much importance on the name which, I had foolishly assumed, placed his ideas somewhere in the no-man's-land between social democracy and neo-liberalism. If it was there that I looked for the Third Way, it was not surprising that I had not found it. My request for advice about where my search should have been located received a less precise response. Giddens's Third Way was a technique, a way of looking at society which transcended the philosophies of right and left by accepting the realities of modern life which they ignored. Of course, he had clear moral priorities—all of which I would recognize as rooted in the traditional values of social democracy. But in the global economy it is important to talk less about how things ought to be and think more about how they are.

There was no doubt that Giddens meant to help me find the Third Way. But his explanation of how Third Way policies are determined was not complemented by a description of what those policies are. He made his work on the subject sound like handbooks—manuals which explain how a motor car works but make no suggestion about the direction in which it should travel. As he spoke, with lucid conviction, about the need to develop a new approach to politics, I recalled the first law of politics which I had learned at Harvard long ago: 'Where you stand depends on where you sit.' Giddens is the sociology man—promoting the discipline in which he works as if, like Joanna Southcote's box, it contains solutions to all the mysteries of the universe. He really does believe that 'more than any other intellectual endeavour, sociological reflection is central to grasping the social forces remaking our lives today'.

No doubt. But in politics, no less than medicine, diagnosis loses much of its point unless it is followed by prescription. Giddens, in the LSE discussion, had angrily rejected judgements on the Third Way which were based on how practising politicians translated it into policies—even though their endorsement of his theories was printed on the jackets of his text. So the search for the ideological content of his Third Way cannot end with a list of those policies which 'Third Way politicians' implement. Indeed Giddens proclaims, as if it proves the contemporary relevance of the Third Way, that 'the German Social Democrats' Basic Values Commission has identified four different Third Ways—the British (market oriented), Dutch (market and consensus base), Swedish (reformed welfare state) and French (state led)'. His conclusion that the various strands of thought are held together by the social democrats' need to choose between modernization and death does nothing to help answer the question. It may confirm that a new 'unifying principle' is needed. But it does not tell us what that unifying principle is.

Perhaps class politics are out of fashion. Capitalism has certainly changed. But does that mean that all politicians can do is accommodate economic changes which the global market has made irresistible? That new technology has produced forces which are beyond political control? Giddens, it seems, would answer yes. In *The Third Way* he wrote:

> The knowledge economy is not yet all-conquering, but it is well on the way to being so. In combination with the broader aspects of

globalization, it marks a major transition in the nature of economic activity...To assess the value of Microsoft, one wouldn't get far by asking about the factors conventionally used to assess value—land, plants, raw materials. The tangible assets of the company are tiny as compared to its market value.

Leadbeater makes exactly the same point in *Living on Thin Air*. But the value of Microsoft was suddenly changed by the Supreme Court's judgement that it was acting in contravention of United States monopoly legislation. The Microsoft example may yet prove—if the judgement sticks—Giddens wrong and Jospin right. 'We are the protagonists, we can lead and not submit...We are the masters of our collective destiny on earth.'

At the end of the LSE discussion, Ralf Dahrendorf—a former director of the LSE and himself a distinguished sociologist— approached the table at which the speakers were still sitting and said that, although he had never shared my view on the moral obligation to promote greater equality, he endorsed my opinion that politicians had a moral obligation to promote something. Suddenly, I realized why Lord Dahrendorf—British citizen and Liberal Democrat Peer—was regarded as the most uncompromising German to adopt this country since Prince Albert married Queen Victoria. When he expressed his surprise that I had taken part in the Giddens benefit event, he told me that I should look further afield. During his time as Warden of St Antony's (the Oxford international studies college) he had been impressed (perhaps he said depressed) by how far the idea had spread.

Of course, I took his advice, but the further afield the search went, the more difficult it was to discern a precise idea. Luiz Carlos Bresser Pereira, lecturing to Oxford's Centre for Brazilian Studies, asserted that the concept of left and right 'will differ from country to country and within a single country from time to time'—a proposition which, if true, changes the nature of political philosophy. Locke, Rousseau, Mill and Marx all believed that what they wrote was true for all places at all times. Hayek and Friedman are equally convinced that their views on the market are universal. Pereira may be right to insist that 'the new left in the developing countries does not make the mistake of imputing its countries' problems to external factors—a mistake of the old left—but understands that the debt requires substantial trade surplus rather than getting still more indebted, as the right still believes possible'. But that is a practical judgement about an immediate crisis. It teaches nothing about the sort of society which applying that principle helps the developing world to become. The underlying principle remains elusive.

The Pereira precept—the legitimate differences in the definitions of what the Third Way really means—is popular if not plausible. Mark Latham, Member of the Australian House of Representatives, speaking to the plenary session of a conference on the Moral Foundation of Government, convened by the Australian Association for Professional and Applied Ethics, described it in purely Antipodean terms. 'The Third Way aims to develop a concept of citizenship suited to post-traditional society. This is what I call multiple-identity citizenship…neither the narrowing of our national identity to the monoculture of white Australia' nor maintaining 'a tribal commitment to economic nationalism'. When he spoke to the Institute of Social Research in Melbourne, his definition was less insular—if a land mass as big as Australia, even when completely surrounded by water, can be so described. It included a concession. 'The Third Way has not been very good at reducing its work programme down to a single statement of ideology.' To my great relief, he went on to provide one. But my pleasure was short-lived. The 'guiding ideology' was, he said, 'the true socialist principle of our time, the dispersal of economic, social and political power'. Of which time was that not the true socialist principle? But he did not even sustain that idea. When Mr Latham said 'a society built around information…makes the spread of know-how, skills and capability more feasible than at any other time in human history', he was arguing (rightly or wrongly) not that the times cry out for a new philosophy but that the conditions of the age make it unusually easy to formulate one. When he went on to argue that 'an information society breaks down all forms of hierarchy' he was making a quite different point. He was suggesting that the now mobile or more equal society which he wants to see is the automatic result of technological progress. No principle or philosophy is needed.

The notion of 'no philosophy needed' is not new—at least to the British Labour Party. During my political youth in Sheffield—

once, but alas no more, famous for both its steel-making and its socialism—I was continually advised not to waste my time on 'theorizing'. But that old-time objection to ideological speculation was based on a different idea from the one which prompts Third Way nihilism. The Labour Party in which I was brought up was built around men and women who had helped to make the 1945 Attlee Government. To them the problems of poverty and deprivation were too urgent and obvious to justify a moment being wasted on ideological discussion. They simply wanted to get on with the job— which is why Labour lost in 1951 when it was no longer clear what the job should be. 'No philosophy' contributed to defeat when I was young. Now it is regarded as the prescription for victory.

Contempt for philosophy is illustrated time after time by Third Way thinkers all over the world. Franke Vandenbrooke, sometime Foreign Minister of Belgium, says—clearly believing his approach to be supremely reasonable—that 'the foundation value in this endeavour is the idea of a fair distribution of burdens and benefits and the political challenge is to find majority support for a distribution that is accepted as fair'. Vandenbrooke—being intellectually more rigorous than many Third Way enthusiasts—then covered his tracks brilliantly. He wants a 'distribution of burdens and benefits' which is 'fair'. But he understands that 'fairness' means different things to different people. So he provides a definition of fairness on which we can all agree—a focus group philosophy. Fair is whatever a majority of the electorate will vote for as fair. The good society is measured against opinion poll ratings.

I had still found nothing like a definition when I was invited to address the Centenary Meeting of the Stockholm Philosophical Society on 'The Meaning of the Third Way'. The secretary's letter referred to the Third Way as if it were a proper philosophy. My letter of acceptance did not disillusion her. I made the trip under false pretences; it was too attractive an invitation to decline. But I had not been to Sweden since the memorable time when a government, committed to subjecting the economy to the rigours of competition, had reduced gross domestic product by five per cent in two consecutive years. Anyway, I like the place and feel at home there. I have Swedish hair—perfectly docile except for a patch which sticks up from my scalp like the cockade on a dragoon's shako. I agreed to go and prepared to admit that my search had been a failure.

There was a dusting of snow on the Stockholm streets and the lights across the harbour sparkled in the clean sub-zero air. On the night before my lecture I was driven to dinner by the director of the Nobel Foundation who corrected (with ill-disguised horror) my mistaken belief that Milton Friedman was a full laureate. Next day, he cycled through a blizzard to the National Museum in which the lecture was to be held and arrived cold but eager, and therefore epitomizing Sweden. It all helped to convince me that, although I had nothing very positive to say, I was right to be there.

The first item on the agenda was a professor from Uppsala who spoke about the origins and history of the society. He spoke for ninety minutes. Much to the quiet pleasure of the members he explained that, when Norway chose separation in 1912, it had been society members who persuaded the Swedish government not to order the bombardment of Oslo. The detail with which he described the society's first hundred years sounded like a reproof to any future speakers who could not match his assiduity. All I could offer was a litany of lost clues, false trails, dubious evidence and erroneous deductions. In the end, I simply confessed failure. 'I have searched,' I said, 'and I have found nothing.' Then I mumbled about there being nothing there to find. In a moment of literary folly, I spoke of trying to hold quicksilver in the palm of the hand and attempting to catch moonbeams in a net. I immediately regretted the images, less because they were so florid than because they might be regarded as complimentary. And moonbeams in a net is a joyously romantic idea.

After some discussion, the rapporteur—always a feature of such occasions—summed up the whole proceedings. The lucky man was Werner A. Perger of *Die Zeit*—a Third Way devotee. At first I thought that his compliments were meant to be ironically offensive. Then I hoped that he was being humorous in a sober German way. It was only when he summed up his appraisal of my lecture that I understood the truth about both his critique and my subject. 'Mr Hattersley,' he said, 'has explained the position precisely. The Third Way is whatever you choose to make it. It is, in consequence, the guarantee of progressive victory. The importance of the Third Way is it means that the centre left can win.'

It was Pat Moynihan who had put the idea of looking for the Third Way into my head. So, when I saw him in Washington in April of this year, I told him of the problems my search had encountered. I have noticed over the years that great men want to discuss subjects of their own choice. Moynihan could think of nothing except a lecture which he had given to the University of Virginia on the rebuilding of Pennsylvania Avenue and a book he had published on the United States Government's passion for secrecy. At the end of our lunch, I laid a restraining hand on his arm and asked him directly, 'What about the Third Way?' He looked at me with undisguised amazement. 'Over,' he said. 'Finished.' I think that he said 'Finished' seven times. Then he asked me, 'Have you read Donald Wilhelm's book?' Before I could admit my ignorance, he told me. 'It's called *The Fourth Way*.' I did not suggest that we found out where it led.

□

NOTES ON CONTRIBUTORS

Paul Auster's most recent book is *Timbuktu* (Faber/Henry Holt). For the past year he has been presenting the *National Story Project* on National Public Radio in the US, a programme devoted to true stories sent in by listeners. An anthology is in the works.

Amit Chaudhuri's 'A Small Bengal, NW3' appeared in *Granta* 65. His fourth book, *A New World*, was published this year by Picador and Knopf. He lives in Calcutta and Oxford.

Gautier Deblonde has been photographing art and artists in Britain since the early 1990s. His first book, on Anish Kapoor, was published by the Lisson Gallery in 1998. *Artists*, a collection of his portraits, was published by the Tate Gallery last year. The British sculptor **Antony Gormley**'s work based on the human body has included 'fields' of tiny terracotta figures, as well as lone, winged figures (of which the largest, *The Angel of the North*, 1997, stands above Gateshead in north-east England). His more recent work includes sculptures made from short steel bars which blur the outline of the body and break up its mass. He is represented by the White Cube Gallery in London.

Fergus Fleming has been a freelance writer since 1991. 'The Oddity of Height' is an extract from his forthcoming book *Killing Dragons* which will be published by Granta Books in October (Grove Atlantic in the US). His last book was *Barrow's Boys* (Granta Books/Grove Atlantic).

Roy Hattersley was an MP for thirty-three years and Deputy Leader of the British Labour Party from 1983 to 1992. He is a journalist and the author of fifteen books, most recently *Blood and Fire: William and Catherine Booth and their Salvation Army* (LittleBrown/Doubleday).

Judith Hermann is a journalist living in Berlin. Her first book, *Sommerhaus, später* [Summerhouse, Later] is published in Germany by S. Fischer.

Ian Parker is a British writer who lives in New York and writes for the *New Yorker*. His piece 'Traffic' appeared in *Granta* 65.

Tim Parks's most recent books are the novels *Europa* and *Destiny* and the essay collection *Adultery and Other Diversions* (all published by Secker and Warburg/Arcade Publishing). He lectures on literary translation at the IULM university, Milan. He has a website: timparks.com.

Elliot Perlman lives in Melbourne where he works as a barrister. 'The Emotions Are Not Skilled Workers' is taken from a novel-in-progress, *Seven Types of Ambiguity* (Faber/Riverhead Books). His short story collection, *The Reasons I Won't Be Coming*, was published this year by Faber in the UK and will be published by Riverhead Books in the US.

Justine Picardie writes for *Vogue* and the London *Telegraph*. She edited *Before I Say Goodbye*, a collection of pieces by her sister, Ruth (Penguin/Henry Holt). She is currently writing a book about the afterlife.

Edmund White is the author of seven novels as well as biographies of Proust and Genet. His most recent novel is *The Married Man* (Chatto and Windus/Knopf). He lives in New York.

The editor would like to acknowledge Paul Sheehan of the *Sydney Morning Herald* as the source of the Olympic statistics in the last issue of *Granta*.